GPS for Mariners

Robert J. Sweet

he   McGraw-Hill

k • Chicago • San Francisco
rid • Mexico City • Milan
n • Seoul • Singapore
• Toronto

The McGraw·Hill Companies

9 0 DOC DOC 0 9 8 7 6

Library of Congress Cataloging-in-Publication Data
Sweet, Robert J. (Robert James), 1942 –
    GPS for mariners / Robert J. Sweet.
       p.   cm.
Includes index.
    ISBN 0-07-141075-9 (pbk. : alk. paper)
    1. Artificial satellites in navigation. 2. Global Positioning
System. I. Title.
    VK562 .S94 2003
    623.89´3—dc21   2002152815

Questions regarding the content of this book
should be addressed to
International Marine
P.O. Box 220
Camden, ME 04843
www.internationalmarine.com

Questions regarding the ordering of this book
should be addressed to
The McGraw-Hill Companies
Customer Service Department
P.O. Box 547
Blacklick, OH 43004
Retail customers: 1-800-262-4729
Bookstores: 1-800-722-4726

Photographs and illustrations by the author unless
otherwise indicated

*To Judy, my lovely bride
and constant boating companion,
and to my sons Rich and Dave,
who often are courageous enough
to go with us.*

Contents

Part 2
Advanced GPS Techniques

Acknowledgments

Many have contributed to this book, whether knowingly or by incidental contact. Those whom I have had the opportunity to work with in GPS classes have, by their questions and interest, contributed mightily. They have been the beta tests that helped me refine the work covered in the book.

A number of individuals contributed directly to the formation of the coursework and this book. Most notable among them is Charles A. Perkins. Charlie, when he learned that I was working on a book, provided the impetus for me to finish it, and then served as reviewer. He has volunteered his time for more than thirty years teaching all levels of boating and navigation. He had the courage to teach me advanced celestial navigation. Charlie has an extraordinary grasp of what material should be presented and then to deliver it.

I worked with others who helped shape my perspectives on how to deliver GPS material. Frank E. Lingard brought me back to boating education, demonstrating a unique and captivating style of instruction. Dick Carey, Fred Cornford, Dan Kelly, Karl McNulty, and Ken Santoro participated in some of the same programs. Earlier in my career, I had the good fortune to manage the business group of the Harris Corporation, one of the companies involved in the original development of GPS. The business group's GPS work brought us in contact with some very talented managers at innovative companies. I thoroughly enjoyed working with Ken Medlin at Rockwell, Dennie Welsh at IBM, Frank Lovaglio at Harris, and many others during exciting times when we never imagined that so many would be using GPS for so much.

I would also like to thank my wife, Judy, and Helen Gores, for their assistance in making sure my words are understandable with some semblance of grammar, and for the many hours they endured while my face was pointed at the computer screen. And, many thanks to the team at International Marine, including Tris Coburn, who made the process of being an author far easier and enjoyable. They put a great deal of effort into converting my original words and pictures into this well-formatted book.

A number of companies have been most helpful in providing information, pictures, screenshots, and demonstration software that I used in compiling the material for the book. Garmin, Magellan (Thales Navigation), Navman, Raymarine, Simrad, and Standard Horizon have graciously allowed me to use images of their products and screens. C-Map, Maptech, and Nobeltec have provided cartography and software that was used to compile screenshots for the book. Maptech, Net Sea (MaxSea), Nautical Technologies, Nobeltec, and Raymarine provided demo navigation software, and their perspectives were used to present graphics and to derive thoughts on the state of the art in navigation software for the book. All of these companies demonstrate the high quality of hardware and software offerings available to you, the recreational boater. It is hard to imagine that you could go wrong with any of their offerings. I also would like to thank the friendly staff at West Marine in Falmouth, Massachusetts, who let me test and demonstrate a variety of GPS receivers to help make this information as accurate as possible.

I supplemented my experience and research with information provided by many government entities and companies, including the U.S. Air Force, the U.S. Army, the U.S. Coast Guard, NOAA, NOS, USGS, Aerospace Corporation, and many useful websites. The resources section in the back of the book presents a representative list of websites for those who would like to further expand their knowledge of GPS and navigation.

How to Navigate This Book

Consumers purchase well over a million GPS receivers every year. Boating navigation is one of the foremost uses for these and for the millions already in service today. GPS receivers have become affordable as well as essential, and no boater should be without one. A wide range of GPS receivers are on the market, many specifically designed for boating. This book is written for anyone and everyone considering the use of GPS for boating, whether experienced or novice, or whether the owner of a small runabout, a sailboat, or a powerboat.

GPS navigation leads to vastly safer boating, but learning it may initially appear daunting. Even those who use a GPS receiver regularly often utilize only a fraction of its capabilities. It is essential to use charts—paper or electronic—with GPS to ensure that the path is clear from a departing location to a destination. While many of you may be put off by navigation, GPS technology makes it vastly easier. This book will guide you through everything GPS can do to aid maritime navigation.

GPS for Mariners is not a buying guide; rather, it is directed primarily at mariners who already own a GPS receiver. (If you are still considering a purchase, however, chapter 5, GPS Receiver Selection and Cost Considerations, provides a capsule summary of what you need to know.) Most boaters first purchase a handheld GPS receiver, as these units are accurate and inexpensive. Using them on a moving boat does present challenges, but part 1 of this book provides

tips to help you overcome them. While part 1 uses a handheld as the model for illustrations, all GPS models share similar buttons, pages, functions, and features. Mariners using fixed-mount GPS receivers will find much of the information useful.

As their desire for more integrated GPS information increases, many boaters acquire an electronic chartplotter, use of which permits you to monitor where you are on a chart at all times. As prices have come down, chartplotters have become far more common, especially on small boats where there is limited space to lay out a paper chart. There are other ways, too, to integrate the information received from your GPS with electronic chart displays. An increasing number of boaters accomplish this by connecting a laptop to a GPS receiver for live navigation. Part 2 of the book addresses the many issues involved in combining the location information provided by GPS with electronic charts.

Now for a chapter-by-chapter breakdown. Part 1 quickly and thoroughly grounds you in using waypoints and routes for basic navigation with your GPS receiver. Chapters 1 and 2 summarize the global positioning system itself—how and why it was developed, how it works, and how the elements of the system affect onboard receipt of satellite information. Chapter 3 introduces the handheld GPS receiver, explaining its buttons, screens, and menus and answering a boater's questions in a way GPS manuals do not. Chapter 4 introduces the practical basics of GPS navigation for mariners and provides how-to examples to get you navigating your boat using many GPS receiver functions with paper charts. This chapter also discusses what to do if your GPS receiver fails. (Appendices 1 and 2 show you further ways to make use of a GPS receiver.) As already noted, chapter 5 covers selection issues. Even boaters possessing considerable experience with GPS navigation will find some useful tips, features, and techniques in part 1.

Part 2 addresses the many issues related to integrating the location information provided by GPS with the world around you. Chapter 6 provides a range of techniques for relating GPS output to your surroundings and to paper charts. You will learn how to use data fields to easily control your boat, and you will find a special emphasis on techniques to avoid hazards and to double-check the accuracy of your GPS. The chapter also shows sailors how to use GPS to determine when to tack toward their destination. (Powerboaters can also use this technique to tack across heavy seas.)

Chapter 7 explores chartplotters and their role on board. This chapter also introduces electronic charts and the differences between raster and vector formats. Chapter 8 shows how to connect your GPS to a computer—at home or on a boat—for planning, uploading, downloading, and editing of waypoints and routes. Waypoint management directly on the GPS unit can be tedious, but a computer makes this task a snap. Almost all GPS models can be connected to a computer, and the variety of relatively inexpensive software available makes waypoint entry and management quite easy and affordable. Chapter 8 also includes an explanation of digital charting software, which enables waypoint and route planning on your computer screen with actual electronic charts. Chapter 9 expands on the issues that arise when connecting computers to GPS receivers, and discusses techniques used to connect GPS to other navigation equipment, such as autopilot and radar, on your boat. Chapter 10 describes GPS receiver performance enhancements, including the Wide Area Augmentation System (WAAS), Differential GPS (DGPS), and antenna placement. That chapter also discusses present and future GPS receiver accuracy and how you can get the most from your investment.

The appendix includes model-specific instructions and a sample exercise section.

As you are reading the book and working with your GPS receiver, you may also find the glossary helpful, as some GPS terminology can be quite confusing.

The resources section identifies a wide range of helpful websites. A wealth of information about GPS navigation for mariners is available on the Internet, and you may well find such supplemental material useful after mastering the information and techniques in *GPS for Mariners*.

GPS technology has greatly enhanced boating. However, as you begin using this book, a few strong words of caution are in order. First, *never rely entirely on any one device such as a single GPS receiver for your safety*. Second, *a GPS receiver only tells you your present location*. GPS does not know what objects or hazards may be in the way as you travel to your destination. That information is provided by charts (paper or electronic) and visual observation.

Part 1

Using Your GPS Receiver

History and Perspective

NAVSTAR GPS (*Navigation Satellite Timing And Ranging*—*Global Positioning System*) began in the mid-1970s. The federal government designated the U.S. Air Force the lead agency for this multiservice program. At that time, some in Congress opposed the development of GPS, so the air force designed the system with a "civil" capability to gain broader support. However, given the anticipated high cost, many considered potential civil applications limited. The military officially downplayed the accuracy potential of GPS to the enemy, and, to hide the system's true capabilities, the air force developed techniques to segregate high-performance military use from what the enemy might be able to achieve using the "civil" mode. Ironically, the military considered it less likely that the enemy would attack GPS satellites if foreign powers were able to use them, too, albeit with degraded performance. While initially the future commercial uses for GPS generated some discussion, nobody envisioned that GPS ultimately would become available to every citizen.

GPS progressed through several phases of development. The air force achieved Full Operational Capability, which was dependent upon a fully deployed constellation of satellites, in 1995. The government launched the initial Block I satellites between 1978 and 1985. The Block I satellites (which were used for development and testing of GPS) provided limited coverage

due to the small number of satellites launched; position "fixes" could be obtained only at finite locations and selected times of day. The government launched the Block II satellites, which provide our current service, between 1989 and 1997. The government is currently replacing these satellites as they age by Block IIR satellites. Block IIF satellites are currently in development. GPS is rapidly becoming a key system supporting not only the military, but other air, sea, and land navigation users. Expanding uses are emerging rapidly for precision surveying, road building, other construction, cartography, truck and train routing, urban planning, and mining. Consequently, the air force initiated studies with Rockwell and Boeing that were meant to enhance the design of the next generation of GPS satellites to better serve these broader markets. It is expected that more frequencies will become available to improve performance and security for a wide range of civil uses and military applications. Clearly, the military has made broad use of GPS, including guiding precision weapons to designated targets.

Today, the military still enjoys performance advantages over what is available to us for marine navigation. However, one of the techniques originally implemented to deny accuracy to civil users, Selective Availability (SA), was turned off by presidential order in May 2000. SA allowed the air force to alter the satellite clocks on the civil frequency so that the user accuracy was degraded to as much as 328 feet (100 m). Since the air force turned off SA, GPS receivers provide us with accuracies typically as good as 33 to 50 feet (10–15 m). Prior to the shutdown of SA, the U.S. Coast Guard implemented a system called *Differential GPS* (DGPS) in our coastal regions, which enabled correction for the SA and some other system errors to improve the accuracy to 16.4 feet (5 m) or better. DGPS was deployed to support commercial boating and is available to the general public. This system remains fully operational, but it is deployed only in coastal areas and some inland waterways. The Federal Aviation Authority (FAA), in response to aviation interest in using GPS for precise navigation, initiated a program called *Wide Area Augmentation System* (WAAS), which extends coverage across the entire country and further improves accuracy to 10 feet (3 m). Meanwhile, a number of companies developed special equipment that produces GPS accu-

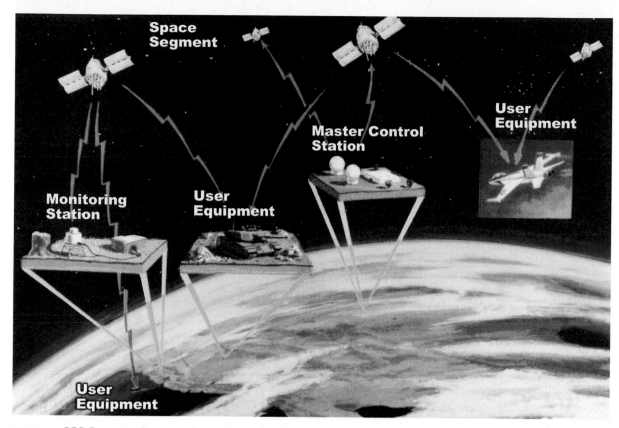

FIGURE 1-1. *GPS Operating Segments: Space, Control, and User. GPS consists of three distinct operating segments. The air force manages the space and control segments. The monitoring stations listen to the satellites and communicate adjustments to the satellites for timing and positioning via the Master Control Station. The User Equipment consists of military and commercial receivers that provide position information to users.* (ADAPTED FROM AN ILLUSTRATION BY THE U.S. AIR FORCE)

racies on the order of centimeters or better for precision surveying used in commercial construction, road building, and other applications for the public and governments.

The Soviets developed their own version of GPS, GLONASS (for Global'naya Navigationnaya Sputnikovaya Sistema), with fewer satellites in slightly different orbits. The precision surveyors and mapmakers often use both GPS and GLONASS together to obtain their high level of accuracy. GLONASS currently provides no useful applications for the recreational boater.

GPS requires substantial government support to remain in operation and to evolve. Figure 1-1 shows the various components of the GPS system. There are three major segments, all funded by the Department of Defense. The space segment includes the artificial

"stars" (satellites) that provide the navigation information. The user segment consists of GPS receivers (User Equipment) that perform a similar function to those we now use on our boats. The control segment (Master Control Station) manages the location and maintenance of the satellites. The control segment uses five Monitoring Stations throughout the world that listen to each satellite and relay information on any errors in accuracy. These error data are routed to the Master Control Station, where computers calculate and transmit corrections to several monitoring stations, which then transmit the new information to the satellites as they orbit overhead. The Master Control Station is located at Falcon Air Force Base in Colorado Springs, Colorado. This station and the one located in Hawaii do not have the capability to communicate directly with the satellites. Only the monitoring stations on Kwajelein Island in the Pacific Ocean, Diego Garcia in the Indian Ocean, and Ascension Island in the Atlantic Ocean "talk" directly with the satellites.

The air force built the GPS program based upon practical experience gained with a predecessor satellite navigation program called TRANSIT. Initial studies and development demonstrated that the concept of satellite-based navigation would work. Figure 1-2 shows an early experimental four-channel receiver built by what is now Rockwell Collins. With these positive results, Congress authorized the development of GPS, narrowly passing legislation funding the project. Soon thereafter, the program proceeded into full-scale development. The initial complement of receivers and antennas for various user applications is shown in figure 1-3. Rockwell Collins was the prime contractor and developed the user segment receivers. Their team partner, Harris Corporation, developed the antennas and associated processors.

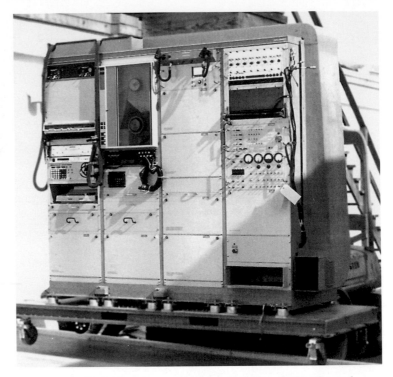

FIGURE 1-2. *An Early Experimental GPS Receiver, Circa 1978. The air force ran tests of GPS using these electronics bays aboard a C-141 aircraft. This is a four-channel receiver with recording capability, which enabled engineers to review the results. At the time this receiver was flown, there were only four satellites in orbit, so the tests had to be planned for locations that had all of the available satellites in view.* (HARRIS CORP.)

FIGURE 1-3. *The Original Complement of GPS Components Designed for the Military. The GPS contract provided for a group of components that could be applied to different military platforms. The Manpack in the center was a single-channel receiver for the army. The black boxes were used on aircraft, and the white boxes on military vehicles. The round object in the center foreground is an antenna that provided jam resistance for aircraft by adapting the antenna pattern to avoid unwanted jamming signals.* (ROCKWELL COLLINS)

Chapter 2

How GPS Works

FIGURE 2-1. *A GPS Block II Satellite. Block II satellites, notable for their extraordinary performance and longevity, represent the current generation of GPS satellites. GPS encompassed the first large constellation of satellites deployed for any mission, and the design of all satellites in use today is based on that used for GPS.* (U.S. AIR FORCE)

The air force has developed and launched several generations of GPS satellites. Figure 2-1 shows a typical Block II satellite. Overall, the performance and useful lives of GPS satellites have exceeded expectations by a substantial margin. A typical satellite weighs over 2,200 pounds (4,840 kg), has a ten-year useful life, generates close to 1,000 watts using solar panels, and transmits signals with an average power of 50 watts each on two frequencies. Two tandem atomic clocks provide precise timing. These clocks are so accurate that it would take over a thousand years for them to be off by as much as a second; however, they are monitored constantly and adjusted to maintain their high degree of accuracy.

The lower-performance civil channel is transmitted on 1,521 MHz on what is known as the *L1 frequency*. This is the channel available to us as individual and commercial users. The signal is very weak by the time it reaches the Earth, so GPS employs a special pseudorandom code (discussed later in this chapter) in transmitting the signal. The receiver stores an image of this code and matches it with the incoming signal.

The military, in addition to L1, uses the L2 frequency of 1,227 MHz, with a longer and more precise pseudorandom code. Even on the L1 frequency, the government considered the GPS performance too good to allow the enemy to use in a conflict. Conse-

quently, the air force had the satellites designed with a means to artificially degrade the clock performance, an application known as *Selective Availability* (SA). However, as noted in chapter 1, SA was shut off in May 2000.

The "constellation" consists of 24 GPS satellites orbiting at almost 11,000 nautical miles above the center of the Earth. The satellites are arrayed in an *inclined polar orbit*. These orbits are inclined 55° from the plane of the equator. The satellites are arranged into six individual orbit planes (four satellites occupy each orbit plane). These orbit planes are spaced at equal intervals around the Earth to provide global coverage, as shown in figure 2-2. Typically, 21 satellites are in use at any given time. In-orbit spares can be moved to fill a gap or to take over for a malfunctioning satellite. Schematically, the GPS satellite constellation appears like a dispersed cluster of bees orbiting the Earth. The pattern is designed such that a number of satellites can be seen at various directions from almost any location on Earth. Any given satellite completes an orbit around the Earth in 12 hours, so each satellite is moving with respect to an observer on the ground.

7

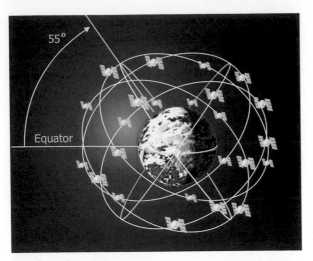

FIGURE 2-2. *The GPS Satellite Constellation Covers the Earth.*
The air force deploys GPS satellites in six orbital planes.
The orbits are inclined 55° from the equator. There are 24
satellites total, with 21 operational at any given time. The air
force controls the satellites and moves the spares to fill holes
in coverage. Each satellite orbits the Earth every 12 hours.

To see how GPS works, let's look at the signal from a single satellite. Each satellite transmits signals in what is known as a *pseudorandom code*. This is a sequence of coded information that reliably can be transmitted at low power and recovered by the receiver. Since the receiver knows what sequence to look for, it can enhance this signal and reject extraneous noise and signals. Within the pseudorandom

coded sequence is imbedded the key information that the satellite is sending to the receiver. That information includes the satellite's identity, its position at the time of the transmission, and the exact time of the transmission. This is depicted in figure 2-3. The receiver, using its own internal clock, compares the time the signal was sent with when it was received and measures how long the signal took to get from the satellite to the receiver. From this information, the receiver calculates the distance, knowing that the signal travels at the speed of light.

The GPS receiver now knows how far it is from the satellite. Imagine if you could tie a string of that length to the satellite and mark every spot on the Earth where that string could reach. You would get a circle on the surface of the Earth. This is called a *circle of position* (COP). The center of the circle is that point on the Earth's surface directly below the satellite. This is depicted in figure 2-4.

Although the GPS receiver knows how far it is from the satellite, a position on the Earth is highly dependent upon the size and shape of the planet, which is not a perfect sphere. A mathematical model called *datum*, described later in this chapter, represents the shape of the Earth. When we draw our COP

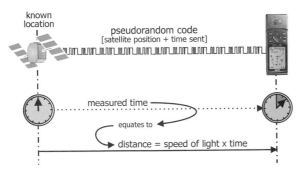

FIGURE 2-3. *Signals Are Transmitted from Satellites to Users.*
The GPS satellites know their position. Each satellite transmits a coded signal to the Earth telling the GPS receiver its identity, its precise location, and the exact time the signal was sent. The receiver compares the time the signal was sent with when it was received to compute the distance from the satellite to the receiver.

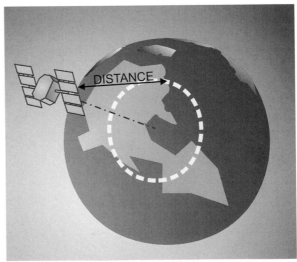

FIGURE 2-4. *The GPS Solution from a Single Satellite. The transit time of the signal from the satellite to the receiver can be converted to distance. All possible points on the Earth at that same distance from the satellite result in a circle with its center directly under the satellite.*

representing all of the possible locations that could meet the distance criteria (called *pseudorange*), it is slightly distorted by the shape of the Earth. In addition, there is some uncertainty about the precise distance from the satellite to the receiver. This uncertainty is caused by the inaccuracy of the receiver's inexpensive clock. Instead of a fine line on the surface of the Earth, this uncertainty produces a band of some width within which you are located. With only one satellite, you know only that you are located somewhere on that circle within the band of uncertainty.

When the GPS unit receives the signal from a second satellite and computes its distance, a second circle results, as shown in figure 2-6. The two COPs intersect at two places. Your position could be at either; however, you generally have information, such as knowledge of which state or body of water you are in, that would lead you to believe which of the intersections corresponds to your location. Because each circle has a band of uncertainty, the two intersecting bands still define a wide region for your position. The GPS receiver still does not have sufficient information to determine a useful fix.

To eliminate the uncertainty, your GPS unit must know time more precisely. It takes only a few hundredths of a second for the signal to travel the entire distance from the satellite to the Earth. To determine position within 50 feet (15 m) along the surface of the Earth, the receiver needs to know time accurately—to within a few hundred-millionths of a second. A complete GPS fix involves four pieces of information defining a three-dimensional (3-D) position in space. The first of these is precise time, the remainder are

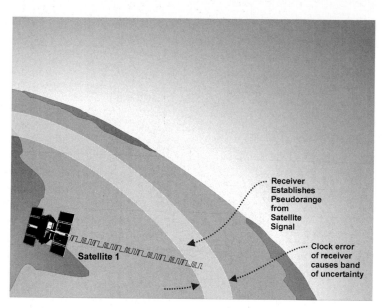

FIGURE 2-5. *Band of Uncertainty Due to GPS Receiver Clock Inaccuracy. Looking closer, you can see that the circle on the Earth is not a line but a wide band. This is due to the imprecision of a GPS receiver's clock in measuring the time of transit for the signal. You know you are located somewhere on the Earth within this band. This is depicted by the wide, light-colored band here.*

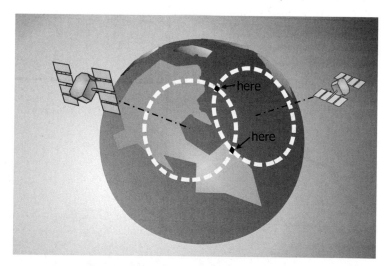

FIGURE 2-6. *The GPS Solution from Two Satellites: Still No Fix. Decoding the signal from a second satellite results in a new distance and a second circle on the surface of the Earth with its center under the second satellite. You are located at one of the two intersections of the two circles. Since the receiver has not resolved its clock calibration, uncertainty leads to circular bands of some width rather than sharp lines. The black areas indicating your possible locations are too large for any meaningful fix, even if you can determine your general location to one of the two intersections. The Satellite screen will indicate that the GPS still is "acquiring satellites."*

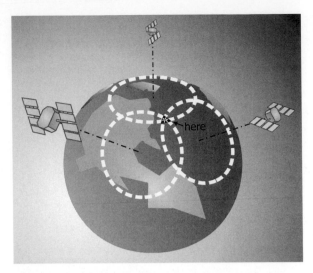

FIGURE 2-7. *A Third Satellite Produces a 2-D Fix. Adding the signal and the corresponding computed distance from a third satellite narrows the region for your location as shown by the black triangle on the diagram. By assuming your altitude to be near the Earth, your GPS unit will adjust its internal clock until the circles formed by the three computed distances converge to a point. This is illustrated by the narrow three white lines within the black triangle. Your 2-D fix position is indicated by the black dot at their intersection. This fix is of degraded quality since it is based on an assumption. Generally, the GPS will provide a position to within 100 feet (30 m) or so. The Satellite screen will indicate that you have achieved a 2-D fix. This fix can be used for navigation with care should the signals from more satellites not be forthcoming.*

FIGURE 2-8. *The 3-D Fix. Signals from a fourth satellite enable the GPS receiver to compute precise time and establish a 3-D fix. The fourth satellite allows the receiver to refine its internal clock further while computing a value for altitude as well as latitude and longitude—thus a 3-D fix. Altitude accuracy is not nearly as great as that for horizontal position due to the geometry of the satellites.*

latitude, longitude, and altitude. The receiver can refine its clock's accuracy with signals from three or more satellites.

The addition of a third satellite produces a third COP on the Earth as shown in figure 2-7. This creates three bands that clearly define the region for your location that would still appear to be a wide area. If a value for altitude is assumed, such as zero (not an unreasonable assumption for a boater), the GPS can adjust its clock until the distances computed from each of the three satellites produce a solution that is nearly a single point. This becomes the computed two-dimensional (2-D) fix. Its accuracy is somewhat limited because it involves some assumptions, but it generally produces reasonable accuracy within hundreds of feet.

By adding the signal from a fourth satellite, the GPS can further refine its accuracy and produce what is known as a *3-D fix*. The receiver further refines the adjustment of the clock until the navigation solution converges to a single precise point, as shown in figure 2-8. This solution provides a highly accurate horizontal position (latitude and longitude), generally to within 33 to 50 feet (10–15 m). It also provides a solution for altitude that is somewhat less precise owing to the geometry of the satellites. Generally, altitude accuracy is poorer by 50 percent or greater than

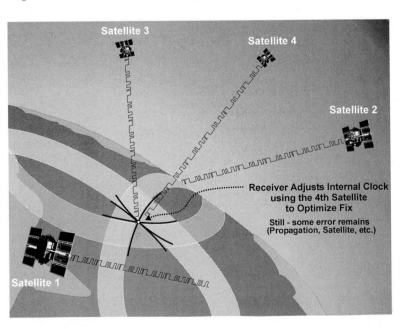

Satellite 3

Satellite 4

Satellite 2

Receiver Adjusts Internal Clock using the 4th Satellite to Optimize Fix

Still - some error remains (Propagation, Satellite, etc.)

Satellite 1

the comparable horizontal accuracy for any fix. The time reported by the GPS is very precise.

As described in the following sections, most current GPS units receive simultaneous signals from a dozen satellites. The GPS receiver selects the four satellites in the best positions to obtain a 3-D fix. The receiver monitors the other satellites and continuously substitutes better-positioned ones to achieve an accurate fix, since the satellites move over time from your vantage point. Also, when a satellite signal is blocked by objects on your boat, the GPS receiver drops the weak satellite and substitutes one that can be "seen."

The Native Language of Navigation

The language of marine navigation is *latitude* and *longitude*. A specific location is represented by a set of *coordinates*. This is your address, much like a street address within a city citing the intersection of east–west streets with north–south streets. Figure 2-9 shows how latitude and longitude are defined. Latitude is measured from the equator at 0° to 90° North or South at the respective poles. Longitude is measured from the prime meridian at 0° in a direction west or east to 180° meeting at the international date line (at which point the calendar day changes by one). The prime meridian (zero longitude) is the longitude of Greenwich, England. The prime meridian at Greenwich also is used as the reference location for time called *Coordinated Universal Time* (UTC). Anyone on the Earth can determine their local time as compared with UTC by subtracting one hour for each time zone they are west of Greenwich, or adding if they are east of Greenwich.

Its ability to tell you your latitude and longitude is why the GPS receiver is so useful to mariners. The GPS unit also provides a value for altitude and precise time. While this is the only information that these expensive satellites tell us, it nonetheless is important information not otherwise easily obtained.

Your GPS unit also provides a wide range of other information useful to the mariner. This information is computed within your GPS receiver by comparing

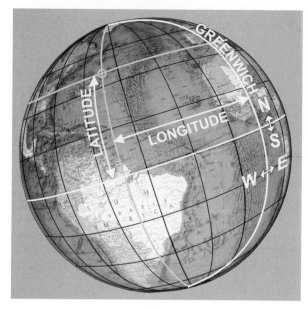

FIGURE 2-9. *Latitude and Longitude: The Street Address of Navigation. The GPS unit presents the boater with two key pieces of information as coordinates: latitude and longitude. These coordinates indicate our location north or south from the equator, and east or west from the prime meridian that passes through Greenwich, England.*

your current position with an earlier position, or by comparing your current position to that of another location that you have stored in the receiver's memory. For example, the GPS unit derives information regarding your direction and speed by comparing your current coordinates to those at a slightly earlier time. The receiver provides the direction to steer the boat to a fixed object, and the object's distance from the receiver, by comparing your current coordinates with those of the object toward which you are headed.

As noted earlier, the Earth is not a perfect sphere — it bulges more at the equator than at the poles, a shape known as an *oblate spheroid*. The Earth's diameter through the equator is some 23 nautical miles greater than through the poles. In order to draw the COPs on the surface of the Earth based on the distance from each satellite, the GPS unit must have a reasonably accurate model for the Earth's shape. This model is known as a *datum*. The precise spot where the computed distance from the satellite intersects the Earth's surface is dependent upon this model. Over the years, scientists have refined the model. The most recent

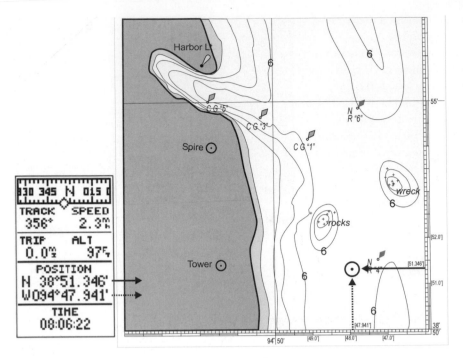

FIGURE 2-10. *GPS Position (Latitude and Longitude) and Charts. The GPS receiver has no idea of the conditions surrounding your present location, so you must plot the GPS-provided latitude and longitude coordinates representing your location on a chart to determine if it is safe to proceed. This is a somewhat tedious process, but it is very important for making navigation decisions and avoiding danger.*

Otherwise, your GPS position will not correspond with charted objects. The datum is listed in the title block of each chart. Most modern-day charts use WGS-84. There are a number of other datum grid systems in use by foreign countries and other applications such as the U.S. Geological Survey charts. GPS receivers can process position using many of these systems.

While the GPS unit tells you your latitude and longitude, it tells you nothing about what is to be found at or near that location. To learn that, you must go to a chart (fig. 2-10) using that same datum and plot the GPS address on the chart. You need the chart to tell you about the local environment such as landmasses, water depth, hazards, aids to navigation, etc. Chapter 4 contains more detailed information about using charts with your GPS receiver.

version is known as WGS-84 (World Geodetic Survey 1984). It is essential that the datum used for the calculation in the GPS receiver corresponds with the datum used to compile the paper or electronic chart that you use to mark latitude and longitude for fixed objects.

Chapter 3

Your GPS Receiver

Your GPS receiver is a marvel of engineering. The core function of the GPS unit is to receive and process signals from satellites, and to compute a set of coordinates for your current position. In effect, the GPS unit is a radio receiver attached to a miniature computer. Manufacturers have expanded the computing functions and created software to provide an excellent set of navigation tools, many of which apply to the mariner. The first portable GPS unit was designed and built for the military (see fig. 3-1). Developed in the 1980s, the entire unit weighed 15 pounds (7 kg) and was worn like a backpack. It cost over $40,000 and could process the signals from only one satellite at a time. We have come a long way since then. Today's handheld GPS unit weighs some 10 ounces (300 g), costs as little as $100, processes a dozen satellite channels at the same time, does a great deal more, and works better and faster than its predecessors.

The quality of a fix is dependent upon good signals from the GPS satellites and the relative placement of the satellites. For a good latitude and longitude determination, you need satellites that are arrayed at various bearings from your location, somewhat away from directly overhead. It is easy to appreciate that two visual bearings on closely spaced objects do not give a good fix. Bearings on two objects almost 90° apart from your location give a far better

FIGURE 3-1. *The Original "Handheld" GPS Receiver. The Manpack weighed 15 pounds (7 kg) and was worn as a backpack. This GPS unit was a single-channel receiver costing some $40,000, whereas today's handheld GPS receivers have 12 channels, cost as little as $100, and do a great deal more.* (ROCKWELL COLLINS)

fix. Figures 3-2 and 3-3 illustrate optimum satellite positioning, or *quality factor*. This factor is called *geometric dilution of precision* (GDOP). Some GPS receivers display the value of GDOP. The closer the GDOP number to 1, the better. The computer within the receiver selects the satellites that produce the best combination of signal strength and GDOP. For most applications, the selection of satellites is optimized to give you an accurate latitude and longitude. For this reason, the altitude value, even with a 3-D fix, generally is not as accurate.

Manufacturers programmed the computer in your GPS receiver to provide an array of functions that may be useful for navigation. This section provides you with an appreciation for how these functions work and what they mean to a boater. Armed with what you learn here, you can determine what you want to use and then figure out how to access that mode on your specific receiver model.

Using Your GPS Receiver

By now, you are itching to turn on your GPS receiver. So, before diving into the details of buttons, pages, and menus, let's look at what happens when you turn it on. At this point you should be aware that the GPS unit has only a few buttons, but many functions. Since practical design and cost limits the number of buttons used on the receiver, the manufacturer relies on menus and submenus to set up and access these preprogrammed functions. Those familiar with computers will recognize the concept of menus, submenus, and drop-down menus. However, the structure of these menus is a source of endless confusion and frustration for many users. It can be exasperating to find that one function you seek may involve working your way through several tiers of menus, as the following example demonstrates.

In this first example, we will set the GPS unit in the Simulator mode. Having the receiver in this mode will be very useful to navigate through the other material in this section. For some GPS models, setting up the Simulator mode can be slightly complex, so we have provided step-by-step in-

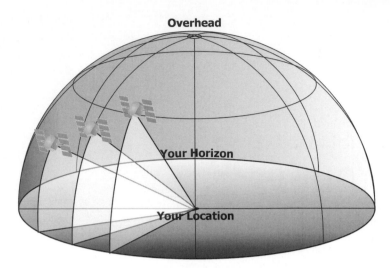

Poor GDOP - satellites too close together

FIGURE 3-2. *Satellites from the Same Region of the Sky Provide a Poor Fix. With all of the satellites bunched together, it is quite easy for an object to block the signals from reaching the antenna. The accuracy of a fix is dependent upon satellite geometry. If the available satellites are all closely spaced, the accuracy of the fix is adversely affected. The GPS receiver attempts to select satellites that are the most widely spaced of those available. The measure of satellite position is called* geometric dilution of precision *(GDOP). The lower the GDOP, the better the fix. GDOP is a number multiplied by the basic accuracy of GPS to indicate the current accuracy. A GDOP of 1 is ideal; 3 is poor.*

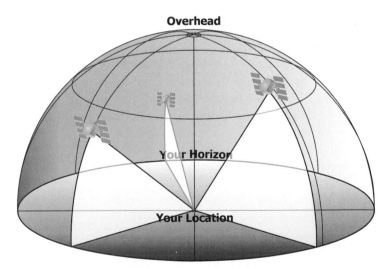

Good GDOP - satellites well spread

FIGURE 3-3. *Widely Separated Satellites Provide a Good Fix. Satellites from widely separated regions of the sky produce a lower GDOP and a higher-quality fix.*

structions for two typical GPS units. If your receiver is very different from those described, you may want to build up the courage to tackle the manual that came with it.

Start-Up: Simulation and Initialization

The GPS unit is turned on using the "Power" button. Typically, after pressing this button and holding it down for a second or two, the receiver displays some instructional or supplier information and disclaimers. Pressing "Enter" acknowledges this screen and advances to the Satellite screen, described shortly. The GPS unit will automatically attempt to "acquire" satellites. If you are indoors it is unlikely that you will have sufficient signal strength to acquire satellites. Indoors and in other situations, however, you can use the Simulator mode, which allows you to practice using all of the functions of the GPS unit under lifelike conditions, or to enter and review data. Appendix 1 provides detailed instructions for activating the Simulator mode on a number of handheld GPS receivers. The next section summarizes the Simulator and how to set it up.

Simulator

At this point, your GPS unit should be turned on.

To enter the Simulator mode from the Satellite screen, press the "Menu" button, if your GPS receiver has one (see the next paragraph if it does not). A submenu should come up with "Start Simulator" as one of the choices. Once you have located the Simulator option, scroll down using the cursor key until this menu item is highlighted, and then press "Enter" to activate. Some GPS units bring up an interim page asking you to confirm that you want to use the Simulator; if this page appears, follow the instructions and

press "Enter" again. There is a reason for all of this caution: the last thing you would want to do is accidentally put the GPS receiver into the Simulator mode when you are attempting to navigate on the water. For the same reasons, most GPS units, once powered down, will go automatically into the Normal mode rather than into the Simulator mode when powered on again.

If you have a Garmin GPS 12 or similar model (fig. 3-4), there is no "Menu" button. You get to the Simulator by paging (pressing "Page" repeatedly) until you reach the Main Menu. On the Main Menu, scroll down and select "Setup Menu" using the up-down motion of the cursor, and then press "Enter." Do the same thing on this next page, selecting "System Setup." On this final page, select the "Mode" field. Scroll down from "Normal" until you see "Simulator." Now press "Enter" one more time to activate.

This brief example shows how complicated the GPS receiver menu structure can seem. Once you get

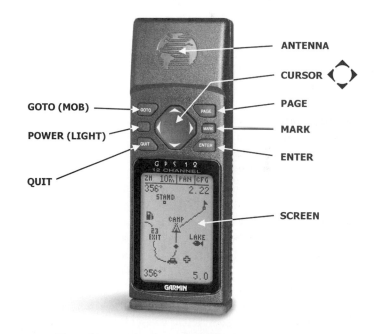

FIGURE 3-4. *Typical Layout for a Basic Handheld GPS Receiver. The buttons, pages, and menus are similar from one GPS model to another, but each has its own particular structure. This Garmin GPS 12 is a basic high-quality handheld. The 12-channel receiver provides quality position information, but the display has moderate resolution and other functions are somewhat limited. The pages from this model provide the baseline for this part of the book.* (GARMIN)

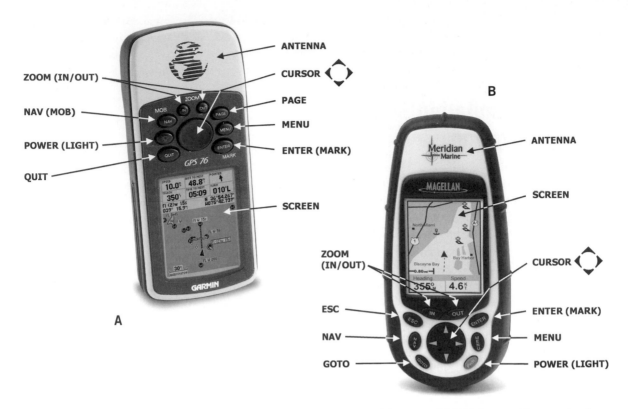

FIGURES 3-5A *and* 3-5B. *Layouts for Other Handheld GPS Models. A newer model Garmin GPS 76 that provides a marine database of buoys and aids to navigation is shown in figure 3-5a. The screen is higher resolution than the GPS 12, and the unit has more buttons. A Magellan Meridian Marine unit is shown in figure 3-5b. This GPS receiver has the ability to display maps as well as the marine database. Functionally, both provide similar marine capability.* (GARMIN AND MAGELLAN)

the sense of how your GPS unit uses menus and submenus, you will find this process less intimidating. Also, understanding the menu structure will enable you to find what you are looking for by trial and error, even if you do not have the manual available. If you had trouble following the scenario, or have a different GPS receiver, check in appendix 1 for a detailed description. Figures 3-5a and 3-5b show two models with "Menu" buttons.

Your GPS receiver is now in the Simulator mode. This means it is functioning much as it would if it had acquired real satellites. The Simulator shuts off the signal-receiving section of the GPS unit and uses a stored position as your current location. If this is the first time you have used the unit, it may think it is in some faraway place, perhaps where the GPS receiver was manufactured. If you have previously used your GPS receiver, it may assume you are at the last position where it was operating with real satellite signals. The process of acquiring satellite signals is described next. In this section, you will be working with the basic buttons and pages. To follow along using your GPS receiver in the Simulator mode, it is not important that it simulate your current location. If it is important to you to have the location correct, the easiest way to do that is to shut it off, go outside, power up the receiver, and let it go through the automatic initialization process described in the next section. Then activate the Simulator mode by repeating the preceding process.

Initialization

If you are outside, you will want to use the GPS receiver in the "Normal" navigation mode. Once you turn on the receiver and clear the disclaimer page, the GPS unit will begin to acquire satellites. By the way, manufacturers use the disclaimer page to remind you that they do not want you to put your life in their hands by relying solely on the GPS receiver for your safety!

Once it's turned on, the first task the GPS unit performs is satellite acquisition, a process known as *initialization*. To do this, the receiver needs an unobstructed view of the sky. If you do nothing other than turn it on, the GPS receiver ultimately will acquire satellites. This is called a *cold start*. Acquiring satellites can take several minutes or more depending upon the model. The reason for this is simple: the GPS unit has no idea which satellites are in view unless it knows roughly where you are. Unless you have previously used it in the same general area, it must go through the repertoire of satellites until it finds one in view. Once this satellite is acquired, data begin to flow, and the receiver now has some idea which other satellites are in view. The GPS unit then tunes to these satellites and acquires them one at a time. Most GPS units give you an option to accelerate the process by selecting a country or state from a menu. After a GPS receiver has once acquired satellites and developed a fix, the receiver will assume this last position the next time it is turned on. This accelerated satellite acquisition process is called a *warm start*.

Buttons, Screens, and Menus

Each GPS model has its own unique structure of buttons, screens, and menus. The buttons are the means whereby you access specific screens and enter data. The screens provide you with information you need for navigation. Many of these screens allow you to customize the presentation of information to suit your specific needs and interests. The menus are special screens that enable you to set up your GPS receiver, select other screens, and set modes of operation. Understanding these screens, what they tell you, how to use them, and which are most useful is a subject of paramount importance to boaters. Once you know what you want, it is simply a matter of how to access and use the appropriate screens.

The major manufacturers learn from each other

and from their customers' reactions as to which features customers find useful. As a result, there are more similarities than differences between current GPS receivers. What may be unique is the exact sequence of buttons you need to press to accomplish what you want. Each GPS receiver model, even two models offered by the same manufacturer, may differ in the way you access functions and features. Ultimately, there may be no alternative to deciphering the manual to access specifically what you want, but most units have a lot in common. Armed with the information in this book, you will likely be able to find what you want even if you don't have a manual in front of you—or possess the patience to read it. In any event, with knowledge of the structure and rationale behind the GPS receiver, you will have a far easier time using your model and a renewed appreciation for what your receiver does.

Many people are concerned that they can somehow break their GPS receiver by pressing the buttons. Be assured that experimenting with the buttons is highly unlikely to inflict damage but is very likely to lead you to the mode you seek. Also, most missteps can be reversed prior to pressing "Enter" by pressing the "Quit" key. Under some circumstances, it may be possible to disrupt a course that you have in progress, which you may not wish to do. Those menu functions that do disrupt a course in progress are highlighted in chapter 4 at Preventing an Accidental Change in the Active Course.

At this point, with your GPS unit turned on, you may wish to follow along with the explanations by pressing the buttons discussed to familiarize yourself with your particular GPS receiver and how it handles. More details on buttons, screens, and menus follow in this chapter (see appendix 2 for specifics on a number of the major handheld GPS models).

Buttons

Most GPS receivers have a limited number of buttons, which control all of the functions. You access these functions through menus and submenus, as demonstrated by your task of setting the GPS unit to the Simulator mode that was described earlier. Typical functions that are deemed important enough to be assigned their own buttons are summarized in figure 3-6 and described below. Not all these buttons are on every GPS model. Typical GPS receiver button names and layouts are similar, with subtle differences. Appendix 2 describes button structures for a number of handheld GPS units and compares them with our baseline list. As can be seen by comparing figures 3-4, 3-5a, and 3-5b, there are differences even within a company's product line. Garmin is selected for presentation purposes because it has a large selection of handheld GPS receivers. Various handheld models from Magellan, Lowrance, Standard Horizon, and others are equally good; choose a receiver based on your personal preferences and what features you want in a GPS unit.

Typical Buttons—not available on every GPS model

• Power (Light)	turns unit on and off and backlight on and off
• Page	scrolls through available screens
• Menu	displays menu of functions
• Enter	similar to "Enter" on keyboard
• Mark	used to mark current position
• Quit	similar to "Esc" key—go back one step
• GoTo (Nav)	used to select places or places to go
• Zoom (In/Out)	sets scale of "Map" and "Highway" pages
• Cursor	used to highlight a field or scroll on the "Map" page
• MOB	Man Overboard for emergencies

FIGURE 3-6. GPS Receiver Buttons and Their Functions. Each GPS unit employs buttons similar to those listed, but any particular unit will use only some of those shown. Manufacturers save on cost and reduce receiver size by using a few buttons to do many tasks, but this makes the GPS a bit more difficult to use. You need to access menus and submenus to find the function you seek.

Typical buttons offered on a GPS unit are summarized below with a brief description of each button's function(s). The button functions are described in greater detail in subsequent sections. Although it's unlikely any unit has all of these buttons, be assured the feature is available even if the manufacturer did not choose to provide a dedicated button for that task. Some buttons perform dual functions. Usually the primary function is labeled on the button, and the secondary function is labeled on the case next to the button, often in a different color. You access the secondary function usually by pressing the button a second time.

Power

The "Power" button turns the unit on and off and turns on the backlight. With most units, you must press the "Power" button for a few seconds to shut off the receiver. Often, a countdown display indicates how many seconds remain until it is powered off. Some GPS units permit adjustment of both backlight and contrast by pressing the "Power" button briefly while the unit is operating. Some units display two slider bars on the screen that you adjust by using the cursor key (usually this is up or down for backlight, left or right for contrast). Other GPS units have several levels of backlighting that are accessed by sequentially pressing the "Power" button until the desired illumination is achieved.

Enter (Mark)

The "Enter" button is used much like the "Enter" key on a computer keyboard. Pressing this button causes the GPS receiver to execute a task. Some GPS units also use this button to mark points of interest (waypoints). If the key is labeled "Enter/Mark," you can store (Mark) a position in the receiver's memory by pressing the key twice.

Quit

The "Quit" button is used much like the "Esc" key on a computer keyboard. Pressing this key will usually return you to the previous screen you were viewing. Some GPS receivers label this button "Esc" or "Clear."

Zoom In/Out

The "Zoom In/Out" feature usually consists of two buttons. They are used for the Map screen and the Highway screen to set the scale of the screens. Each press of either key advances the scale by one increment, as determined by the setting on the individual GPS receiver.

Mark

"Mark" is sometimes available as a separate key. If it is not, you will access "Mark" using a dual-function key (such as "Enter"). Pressing it "marks" the current position and stores it in the receiver's memory, usually assigning it an identifying number.

GoTo

"GoTo" is often assigned its own button. This function is used to tell the GPS unit where you want to go. Pressing it will usually bring up a list of stored waypoints from which you make a selection. Alternatively, it will assume you want to go to the point under the cursor that you have scrolled to on the Map screen (this is described later in this chapter). Pressing the "GoTo" or "Enter" button at any time that a waypoint is highlighted will cause the GPS receiver to compute the course and distance to that waypoint and begin navigation. This action will replace any previous navigation that was in process.

Nav

Some GPS units have a "Nav" button instead of "GoTo." If your receiver has a "Nav" button, you press that key to get to a submenu that usually contains "GoTo" and other navigation functions such as "Route" and "Find." Advance to the desired submenu by scrolling with the cursor and then select it by pressing the "Enter" button. Activating "GoTo" a waypoint by pressing "Enter" replaces any prior navigation process.

MOB

Your GPS unit may have a separate "MOB" (man overboard) button. When you press this button, the GPS receiver records your current position and displays steering directions, so you can return to that exact spot to pick up someone who fell overboard. On some GPS receivers, "MOB" is a secondary function of another button such as "Mark" or "Nav." On these receivers, "MOB" is activated by pressing and holding down the dual-use button, or by pressing it twice—

check your manual. The "MOB" button is more often found on fixed-mount GPS receivers, which are larger than handhelds and can accommodate more buttons. Once activated, MOB supercedes any previous navigation process that was underway.

Cursor

The "Cursor" usually is a large, four-way rocker switch around which the other, smaller buttons are arrayed. On most screens, you can access individual functions by scrolling the cursor to highlight that function and pressing "Enter" to get to the next screen. You can also use this key to scroll around the Map screen and to select data to enter into the GPS receiver.

Menu

The "Menu" button may be used for direct access to the menus that control the GPS unit. There may be more than one screen of menus that can be accessed by repeatedly pressing the button until the desired screen is reached. You select the desired function from the menu by highlighting it using the cursor and pressing "Enter."

Page

The "Page" button is used to scroll through a sequence of screens (or pages) that display different information. Some Magellan units use the "Nav" button to select the appropriate screen.

Find

The "Find" button is offered on some newer GPS units. It facilitates finding points of interest, usually through submenus. Points of interest may include prestored lists of cities, services, or locations usually provided with the GPS unit.

Screens

Most GPS receivers use screens, or pages, similar to those shown in the photos in this section. The layout and presentation may vary, and in some cases, you may have options as to what they display. On some models, you can select data fields to suit your navigation needs and preferences. This section is intended to provide you with an understanding and overview of

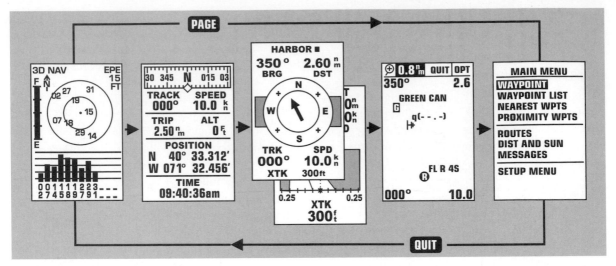

FIGURE 3-7. GPS Screens Are Accessed Sequentially by Pressing "Page." The GPS receiver provides a number of different information presentations to the user. Each screen provides a different perspective and different information. The screens are accessed sequentially on this Garmin model by pressing the "Page" button. The process can be reversed using the "Quit" button to return to the previous screen. (ADAPTED FROM IMAGES BY GARMIN)

the purpose and utility of each screen as it relates to marine navigation. Figure 3-7 shows typical screens of a Garmin GPS receiver. Each time the "Page" button is pressed, the receiver jumps to the next screen. Once the last page is selected, pressing "Page" returns you to the first screen. Conversely, each time that the "Quit" button is pressed, the receiver returns to the previous screen. The next chapter includes further details about using these displays for navigation. Some of the figures that follow provide examples of comparable screens on different GPS models.

Satellite Screen

Figures 3-8a and 3-8b show the satellites visible to the receiver by satellite number (each satellite is assigned a unique number) on a sky-view map centered on you. Concentric circles generally indicate the horizon, 45° above the horizon, and a point or cross for directly overhead. (Figure 3-9 shows the relationship between the satellites and circles in 3-D.) The height of each bar indicates the relative signal strength from that particular satellite as identified by its satellite number. A hollow bar indicates that the GPS unit is receiving a signal from a specific satellite. A darkened bar indicates that the receiver has acquired this satellite and is receiving navigation data from it. If a satel-

lite number is shown but no bar, the satellite is in view, but you're not receiving a signal from that satellite.

This screen also may show the relative battery power remaining, and possibly a geometric dilution of precision (GDOP), which was discussed earlier in this chapter, and/or *estimated position error* (EPE) indicating an approximate accuracy in feet. Some GPS models also provide your current position on the Satellite screen, as shown in figure 3-8b.

As a user, you should check this screen to verify that the GPS unit indicates that most of the satellites shown have been acquired. If a sector of satellites has not been acquired, check the antenna placement to ensure that its visibility to the sky has not been blocked. Usually, the screen provides an indication of "Acquiring Satellites," "2-D Nav," or "3-D Nav" to let you know the GPS receiver's operating status. Alternatively, it may indicate "Simulator" if you are in that mode. The EPE gives you a good indication of the accuracy that the GPS unit believes you should be achieving.

Position Screen

The Position screen is for informational purposes. This screen typically has the most data fields compared to

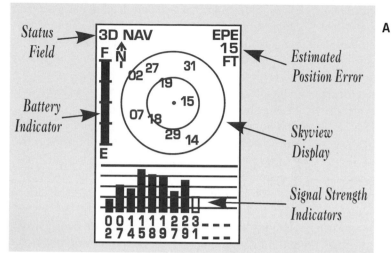

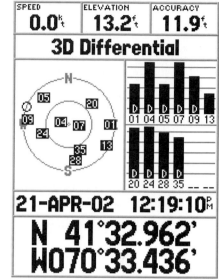

FIGURES 3-8A *and* 3-8B. *Satellite Screens. The "Satellite" screen tells us information about the signals received by the GPS receiver. Circles represent the horizon and the sky with potentially visible satellites identified by direction and altitude. The signal strengths of these satellites are shown as vertical bars on both screens. Hollow bars (as shown in fig. 3-8a) represent a satellite signal being received. Solid bars indicate that the satellite is providing navigation information. The higher the bar, the stronger the received signal. Some GPS units provide an indication of battery strength on this page. The status field indicates the current mode, such as "Acquiring Satellites," "2-D Nav," "3-D Nav," or "3-D Differential." Most units provide a measure of estimated position error (EPE) as a computed measure of the current horizontal accuracy. Figure 3-8a shows the Satellite screen from a Garmin GPS 12, and 3-8b shows the Satellite screen from a Garmin GPS 76. The GPS 76 has a higher resolution screen and therefore can display data in greater detail. The D's in some of the bars indicate that these satellites are providing a WAAS differential quality signal, explained in chapter 10.*
(ADAPTED FROM IMAGES BY GARMIN)

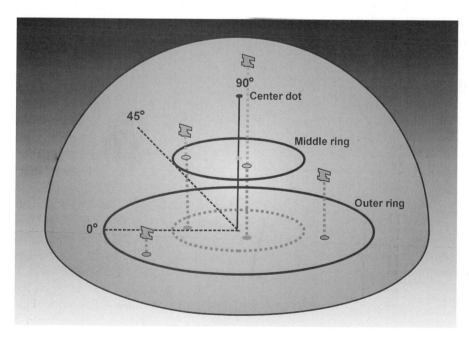

FIGURE 3-9. *A 3-D Depiction of the Sky-View Display. The sky-view display shows a top view of where the satellites are located. The concentric circles of the sky-view display, viewed in three dimensions as in this illustration, present the azimuth and elevation of individual satellites as viewed from your current location.*

other GPS receiver pages. Figure 3-10 shows a graphic display on a Position screen. The display appears similar to the edge face of a standard magnetic compass—but it's not a compass. The center of the display indicates your current course over ground. From the Setup Menu, you can set the direction to either true or magnetic north. The Position screen also provides the current latitude and longitude, as well as GPS time. The time can be adjusted to local time or UTC (Coordinated Universal Time) in the Setup Menu. Other data fields provide current course over ground and speed over ground. This particular GPS model offers two user-selectable data fields: in figure 3-10, trip odometer and altitude. Other data fields are described later in this chapter. Not all GPS units present a Position screen per se, but the same information is available on one or more other pages. For example, the GPS 76 (fig. 3-8b) provides position on the Satellite screen.

The Position screen provides the principal information in data format that you need to navigate. The ribbon display provides information in graphical format, scrolling left or right as you navigate to maintain the current course in the center. The direction indicates the direction of the boat over ground (called "course over ground"—COG—or "track"—TRK). This display looks a great deal like your boat compass, especially if you use the magnetic mode. However, this screen may not match the ship's compass, which displays the heading of the boat, not its direction over the ground. Heading is the direction in which the bow is pointing. To illustrate the difference, note that on the water, wind or the current is often pushing the boat to one side. The course over ground is a product of both the power supplied to the boat and the effects of the wind and/or current. Consequently, *do not use the GPS unit as a substitute for your compass unless you do so under conditions with no wind or current.* Similarly, the speed indicated by the GPS receiver is "speed over ground" (SOG) rather than speed over the water. The receiver does not know what the wind and current conditions are around you, so it calculates your actual motion over the ground (and on the chart). Speed instruments on the boat measure the boat's motion through the water and do not take into account the fact that the water may be moving in a current. *Do not use the GPS unit to calibrate your speed log or vice versa.*

The GPS receiver determines speed and direction by comparing your current position with your earlier position, and by computing the course and speed from the change in position over the elapsed time. It is important to recognize that a GPS unit provides accurate direction only if you are moving. *Do not attempt to use a GPS receiver for current direction while on a stationary boat.*

Many Position screens also provide bearing and distance to the active waypoint. The GPS receiver will tell you

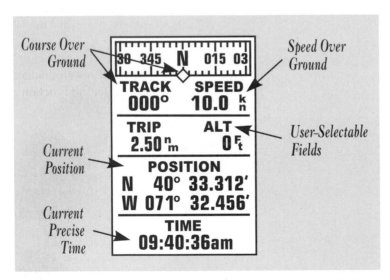

FIGURE 3-10. *The Position Screen. The Position screen provides a lot of information useful to the navigator. An analog representation of COG is prominently displayed. The current track is shown in the center. The GPS receiver does not present boat heading, but does provide the direction or course of the boat over ground, also known as "Track." Track can be shown as true or magnetic based on how the receiver is set up and the user's preference. GPS is not a substitute for a compass. The current coordinates are shown, along with a number of other data fields. Some of these data fields are user selectable (in this case, trip distance and altitude). With a 3-D fix, the GPS provides very precise time. Not all GPS receivers have a Position screen, but, if not, the same data can be found on other screens.*

Typical user-selectable data fields

- **Position Page**
  - Trip Odometer
  - Trip Timer
  - Elapsed Time
  - Average Speed
  - Maximum Speed
  - Altitude

- **Highway Page**
  - Est Time Enroute
  - Est Time Arrival
  - Course to Steer
  - Crosstrack Error
  - Velocity Made Good
  - Turn (degrees)

FIGURE 3-11. Some Typical Optional Data Fields. A GPS unit includes a course computer attached to the signal receivers. A GPS receiver calculates a variety of useful information by comparing your current location with that of a short time earlier. A receiver presents this information in optional data fields. The figure lists typical data fields from Garmin and Magellan GPS units. The selection of data fields depends on the user's application. Boaters are interested in trip information, crosstrack error, and velocity made good, among others. Optional data fields permit the user to select which information is displayed. These data fields can be changed at any time, and the current information will be displayed for that field.

the direction and distance to that waypoint as a bearing and as a distance in degrees and nautical miles (or other format you select). Chapter 4 describes waypoints in more detail.

This Position screen provides a number of data fields, some of which are user selectable. Figure 3-11 shows typical user-selectable fields available on some of the GPS screens. Some Position screen user-selectable fields include the following.

Trip Odometer

The Trip Odometer provides a resettable value of the distance traveled since "Trip" was last reset. The odometer can be reset by moving the cursor down to highlight the Trip Odometer field and pressing "Enter" to get a menu of options, one of which is "Reset." You can use this reset technique on the other user-selectable data fields below.

Trip Timer

The Trip Timer provides a resettable value of the elapsed time that the boat has been moving since "Trip" was last reset.

Elapsed Time

Elapsed Time provides a value of the elapsed time since it last was reset. Elapsed Time operates independently from the Trip Timer.

Average Speed

Average Speed provides an aggregate average speed of the boat since average speed was last reset.

Maximum Speed

Maximum Speed provides a peak value of speed over ground since maximum speed was last reset.

Altitude

Altitude provides a value corresponding to the altitude of the GPS unit above mean sea level. This value is not as accurate as a horizontal position due to the geometry of the satellites that have been selected to optimize horizontal position. This value may vary by 100 feet (30 m) or so from the actual altitude, and may continue to change. You'll find you don't have much use for this function while boating!

Map Screen

Figures 3-12a, 3-12b, and 3-12c show the Map screens of several GPS models. In fig. 3-12a, your current location is indicated by a cross or a symbol such as a triangle (some units let you select the symbol). A dotted-line trail indicates your past course over ground (if the track function has been activated). Waypoints and other objects whose coordinates have been preloaded into the GPS receiver also will appear if they are within the field of view of the current screen. The field of view usually is selectable with a zoom feature. Zoom is controlled either with dedicated buttons or through menu options on the Map screen.

Data fields indicate current course over ground and speed over ground. Two other data fields indicate the bearing and distance to the waypoint you have selected. The display also indicates the level of

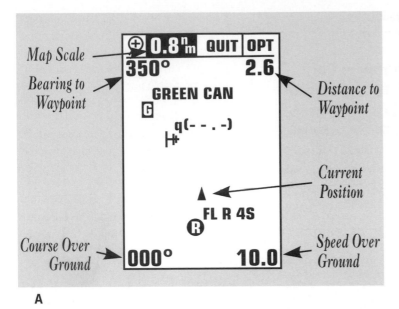

Map Scale

Bearing to Waypoint

Distance to Waypoint

Current Position

Course Over Ground

Speed Over Ground

A

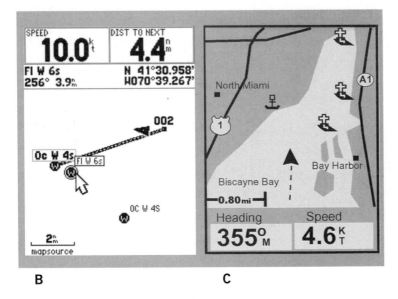

B

C

FIGURES 3-12A, 3-12B, and 3-12C. Typical Map Screens. The Map screen presents current position and other objects within view. This is one of the most useful GPS receiver screens, provided that other objects of interest have been pre-entered into the receiver. This screen also provides data fields—typically the bearing and distance to a selected point called a waypoint. The Map screen can be zoomed in or out to different scales showing more or fewer objects. Figure 3-12a shows a Garmin GPS 48 Map screen, which contains the least information of the three Map screens shown. Figure 3-12b is from a Garmin GPS 76. This figure demonstrates the effectiveness of a higher-resolution display with a database of aids to navigation. Figure 3-12c shows a Magellan Meridian Marine Map screen with display of streets and aids to navigation. (SCREENSHOTS COURTESY GARMIN AND MAGELLAN)

zoom and scale in miles of the map display.

The Map screen is one of the most useful displays on a GPS unit, especially if utilized effectively. To be useful, the map needs to have objects other than the boat displayed. The map will show all waypoints (and, in some models, stored data) entered into the GPS receiver that are within the field of view of the current zoom. Chapter 4 includes a great deal more information about the Map screen.

If you have selected a waypoint and your location, the GPS receiver draws a line from your location directly to that waypoint. That course line stays on the page in its original position until you select that waypoint from another location or select a different waypoint. The bearing and distance to the selected waypoint is constantly updated to reflect your current position.

Compass Screen

Figures 3-13a, 3-13b, and 3-13c show typical Compass screens from three different GPS models, with a compass rose indicating the cardinal course (N, S, E, or W) on top, track (course over ground) and speed over ground, and information regarding the bearing and distance to the user's selected waypoint. On some models, the name of the waypoint is also displayed, as well as a user-selectable field for XTK or XTE (Crosstrack Error). The Compass screen uses an arrow to indicate the direction to the selected waypoint relative to your current course, which is straight up on the display.

The Compass screen provides a rough graphical interpretation of COG or Track direction. It is not as detailed as the ribbon compass presentation on the Position screen. Data fields on other screens may show the same information. The selection of any screen for navigation is a matter of personal preference. The Compass screen may be more useful to hikers than mariners, since hikers are more likely to prefer the simplified pointing information on this display. For mariners, an alternative known as the Highway screen may be more useful.

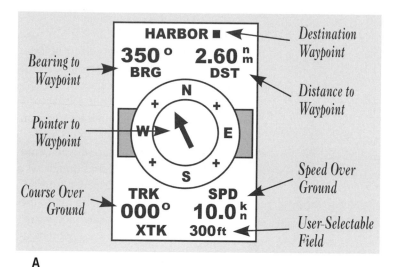

A

B   C

FIGURES 3-13A, 3-13B, and 3-13C. Compass Screens. The Compass screen shows general direction of motion (COG and Track) and a pointer to the selected waypoint. The Compass screen for the Garmin GPS 12, shown in figure 3-13a, shows the information in a different format. The compass is circular with ordinal directions. An arrow in the middle shows the relative direction to the selected waypoint. Bearing and distance to that waypoint are shown digitally. Other data fields are also available. Figure 3-13b shows the same screen on a Garmin GPS 76, which features a more refined compass card. Figure 3-13c shows a similar presentation on a Magellan Meridian Marine unit.
(SCREENSHOTS COURTESY GARMIN AND MAGELLAN)

Highway Screen

Figures 3-14a, 3-14b, and 3-14c show the Highway screens of three different GPS models. On some GPS units, you can display either the Compass screen or the Highway screen in the paging sequence, but not both. To select the other, you press "Enter" while viewing one of these two screens. The GPS receiver will present you with the option of selecting the alternate display. The receiver will present the selected choice in the page sequence until the selection is changed by the user.

The Highway screen shows a 3-D depiction of your position on an imaginary highway. The viewpoint is from a spot somewhat above your current location and looking in the direction you are moving. The centerline on the highway represents the original course line drawn when you selected the active waypoint. The highway's width is provided to give you a perspective on the degree of zoom on the display and does not correspond to the relative width of any object. The centerline represents the same course line as presented on the Map screen. In figures 3-14b and 3-14c, you are shown to be "on course." The centerline of the highway lines up with center of the display, and it appears as if you are located in the middle of the highway. The highway stretches straight ahead of you, indicating that you are heading directly toward the waypoint. If you were to port (left) of the track, then the center of the highway would appear to be off to the right. The scale below the highway on this GPS model is set to show the *course deviation indicator* (CDI), or the distance

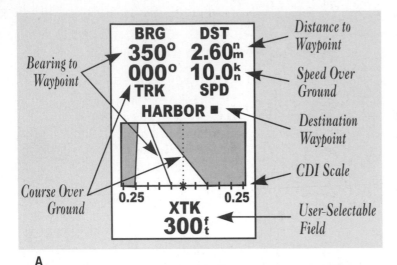

A

Bearing to Waypoint

Course Over Ground

Distance to Waypoint

Speed Over Ground

Destination Waypoint

CDI Scale

User-Selectable Field

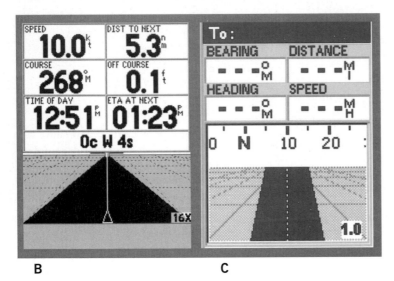

B

C

FIGURES 3-14A, 3-14B, and 3-14C. *Highway Screens. The Highway screen is one of the most useful pages for boaters. This screen appears as an imaginary 3-D highway. In figure 3-14a, you are positioned to the right of the highway center and moving farther off course to starboard (right). The course to steer is 350°, but the current track (TRK), or course over ground, is 000°. If no other action is taken, you will diverge farther from your intended course. The figure represents the Highway screen of a Garmin GPS 12. Data fields show the bearing and distance to the selected waypoint, and your current course over ground, or track, and speed over ground. A user-selectable data field at the bottom of 3-14a shows the number of feet that you are off course (the center of the highway). The helmsman using this display simply maintains the view shown in figures 3-14b or 3-14c to stay on the original course line. Figure 3-14b shows a Highway screen with higher resolution on a Garmin GPS 76. This display can also show other waypoints within the 3-D window. Figure 3-14c shows a Highway screen for a Magellan Meridian Marine. (SCREENSHOTS COURTESY GARMIN AND MAGELLAN)*

by which you are to either port or starboard of the highway centerline. The scale is user selectable. Many manufactures have eliminated CDI on newer GPS models because the *crosstrack error* (XTK or XTE) data field provides the same information.

The Highway screen is one of the two most useful screens for boaters available on a GPS receiver (the Map screen is the other). While the Position screen provides much of the same information, the Highway screen presents information in a graphical format that is easy to visualize and understand. The graphical display is intuitive; the information can be interpreted without consciously processing digital information. You simply navigate so that you remain in the center of the highway with the highway pointed straight ahead.

The Highway screen also provides specific numeric data, such as the bearing and distance to the waypoint, in addition to the current track (course over ground) and speed over ground of the boat. Comparing the bearing to the waypoint from your current position with the track tells you if you are on course.

Typical user-selectable data fields on the Highway screen are given in figure 3-11. You can display additional data fields on the Highway screen; the various options follow. These fields would appear in the place of the "XTK" field shown in figure 3-14a, and provide the following information.

Estimated Time En Route (ETE)
ETE provides the amount of time you can expect it will take for you to reach your current waypoint based on your speed over ground and course over

ground. ETE will change if either (or both) are changed.

Estimated Time of Arrival (ETA)

ETA provides a time estimate of your arrival based on your current speed over ground and course over ground.

Course to Steer (CTS)

CTS provides a recommended course that will bring you back to the original course line efficiently based on a programmed calculation provided by the manufacturer. The GPS receiver makes no automatic adjustments for obstacles that may hinder your path. You need to look for these on your chart and adjust your course accordingly.

Crosstrack Error (XTK)

XTK (XTE on some models) tells you how far (in distance, e.g., nautical miles) you are from the center of the course line. This is a numeric value of the information displayed by the center of the highway on the Highway screen graphic.

Velocity Made Good (VMG)

VMG provides the effective speed of the boat toward your active waypoint. As an example, you may be moving at 10 knots on a track 45° away from the bearing to the waypoint. The VMG, or the effective motion in the direction of the waypoint, is only 7 knots. VMG is especially useful for sailboats wherein you may not be able to sail directly toward your destination, but must tack back and forth toward your objective.

Turn (TRN)

Turn is the angular difference between the current course over ground and the bearing to the waypoint. Turn indicates the number of degrees and the direction (left or right) you must turn to get back on course.

Trip Computer Screen

Some GPS units offer a Trip Computer screen. On some models, the Trip Computer does not appear in the page sequence but is accessed via the menu functions. Generally, the Trip Computer provides a single screen of data that presents many of the data fields outlined previously. Typically, you can reset a group of Trip Computer screen fields for distance, maximum and average speed, time of travel, time in motion and time stopped, and other information. This screen can be very useful for reviewing a day's cruise or for calculating fuel consumption.

Menus

Menus represent the primary means of controlling a GPS receiver. Each receiver has multiple sets of menus and submenus. One set is used to access the navigation functions of the receiver, such as waypoints and routes. A second set is used to control how and what the GPS unit computes and displays. Another set controls the interface between the GPS unit and other devices. The menu structure probably is the source of greatest confusion to new users. The greatest frustration comes when the desired setting is three submenu tiers away, and you cannot remember the first two selections necessary to get there. This section is intended to help you navigate the menus and submenus to find what you seek.

Various GPS units each have a different way of accessing the Main Menu; however, the basic functions of the Main Menus are very similar. Typically, the Main Menu of a specific GPS model is accessed one of two ways. Some GPS receivers have a "Menu" button that facilitates the process. Others enable access to the Main Menu via the "Page" button, with Main Menu being one of the screens in the screen sequence.

Most GPS receivers have multiple menu pages, with functions generally divided into the following categories.

Main Menu—most other functions are accessed through this screen, including the following:

→ Waypoints—*destination points used for navigation*

→ Routes—*sequences of waypoints for navigation*

→ Setup—*controls the GPS receiver and is usually divided into further submenus:*

• System Setup—*controls the GPS unit*

• Navigation Setup—*controls how the GPS receiver computes navigation data*

- Interface Setup—*controls how the GPS receiver talks with other devices*
- Alarms Setup—*allows you to set alarms for various navigation tasks*

This section concentrates on the Main Menu and the Setup submenus. Waypoints and routes are presented in subsequent sections. When you first use your GPS receiver, you will need to set it up to function and display properly depending on your intentions. Boating is fundamentally different from hiking, so you need to set the proper datum (see page 11). Most coastal and offshore mariners use the *magnetic north reference, nautical miles*, and a *position format in degrees, minutes*, and *tenths* as their datum. Most of us prefer to refer to local time rather than UTC, so you will need to enter the *offset* appropriate for your location (the offset is simply the number of hours difference between your current time zone and that of Greenwich, England). The specific selections for position format (e.g., latitude, longitude), map datum, and units depend significantly on where you are using the GPS and the charts or maps that you plan to use with the GPS. For example, boaters on the Great Lakes may be using charts with statute miles and charts calibrated in degrees, minutes, and seconds.

Consequently, you would be better served to set the GPS accordingly. If you are boating on lakes or rivers using USGS topo maps, you will want to set the position format to UTM (Universal Transverse Mercator) to match that unique grid structure. If you're boating in certain areas, such as Alaska, where the charts have not been updated to WGS-84, you will need to check the chart and may find that they may use NAD-27 instead for map datum. All of these are set through the various Setup submenus.

Depending on your GPS model, you can access the Setup submenus either by multiple presses of the "Menu" button or through subordinate screens accessed via the Main Menu. Figure 3-15 shows a typical Main Menu. In the case of the Garmin models GPS 12 or GPS 48, you can access this menu by paging through the various screens until you reach the Main Menu screen. With many other GPS units, you can directly access a similar screen simply by pressing the "Menu" button. You make individual selections on a menu screen by scrolling down to highlight that choice and pressing "Enter." This presents the subordinate functions under that selection, which you can in turn select by scrolling down and pressing "Enter." Usually, you can reverse any step and return to the prior screen by pressing "Quit."

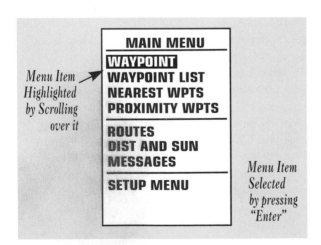

FIGURE 3-15. *The Main Menu. The Main Menu allows access to both the Navigation and Setup screens. Most functions on a GPS receiver are accessed through menus. The Main Menu offers options for selecting waypoints, routes, or setup functions to control the way the GPS receiver operates.*

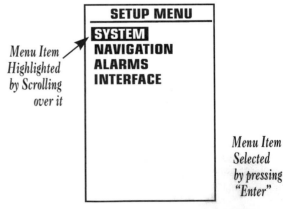

FIGURE 3-16. *The Setup Menu. From the Setup Menu, Setup submenus can be accessed for the system, navigation, and other functions. Separate submenus permit the user to set the way the GPS performs and displays navigation information, to set alarms, to set up interfacing with other devices, and to control how the GPS unit itself functions under the heading "System."*

Setup Submenus

The Main Menu provides access to the Setup Menu, as shown in figure 3-16. GPS units typically have several setup submenus divided by the functions they perform. Most receivers provide a System Setup Menu to control the operations of the GPS unit, a Navigation Setup Menu to control how the GPS unit computes and displays navigation data, an Interface Setup Menu to control how the GPS receiver talks to other devices, and an Alarms Setup Menu to control warning alarms. Each of these submenus is accessed through the Setup Menu. Figure 3-17 illustrates the Setup submenus of several GPS models. Each Setup submenu is described in greater detail below.

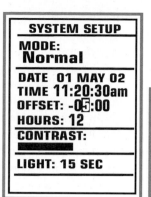

Set "Normal" or "Simulator"

Set time offset for local time

Set format, datum, nautical vs. statute compass - true or magnetic

Set interfaces & DGPS (advanced)

FIGURE 3-17. *Setup Submenus. Submenus are used to control the ways the receiver processes and displays functions. The figure shows three typical submenus: System Setup, Navigation Setup, and Interface Setup. The System Setup Menu offers Normal or Simulator mode, the time offset from UTC for local time, and display contrast and lighting. The Navigation Setup Menu enables selection of the format of the coordinate data. A chart-friendly format of degrees, minutes, and tenths is recommended for coastal or offshore boating. The map datum is set to match the chart you are using. Magnetic or true tracks are selected along with the choice of automatic variance or manual. The units should be set to "Nautical" for boating navigation (rather than "Statute" miles). The Interface Setup Menu controls how data are input to or output from the GPS receiver.*

System Setup Menu

The System Setup Menu controls the operation of the GPS unit. It enables the choice of mode: Normal or Simulator. Normal mode is the active mode for GPS navigation. Simulator mode shuts off the antenna and receiver and operates the GPS unit with simulated satellite signals, usually captured at the last location that the unit was operated. Simulator mode is invaluable in planning and practicing with the GPS receiver, but it is very important to *make sure the GPS receiver is in the Normal mode when navigating*. To ensure that this is the case, most GPS units return to Normal mode each time the set is turned off. Also, the Satellite screen usually displays the mode of operation.

The System Setup Menu also permits entering the offset from UTC for local time, the selection of 12- or 24-hour time presentation, display contrast, and the timeout for the light. As on the other pages, you can select these fields by moving the cursor up or down until the desired field is highlighted and then pressing "Enter," as shown in figure 3-18 and described later in this chapter under Data Entry and Options Selection.

Navigation Setup Menu

The Navigation Setup Menu permits the selection of format for position. Most coastal mariners use degrees, minutes, and tenths of minutes, because the latitude and longitude scales on a chart use these same formats. Using these measurements facilitates direct transfers of location from the GPS receiver to electronic charts, and easy plotting of locations on paper charts.

You can also select map datum, described at the beginning of this section, in the Navigation Setup Menu. In figure 3-17, the GPS datum is set to WGS-84, which is appropriate for most NOAA (National Oceanic and Atmospheric Administration) charts. The selected datum *must* correspond to the chart that you are using or your plotted GPS coordinates will not be in the right spot. CDI for the Highway screen also is set on this menu. As noted earlier, many newer GPS receivers have dispensed with the CDI scale since the same information is presented by the crosstrack error (XTK) data field.

You can choose to display the heading in either true or magnetic direction. When the magnetic variation is selected, the GPS unit automatically computes the variation for magnetic north at your current location and sets the receiver based on that information. Some boaters prefer to use "True" setting on their GPS units. Since chart grids are calibrated to True, this simplifies plotting on the chart. Since most boaters use a compass for steering, it usually is easier to set the GPS on Magnetic than to convert back and forth between the GPS in True and the compass. However, you must be certain that you plot the track and bearings using the magnetic compass rose on the chart rather than the grid lines.

The Navigation Setup Menu also permits the selection of units of measure as statute or nautical miles. Mariners generally use nautical miles, since one minute on the latitude scale is equal to one nautical mile of distance. Most marine charts are plotted using the Mercator projection. In order to print a spherical world on a flat chart, cartographers distort the scales so that landmasses retain their shape, local linear distance scales, and directional relationships for convenient plotting. The chart's latitude (vertical) scale is calibrated in minutes and tenths of minutes corresponding to nautical miles and tenths of nautical miles for distance. You can use the vertical (latitude) scale for measuring distance. However, do *not* use the longitude scale for distance. The longitude scale varies with higher latitudes, so it does not correspond to nautical miles.

Interface Setup Menu

The Interface Setup Menu sets up the protocol for data exchange. This allows you to connect the GPS unit to other devices for the exchange of data. These interfaces are further described in chapter 8. On the sample screen shown in the far right box in figure 3-17, the receiver is set to RTCM (Radio Technical Commission for Maritime Services) *in* and NMEA (National Marine Electronics Association) *out*. This setting is used to accept data, in SC-104 format (see glossary) from a Differential GPS (DGPS) receiver (described in chapter 10). This GPS receiver has one data line for outgoing messages (set to NMEA) and one for incoming (set to RTCM), and each can be set separately. The data-out mode is used to exchange navigation data in NMEA 0183 format (see glossary). In this example, the speed of transfer selected is 4,800 baud (bits per second). The most common output choices are NMEA, Text, and GARMN. GARMN is a proprietary protocol for data exchange unique to Garmin GPS units. Generally, other devices will use NMEA. Some software programs written for Garmin receivers use GARMN.

The Interface Setup Menu, when RTCM is selected, displays fields for the DGPS Beacon Receiver, as shown in figure 3-17. The DGPS receiver is tuned using the GPS for control in this Garmin unit.

Alarms Setup Menu

The Alarms Setup Menu (not shown) enables the user to turn various alarms on and off. Typical alarms include waypoint arrival, off-course, and proximity to waypoint. Some units offer an anchor watch alarm to alert you when the boat has moved more than a preset distance. Other units interface with depth sounders and offer depth alarm settings.

Alarms are individually set based on their function. Most GPS receiver alarms have selectable thresholds for distance, and the values are entered using the cursor key. Waypoint arrival alarms generally are set for very small values down to 0.01 nautical mile (60 feet or 18.2 m), as are anchor watch alarms. Crosstrack Error alarm settings are based on just how tightly you want to track the course line. Once any alarm threshold is set and exceeded, the GPS receiver emits a beeping sound and instructs you to press

"Page" to discover what the alarm means. Some fixed-mount receivers have the ability to sound an external alarm using the GPS as a switch to close an alarm circuit for a device of your choosing.

In addition to the Main Menu and its submenus, specific menus are available on many screens to set options unique for those screens. These menus are accessed in one of two ways—by pressing "Menu" or by pressing "Enter." If you do not have your manual in front of you, try the former; if you do not see what you want, press "Quit" to go back, and then try the latter.

Data Entry and Options Selection

You can select options and enter data into your GPS receiver with the cursor key, once the desired menu or screen is located. While on the screen or menu of choice, you select a field by scrolling down until that field is highlighted and pressing "Enter." Once you have selected the highlighted item, the GPS unit either activates the selected function, presents a subsequent submenu from which you select, or puts you into a data-entry mode.

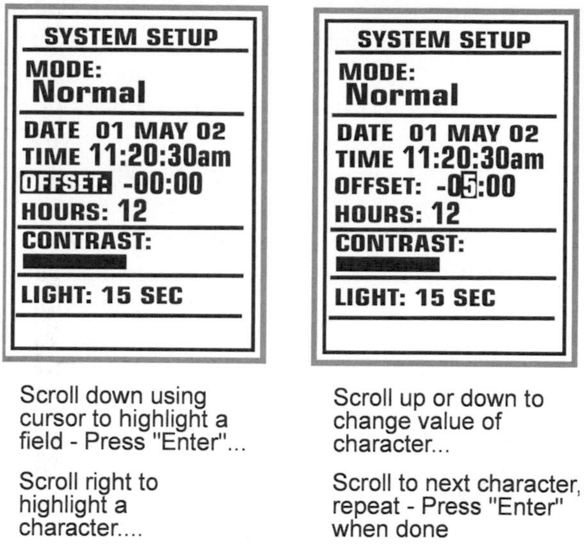

Data Entry

Figure 3-18 shows the typical method of data entry. A data-entry field is usually identified by a field parameter with accompanying alphanumeric fields. In this example, we are viewing the System Setup Menu, and we want to change the time offset used by the GPS receiver to show local time instead of UTC. Generally, mariners navigate using local time for their time zone. If on a long voyage, they will adjust their watches as they transit each time zone. While on this screen, we scroll down to the field labeled "Offset." Since this is the field we want, we press "Enter." This takes the cursor to the data field, highlighting just one character. Usually you will be prompted to start with the character on the left. This is your cue that you can alter the value in this character field using the cursor key. By scrolling up or down, you change the value in that particular character field. Depending on the field, the values will be numerals,

Scroll down using cursor to highlight a field - Press "Enter"...

Scroll right to highlight a character....

Scroll up or down to change value of character...

Scroll to next character, repeat - Press "Enter" when done

FIGURE 3-18. Entering Data. Data are entered by first selecting the field and then scrolling through the choices. Within any Setup submenu, you can use the cursor key to scroll through the fields. Pressing "Enter" either offers a menu of choices or places the highlight within the data field. In this mode, you scroll up or down to change the character, or left or right to move to another character. Pressing "Enter" activates the selected entry and enables you to move to other data fields.

plus or minus signs, or alphabetic characters. By scrolling left or right, you move to different character fields. When you are satisfied with what you have input, you simply press "Enter." The change takes effect, and the cursor again highlights the main field, "Offset." From here, you either scroll up or down to another main field, or press "Page" or "Quit" to move to one of the regular pages.

Screen Options

Most GPS units provide options for how each screen is presented. This ranges from the layout of the screen to the specific data fields that are presented. Typically, these options are accessed while the screen is showing on the GPS. If your GPS has a "Menu" button, pressing it generally brings up a screen-specific menu first. In many cases you can change the number of data fields offered, their sizes, and their locations.

On the Map screen you will be offered options such as the amount of screen detail presented, grid lines, screen orientation (North-Up or Course-Up), zoom features, an accuracy circle option (presents the EPE graphically), line characteristics, point and waypoint features, text size, and how database information is displayed (such as cities).

On the Highway screen you will be given options such as the degree of other detail presented on the screen, for example for other waypoints, tracks, text sizes, and other fields, such as a ribbon compass on some units.

Many newer units offer almost universal control over the selection of the data fields beyond that described earlier in this section. A default option is generally available, but many boaters want to customize the way each screen is presented. Additionally, these screens can be changed to present different data fields. For example, the GPS 76 series offers options such as the following choices for data fields on virtually any screen. These choices are accessed via the "Menu" button from the selected screen. Select "Change Data Fields." Then scroll to highlight the field you want to change and press "Enter" to view the choices; then press "Enter" to select the one you have highlighted.

- Accuracy (or EPE)
- Bearing
- Course
- Depth (if connected to a depth sounder)
- Distance to Destination
- Distance to Next [Waypoint]
- Elevation (or Altitude)
- ETA at Destination
- ETA at Next [Waypoint]
- Maximum Speed
- Moving Average Speed
- Moving Trip Timer
- Off Course (XTK or XTE)
- Pointer
- Speed (or Speed Over Ground)
- Time of Day
- Time to Destination
- Time to Next [Waypoint]
- To Course
- Track (or Course Over Ground)
- Trip Odometer

Chapter 4

Using GPS to Navigate

Boaters operate in a unique environment where GPS is especially useful. Operating a boat on the water is quite different from driving a car on land. On land, your paths are laid out for you in the form of roads and highways. On the water, you appear to have infinite possibilities in how you go from one place to another, but, in actuality, this is not the case: you must choose your paths with care. A GPS receiver will tell you where you are, but you need additional information in order to navigate safely.

Most recreational boaters operate in nearshore, coastal, or inland waters; landmasses, aids to navigation, towns, and other landmarks provide many indications as to location for most mariners. Although this may appear to be a distinct advantage, these same waters present a myriad of hazards, ranging from shallow water to rocks, that impact your available paths in the water. Coastal regions also experience fog that obscures visibility. Within these coastal, nearshore, and inland waters, it is essential to have highly accurate information regarding your position, as well as the locations of any hazards or restrictions.

Offshore boating presents few landmarks, but also fewer navigation hazards, generally speaking. Offshore navigators historically relied upon the celestial bodies to determine their position. GPS technology is accessible worldwide, so offshore navigators have taken to this new technology as their primary source

of position data, with celestial navigation as the backup. Nonetheless, every offshore boater begins and ends his journey in a coastal situation where hazards abound, and most would admit that coastal navigation is their greatest challenge.

Fixes are positions established with a high degree of confidence. In between these fixes, the navigator determines his or her *estimated position*. Traditional navigation using charts, plotting tools, compass, speed, and time is called *dead reckoning*. Now, with GPS data, the mariner has access to constantly updated position information of high quality, as long as the GPS receiver is functioning properly and receiving satellite signals. The GPS system forms the heart of a new type of navigation: *electronic navigation*. However, a GPS receiver alone does not tell you all you need to know, and it cannot be relied upon as the only source of position information. A basic knowledge of traditional navigation is essential for safe boating, and the following brief overview of the approach and terminology will provide a good foundation for understanding what the GPS unit is telling us.

Charts of various scales for the region of operation display information about aids to navigation and hazards. A GPS receiver greatly facilitates determining your current location, which can be transcribed to the relevant chart. The receiver also provides range and heading data to specific places that you select, called *waypoints*, which are defined later in this chapter. However, the GPS unit will point you toward a waypoint without consideration of what lies along the path between your current location and your destination. Consequently, it is very important to note that *the GPS receiver is a supplement to and not a replacement for basic plotting and charts.*

GPS and Electronic Navigation

A GPS receiver provides continuous data regarding the position of the boat over ground. The quality of these position data is equivalent to having constant fixes. If this information were plotted on a chart, it would be extremely valuable; however, it comes from the GPS unit as sets of coordinates. It is up to the navigator to transcribe these positions onto the chart. Clearly, you need the chart to plan and navigate your voyage safely with respect to obstacles, water depth, hazards, aids to navigation, and restricted areas. Without the chart, GPS coordinates are just numbers, subject to error in interpretation. For a variety of reasons, the GPS data can become faulty—usually as a result of equipment failure or mistaken entry/reading of data. It is imperative that you maintain a "physical" relationship between the actual position of the boat and what the electronic devices are telling you.

Typically, the GPS receiver is the primary means of determining position in electronic navigation. Other instruments such as radar and electronic compasses provide information regarding the surrounding environment and the related heading of the boat. The GPS unit computes bearing and distance to waypoints; however, as noted earlier, it is not a compass. All these devices may be connected to an autopilot, which interprets the incoming data and converts them to steering directions to the wheel. Such interconnections are described in greater detail in chapter 9.

Special devices can be used to plot position automatically on a chart with related course lines, planned courses, and bearings. These devices, which utilize electronic versions of charts, are called *chartplotters*. Chartplotters are described in chapter 7.

Using a GPS Receiver with a Paper Chart

Planning Your Trip on a Chart

The prudent boater won't venture onto the water without the appropriate chart of the area. It is also good practice to preplan trips by plotting intended courses ahead of time. By carefully following these intended courses on the water, you can proceed with confidence and without constant reference to the chart. The simplest course to plot has a starting point and a destination, as shown in figure 4-1. By plotting a line from this starting point to the destination, you can determine the course direction. Charts are

printed with grid lines running north–south (called *meridians of longitude*) and east–west (called *parallels of latitude*). Using a course plotter—a transparent template you place over the course line to measure angle or over a waypoint to plot a course—you can measure the angle between true north indicated by the grid line and the plotted course line. With this information, you can steer the boat and eventually will reach your destination.

Second, you can measure the distance from the starting point to the destination using the distance scale on the chart. Alternatively, you can use the latitude scale on the left or right side of most charts. One minute of latitude is equal to one nautical mile (nm). The scale on the side of the chart is printed in degrees, minutes, and tenths of minutes; therefore, you can use this scale to measure nautical miles and tenths of nautical miles directly. If you are interested in how long the trip will take, simply divide the distance by the intended speed. The answer will be in hours or fractions of hours.

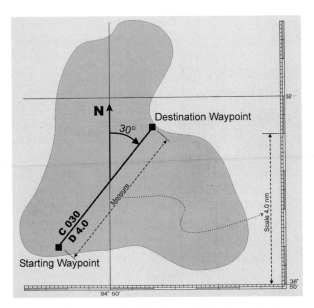

FIGURE 4-1. *Navigation Involves Course Direction and Distance to a Destination. In order to plan a cruise, you draw a course line on a chart, from the starting waypoint to the destination waypoint. You determine the distance using dividers, measuring from start to destination and then reading the distance from the latitude scale. Label the course direction and distance on the course line. The course direction shown in this figure is 30° (030), and the distance is 4.0 nautical miles.*

Example: In figure 4-1 your destination is 4.0 nm distant from your starting point. Let's say you are traveling at 8 knots. With this information, we can determine how long it will take to reach your destination using the following equation:

$$\text{Time (hours)} = \frac{\text{Distance (nm)}}{\text{Speed (kn)}}$$

$$= \frac{4.0 \text{ nm}}{8.0 \text{ kn}} = \frac{1}{2} \text{ hour} = 30 \text{ minutes}$$

A GPS receiver simplifies the process. Instead of measuring the course angle and the distance, you simply enter the coordinates of the starting waypoint and the destination waypoint into the receiver. A *waypoint* is any spot of interest for which you enter latitude and longitude coordinates. The GPS unit will then determine the course direction and the distance.

You measure the latitude and longitude of each waypoint on the chart using a pair of dividers. Latitude is measured between the starting waypoint and the nearest horizontal grid line, as shown in figure 4-2. Latitude is determined by transferring that mea-surement to the latitude scale on either side of the chart. Similarly, longitude is measured between the waypoint and a vertical grid line, and read on the horizontal scale at the top or bottom of the chart, as shown in figure 4-2. The latitude and longitude are indicated by degrees, minutes, and tenths of minutes. Make sure you are reading in the proper direction on each scale. Next, the coordinates are measured in the same way for the destination waypoint, as illustrated in figure 4-3. These steps represent the greatest potential source of error using a GPS receiver. Be sure to double-check your coordinates.

Example: Using figures 4-2 and 4-3, you can determine the coordinates of your starting and destination waypoints to be as follows:

Starting Waypoint	latitude	38°51.0′ N
	longitude	94°51.2′ W
Destination Waypoint	latitude	38°54.2′ N
	longitude	94°49.0′ W

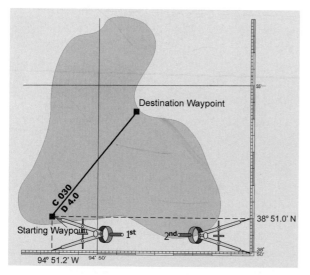

FIGURE 4-2. *GPS Navigation Involves Waypoints. The GPS receiver needs the coordinates of the waypoints to navigate. The starting waypoint coordinates are measured on a chart using a pair of dividers from the starting waypoint to the nearest grid line first for latitude, then longitude. Measuring latitude is shown here; longitude is measured the same way in the horizontal direction.*

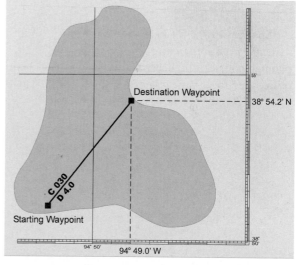

FIGURE 4-3. *The GPS Receiver Computes Course Direction and Distance. After you enter the coordinates of the destination waypoint, the GPS unit computes the course and distance from your current position to the destination waypoint and displays this information on the screen. If you're located at the starting waypoint, you can begin navigation by pressing "GoTo" and selecting the destination waypoint. This puts the bearing and distance on the GPS receiver screen.*

Magnetic North and the Compass

Since most boaters steer using a magnetic compass, it is useful to set up the GPS receiver to use magnetic reference. However, whenever you refer to the chart grid for a measurement, it is important to convert from true to magnetic north. This can be another source of potential error. One approach to prevent errors is to plot and label your courses on your charts with reference to magnetic north.

The compass does not point to true north but to magnetic north. The precise location of magnetic north in May 2000 was 79°19´ N, 105°26´ W, located near the northern reaches of Canada slightly west of Hudson Bay, as indicated by the "M" in figure 4-4. At almost any location on the Earth, there will be some variation between true north and magnetic north. This variation is indicated by the number of degrees difference between the two and whether magnetic north is to the west or east of true from that lo-

cation. Lines of equal variation called isogonics may be found in various reference materials. The amount of variation for your area of boating can be found on the chart. A magenta-colored compass rose appears at various locations on a chart. The outer rose is based on true north. The inner rose is based on magnetic north. The variation between the two is printed inside the inner rose as so many degrees west or east. The location of magnetic north is moving continuously, albeit slowly, so the chart indicates the amount that the stated value should be adjusted for each year following the printing of the chart.

Magnetic Courses

Many mariners choose to plot their courses using magnetic north instead of true north. This makes a great deal of sense if you usually boat in a particular region. Professional mariners who cruise offshore are

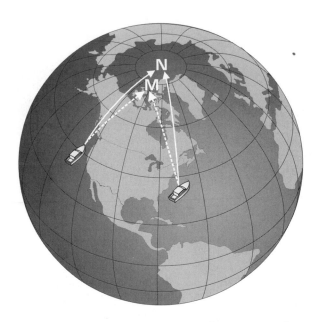

FIGURE 4-4. *The Magnetic North Pole Differs in Position from the True North Pole. The Magnetic North Pole is located in northern Canada. If you are on a boat in the Atlantic, you will find that the compass indicates north is to the left (west) of true north. This is called a* westerly variation. *Conversely, if you are in the Pacific, the compass shows you to be to the east of true north. This is called an* easterly variation. *These variations must be corrected to use the grid lines on a chart for navigation.*

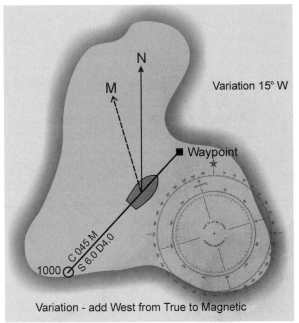

FIGURE 4-5. *Magnetic Course Lines. Magnetic course lines make it easy to steer with a properly compensated compass. The magnetic course is different from true by the local variation. Charts have compass roses (printed in magenta) that provide true directions on the outer circle and magnetic on the inner circle. The rose also provides the value of the variation. This example shows a westerly variation with magnetic north to the west of true north. If you plot magnetic headings, you should annotate your course value with an "M," as shown.*

taught to plot courses and navigate using true north, as they are likely to move across regions with differing variations. Generally, they translate these to magnetic headings to guide the helmsman who steers based on the compass. If you plot magnetic courses, you indicate this by adding an "M" following the number of degrees on three digits and no degree symbol as shown in figure 4-5 (degrees are the only number expressed as three digits and no decimal). For boaters along the Atlantic coast of the United States, the variations are west, as can be seen in figure 4-4. In other words, the magnetic north pole is farther west than the true north pole. Westerly variations are added to "true" bearings to get "magnetic" bearings. Some remember this by the line, "west is best." Conversely, if you are on the West Coast, you can see from the figure that the magnetic north pole is farther to the east than the true north pole. In this case "east is least," so subtract the variation from the true bearing to get the magnetic bearing.

Many of the commercial chart books available to boaters preprint selected point-to-point courses between popular waypoints using magnetic north as the reference and list the distance between these points in nautical miles. The courses are labeled at each start and end point. The course heading listed near a starting waypoint corresponds to the heading to reach the ending waypoint. At the other end of the course line, the indicated course differs by 180°. This is called the *reciprocal course* for steering from the second point back to the first. Any time you measure a course using the grid lines, remember that you must correct for variation before plotting or steering a magnetic course. As an alternative, many mariners will use parallel rulers to transfer course direction and read its magnetic direction directly on the inner compass rose.

Plotting Your Course to Check for Hazards

The primary reason for preplotting your course on a chart is to check your intended path for obstacles or hazards. The chart provides an indication of depth, wrecks, rocks, and other objects. The chart also provides the locations of aids to navigation.

Usually, you will not find a straight-line path from your starting point to your destination. Figure 4-6 illustrates a situation wherein you cannot go directly to your destination (your slip). You will need to break the path into a series of straight-line segments, as shown in figure 4-7. Each of these segments, or legs, is defined by starting and ending points that will be entered into your GPS receiver as waypoints when you are planning your cruise. Although it is possible to enter waypoints while underway, preplanning is preferred, because entering waypoints on a boat with the motion of the water can be tedious and potentially distract you from operating the boat.

Navigating the Course with a GPS Receiver

Once the waypoints are entered into the GPS receiver, one of the simplest ways to begin navigation from your starting point is to use the "GoTo" button to bring up a list of your stored waypoints. As soon as you select the destination waypoint, the receiver computes and displays the bearing and distance to that waypoint.

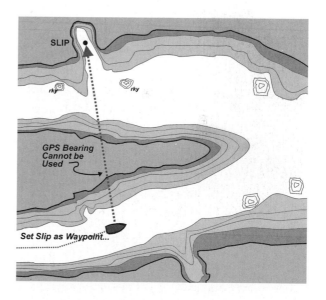

FIGURE 4-6. *Using the GPS Bearing Is Not Always the Best Way to Reach Your Destination. Activating a waypoint does not mean you should go in the direction indicated by the GPS bearing. This example shows a potential extreme, but under no circumstances should the skipper follow a bearing directly toward a selected waypoint without understanding the chart features.*

As you sail the course, the GPS unit continually updates the display of bearing and distance to the waypoint. It also displays your current course over ground (track), and it provides a continuous update of your current coordinates. As long as the GPS unit is functioning properly, it will provide a quality fix at every spot along your cruise.

Piloting: What to Do When the GPS Receiver Fails

Piloting is the art of navigation with the aid of visible landmarks and aids to navigation. Typically, these are available near shore and within inland navigable waters. Piloting is the means by which mariners have navigated for centuries. Underway, piloting can be used to determine your approximate position at any point in time. With your GPS receiver working, you will know where you are with greater accuracy than you may achieve by piloting alone. But what happens when the GPS unit fails? An even larger question is, how do you know that your receiver is working? The prudent navigator never relies upon a single source of information, so it pays to use some tried-and-true

techniques to double-check position, or to navigate when the GPS receiver is unavailable. Some GPS units will default to a dead-reckoning mode using the last course and speed if they lose the satellite signals.

Dead Reckoning

Traditionally, a position at any point in time can be determined by using the process of *dead reckoning*. A dead-reckoning position of your boat at any specific time, called a *DR*, is determined by adding, to the last known fix, the distance traveled based on the boat's speed and time along the course steered, as shown in figure 4-8. At any time, the current dead-reckoning position is established by plotting the appropriate distance along the steered course line. The accuracy of your current position is based on how well you steered the course, how accurately you know the dis-

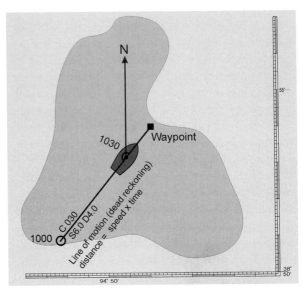

FIGURE 4-8. Dead Reckoning. Plotting a course using direction, speed, and time is called dead reckoning (DR). Basic
piloting uses direction and speed to establish a current position on a chart. Using the compass and a speedometer you
can approximate your position at any time by measuring
time and calculating distance traveled. The compass heading must be converted to a true heading to plot on a chart
using the grid lines. By common practice, the course heading
is shown above the line with a "C," for course, and the compass reading expressed in three digits. Speed and/or distance
are shown below the line in units and tenths of units following either an "S" or "D," respectively. The course or DR line
is considered the boat's "line of motion." Note that the time
is written per the 24-hour clock (military time).

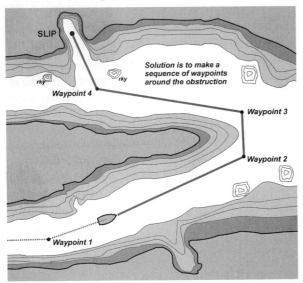

FIGURE 4-7. A Route Can Be Preplotted to Your Destination.
Each turn during the route is marked by a waypoint. The
navigator will take her current position and plot a point-by-
point series of straight-line segments to get to the destination.
The end points of the segments are waypoints. The helmsman can navigate from waypoint to waypoint to reach the
destination.

tance traveled, and external effects on the boat such as wind and current.

The course is steered using a magnetic compass. Course is measured by the number of degrees clockwise from north to the direction in which you are heading. Distance can be determined by multiplying your speed by the time traveled (see formula on page 35). Speed is determined by a variety of means. Some boats are equipped with paddlewheel speedometers or similar instruments. Some boaters develop "speed curves," setting an engine rpm and knowing how fast the boat goes through the water at that rpm. Given that the helmsman maintains that course and speed, it is a simple matter of calculating how far you should have gone in the time since you left.

The line representing the course is called a *line of motion*—the line that the boat is assumed to be *moving* along. As noted on figure 4-8, the course (C) is labeled above the line. Speed (S) and distance to the destination waypoint (D) are labeled below the line. The current position at any time is calculated using the formula: distance = speed x time. Distance is in nautical miles, speed in knots, and time in hours. Alternatively, some boats are equipped with logs that directly measure distance. In one type, the log is tied to the paddlewheel that measures speed. By counting the total number of revolutions, the log can estimate distance. The current position is plotted along the course line at the estimated distance traveled from the fix. The DR is labeled on a diagonal with four digits representing the time of the DR. (By the way, the term *log* comes from ancient mariners, who would throw a log tied to a rope into the water at the bow and count how long it took to travel the length of the boat.)

Example: Using figure 4-9, you want to mark your current DR position

You departed at	1000 hours (10:00 A.M.)
The current time is	1030 hours (10:30 A.M.)
The elapsed time is	0030 = 0 hours, 30 minutes
	= 0.5 hours
Your speed has been	6.0 kn

To determine your distance traveled use:

Distance (nm) = Speed (kn) x Time (hours)
= 6.0 kn x 0.5 hr = 3.0 nm

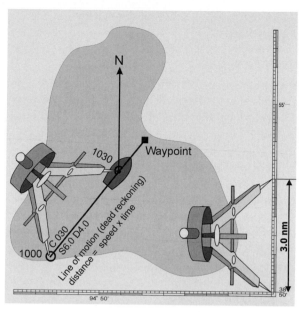

FIGURE 4-9. *The DR Position. The DR position is easily obtained. By calculating how far you have gone from 1000 to 1030 based on a speed of 6 knots, you can determine that you have traveled 3.0 nautical miles. Using a pair of dividers, you measure 3.0 nm on the latitude scale and transfer this measurement to the course line as shown. Where the divider tip indicates 3.0 nm, place a mark and a half circle. This is your DR position.*

Using the latitude scale, measure 3.0 nm using dividers. Place one end of the dividers on the starting waypoint and place a dot at the point where the dividers touch, mark with a half circle and the time. This marks your DR position.

These plotting and labeling conventions are especially important if more than one person will be handling the boat. They provide a commonly recognized format that all experienced navigators understand, so anyone on board can immediately understand them. Also, it is good practice to preplan your routes and label them on the charts. Then dead reckoning is reduced to observing variances from these paths. Since most boaters operate at times in uncertain waters, these plots make safe navigation an easier task. These routes and their accompanying waypoints can be transferred into the GPS unit where chart data may not be present. By staying with charted routes and waypoints, you can use the GPS unit to navigate safely. Still, you will want to keep your charts handy to cross-check your current position with respect to local hazards.

Your Compass

Compasses aren't perfect; they operate in environments where the magnetic fields can be disturbed by local influences. As a result, the compass reading may not reflect magnetic heading accurately. The difference between the magnetic bearing and the equivalent compass reading is called *deviation*. Compasses come with compensating magnets that can be turned to eliminate most deviation. It is advisable to have a professional make these adjustments. Once adjusted, your compass is unlikely to need recompensating unless you move it or add metallic objects to the boat. A professional will use another reference, such as a gyrocompass, to determine the deviation and adjust to minimize it. The compass adjuster will also provide you with a table of what error remains. If this is less than a degree or two, there's no need to worry about it. A one-degree error will put you off course up to 100 feet in a mile (17 m in 1 km). Most compass scales are calibrated in 5° increments and cannot be read as accurately as one degree. Also, the motion of the water will cause continual variations in heading. This does point out the need for regular position checks, because after a ten-mile (16 km) run without correction, you could be off course by as much as a thousand feet (305 m). That's not good if there are rocks or hazards in the area.

Lines of Position and Bearings

At various points while underway, the boater may choose to take a bearing on a fixed object to help verify position. This is a good practice even if you are using your GPS receiver, since it gives you a means of checking the receiver for accuracy. A *hand-bearing compass* is a convenient tool for these measurements. Keep in mind that the reading of the hand-bearing compass, like any compass, is subject to local influences on the boat, such as engines, electrical wires, and other metal objects. A quick check can be made by sighting toward the bow and comparing the hand-bearing compass reading with that of the ship's compass. Adjust your readings accordingly.

You can compare your hand-bearing compass

readings with bearings to the same objects listed on the GPS receiver. However, these objects must have been previously entered as waypoints in the GPS unit. The following sections explain how to do this. If the bearings agree, you will have increased confidence that your GPS receiver is functioning properly.

Alternatively, you can plot the bearing measured with the hand-bearing compass. This line is known as a *line of position* (LOP), because you know with a high degree of certainty that the boat's current position lies somewhere along that line. The line of position is labeled as in figure 4-10. The line extends from the boat to the measured landmark. Time is shown on the top and the bearing below. If you use magnetic follow the bearing with an "M."

Example: Using figure 4-10 as a reference:

- You read 125° Magnetic on your hand-bearing compass to the landmark.

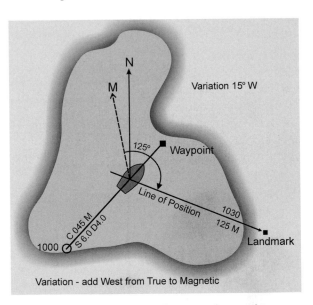

FIGURE 4-10. *Line of Position. Sighting on a known object gives you a line of position. The DR line of motion is an approximation of your actual path. When the opportunity permits, you can take a bearing on a known object. By plotting this bearing from the boat to the object, you draw a line of position. You know with certainty that you are somewhere on that line, but you do not know specifically where. Lines of position are labeled with a four-digit time (24-hour clock) on top and the bearing in three digits below. In this example, you sighted on the landmark at a bearing of 125° Magnetic at 10:30 A.M.*

- Locate the magenta compass rose nearest your current location on the chart. The outer rose is calibrated in true direction. The inner rose is calibrated in magnetic direction.

- Using the inner rose and a parallel rule, align the rule with the 125° graduation and the center of the rose. Transfer this angle and draw a line from the boat area extending directly through the landmark.

- You are somewhere on the line, most probably close to your DR track line (line of motion).

If you prefer to use true north as a reference, you will need to convert the magnetic hand-bearing compass reading to true. Remembering that you used "west is best" and added the westerly variation from true to get magnetic, you must do the opposite to go from magnetic to true. With true bearings, you can measure angles directly from the vertical grid lines on your nautical chart.

If two lines of position are determined from two widely separated landmarks or aids to navigation at roughly the same time, the point at which they cross represents a fix. This is illustrated in figure 4-11. The first line of position was drawn as shown in figure 4-9. You measured a second magnetic bearing to another landmark with your hand-bearing compass indicated to be 185° Magnetic, as shown in figure 4-11. You plot this by determining this angle on the inner compass rose with your parallel rule and transferring it to a line going from the boat through the second landmark as shown. Where they cross is your known position. This fix is indicated by a dot surrounded by a circle, and the time of the fix, 10:30 A.M., is labeled as shown ("1030 FIX").

Relative Bearings

Often, it is easier to use the boat as a frame of reference in measuring bearings. This is called taking a *relative bearing*, which is executed by measuring clockwise from the bow of the boat (boat heading). A relative bearing relates directly to your visual horizon from the boat. Radar usually presents relative bearings on the screen, since the boat is also its frame of reference. There are some quick-reference relative bearings that may be useful even without instru-

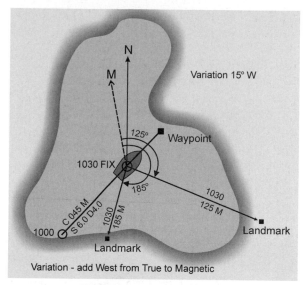

FIGURE 4-11. *Use Two Lines of Position to Get a Fix. Two lines of position from two known objects give you a fix on your current position. If you are so fortunate as to have two nearly simultaneous lines of position from different fixed objects, you can determine you are at the intersection of the two lines. This is called a* fix *and is used to update your position. The DR plot is begun anew from this point. In this example, you sighted on a second landmark at a bearing of 185° Magnetic, also at 10:30 A.M. Where the two intersect, draw a circle and label the time of the fix.*

ments. Using objects on the boat to sight along, you can measure bow, beam, stern, or other relative bearings quickly and easily to provide a check on your position.

However, to use these bearings with a chart or a GPS receiver, you need to convert them to true or magnetic bearings. This can be done quickly as follows, and then they can be plotted in the same manner as you did in the previous example.

True Bearing (fig. 4-12)
    = Sighted Relative Bearing (RB)
        + True Heading (TH) of the Boat 110°T
    = 80°RB + 30°TH

or

Magnetic Bearing (fig. 4-13)
    = Sighted Relative Bearing (RB)
        + Magnetic Heading (MH) of Boat 125°M
    = 80°RB + 45°MH

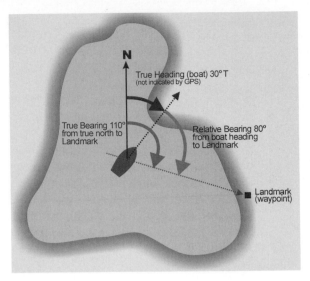

FIGURE 4-12. *Measuring Bearings Relative to the Boat. Often, it's convenient to reference the bearing to an object relative to the heading of the boat. Many mariners will have reference points on the boat so they can quickly estimate the relative bearing to that object by sighting across that reference point from the helm. In order to plot these bearings on a chart, you will need to add the Heading of the boat to the relative bearing. This example shows a true heading (boat) of 30° and a relative bearing of 80°. Adding the two gives you a true bearing to the object of 110°. Note that true heading is used here. You must convert your compass course (heading) to true.*

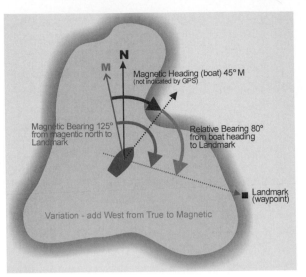

FIGURE 4-13. *Using Magnetic Reference with Relative Bearings. Usually, the person at the helm uses a compass to steer the boat. Thus the heading of the boat is presented as a magnetic heading. In this example the helmsman determines that the magnetic bearing (125°M) is the sum of the magnetic heading (45°) and the relative bearing (80°). This is plotted on a chart using parallel rules and the inner compass rose.*

An alternate technique is to turn the boat temporarily to measure a bearing quickly. You turn so that you are heading toward a landmark, abeam of it, or away from it. By simply reading the compass, and adjusting for beam or stern direction if appropriate, you have your bearing.

Using the Chart to Look for Hazards

The prudent boater will track on the chart his or her position and intended path, continually evaluating the path for risks or hazards. Unfortunately, the basic readout on a GPS receiver is nothing more than two sets of numbers—one for latitude and one for longitude. For example, figure 4-14 shows a receiver providing latitude and longitude coordinates. Taking the time to mark the latitude and longitude on the chart, you are led to believe that you are in safe water outside the entrance to Hyannis Harbor, shown in figure 4-15. From this spot, you should have a clear shot into

FIGURE 4-14. *An Example of Charting Position with GPS Coordinates. The GPS unit gives you a position, in this case a set of coordinates for your current position. But latitude and longitude are just numbers with no intuitive feel for position.*
(GARMIN)

the entrance. Unfortunately, if someone makes a transposition error from the GPS screen to the chart, as shown in figure 4-15 (70°17.6′ N for 70°16.7′ N), an erroneous location is the inevitable result. Checking again with the correct coordinates (fig. 4-16), you will find yourself amidst rocks farther east. This type of error is all too common, especially under stress of being on the water with other boats, chop, wind, and passengers. This brief example shows that latitude and

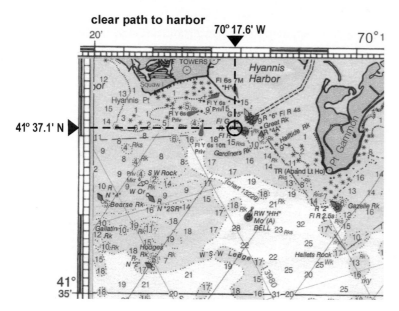

FIGURE 4-15. *Charting the Coordinates. You locate your position on a chart. You need to plot the latitude and longitude indicated on the GPS receiver in figure 4-14 on your chart to see if you are in a safe location. Using the indicated coordinates that you transcribed from the receiver, you find that you should be located just outside the entrance to Hyannis Harbor, as shown. But . . .*

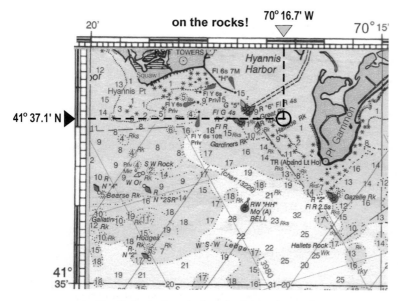

FIGURE 4-16. *Are You Safe? A closer look at the GPS screen in figure 4-14 shows that you made a transfer error by transposing two digits in the longitude coordinate. Instead of marking your position at a latitude of 70°17.6′ W, you should have marked it at 70°16.7′ W. You are really on the rocks! This is a common mistake, one that is very easy to make at sea.*

longitude are just numbers without any physical frame of reference. You must check and double-check coordinate numbers whenever you read them from the chart to enter into your GPS or vice versa. The example also illustrates why you need to maintain an awareness of your position using the chart and the GPS. This chapter provides a number of techniques for using your GPS to stay on course. Chapter 6 expands on situational awareness demonstrating a number of additional techniques using your GPS and charts to verify your position and avoid danger.

GPS Receiver Functions

The GPS unit provides several basic functions invaluable to the boater: waypoints, routes, and tracks. These functions are described in some detail in the following subsections. Now that we have learned all about menus and pages, it's time to focus on what the GPS receiver really does.

The basic function of a GPS receiver is to provide a latitude and longitude at any instant of time. By keeping track of that position over a period of time, the receiver can compute course over ground and speed over ground. However, one of the most practical uses of the GPS unit is to enter the coordinates of your destination or some other point of interest (waypoints). The inclusion of waypoints converts the GPS receiver into a navigation computer. Waypoints are probably the most popular and valuable tool available to the mariner (see next page, top).

By stringing together a group of waypoints into a sequence, you create a route. The GPS unit will automatically ground, speed over ground, and distance traveled in addition to the bearing and distance to waypoints. It also will provide course correction and steering information, as well as estimated time of arrival and other time information. Many of these functions are described in the next section.

Waypoints

A waypoint is simply a point on the Earth that you designate by its coordinates, such as:

These coordinates, when plotted on a chart, mark a definitive location.

For navigation, waypoints represent a spot where you will take an action, such as changing course to the next waypoint. Often, mariners associate waypoints to objects such as buoys, so they can crosscheck where they are on a chart. However, waypoints do not need to correspond to physical objects. It is not uncommon to identify a convenient set of coordinates for a course change where there are no other visual cues or landmarks. These waypoints can be labeled as "TURN1" or some equivalent. Alternatively, waypoints can be used to mark objects that you wish to avoid or landmarks for visual reference. Waypoints can be used in the GPS receiver for a myriad of purposes, as will be described in the next section. In using the receiver, you need to be able to enter waypoints into memory and be able to access preprogrammed waypoints when you need them.

guide you as you steer each leg of the route. This saves the effort of entering individual waypoints while underway.

A history of where you have been, and when, is recorded as a track. The track is displayed on the Map screen and can be downloaded for a historical record or for plotting on a map or chart. The track on the page also provides a ready reference for a return trip.

The GPS receiver provides a number of related functions that make it into a very capable course computer. As already noted, it can tell you the course over

Entering Waypoints into Your GPS Receiver

There are several ways to enter waypoints into a GPS receiver. Some techniques are suited to preplanning while off the boat and some are done while on the boat. The four basic waypoint entry options are

• *manual entry*: using the Waypoint screen and cursor to enter numbers

• *mark*: entering a waypoint at the current location

- *scrolling*: scrolling the cursor on the Map screen and "Mark"

- *computer*: entering and editing data off-line using a computer and transfer cable

This section describes each technique in some detail with the exception of the computer approach, which is described in chapter 8. The manual entry and the computer methods are ideal for off-line planning. The mark and scrolling methods work well on the boat.

Manual Entry

The most direct method of entering waypoints is via the Waypoint screen. Using your charts, you will predetermine the location of waypoints to enter into your GPS receiver. Some charts provide the coordinates for prominent aids to navigation such as beacons. Otherwise, you will need to use your dividers and measure the coordinates on the latitude and longitude scales.

Tip: *Be sure to read the latitude and longitude scales carefully.* For example, in North America, latitude increases upward toward north and longitude increases to the left toward west. Usually there is an additional bar marking alternate minutes of arc running along the scale, as seen in figure 4-16. This makes it easier to distinguish minutes. It pays to count the number of minutes segments to make sure you enter the correct number. Then count the number of tenths between the minute marks. Remember that old carpenters rule, "measure twice, cut once."

Tip: *When manually entering waypoints you must use an up-to-date chart, particularly for floating aids.* Many aids to navigation are moved, added, or removed based on current conditions. These actions are reported in the U.S. Coast Guard's *Local Notice to Mariners*, which is published weekly. Updates are reported by chart number. Having the most-recent edition of the charts for your cruising area is essential, but even they may not reflect the most-recent changes. You can access the *Local Notice to Mariners* on-line at the U.S. Coast Guard's Navigation Center website (see the resources section at the back of the book). Alternatively, many chart publishers update their information every week based on

the USCG notices and provide subscription services.

To enter waypoints manually, first, go to the Main Menu, scroll down to "Waypoint," and press "Enter." This produces the Waypoint screen. If your model has a "Menu" button, press it instead. This produces a list of installed waypoints. Next press "Menu" and select "New Waypoint" to get to the Waypoint screen.

Tip: *Some models such as the Garmin GPS 76 make entering a new waypoint manually more difficult.* The GPS 76 series of units does not offer a direct means to access the waypoint screen to enter a new waypoint. On these units, go to the Map screen as described further under "Scrolling," below. When you move the cursor to any position and press "Mark," the waypoint screen will appear with an assigned number and the coordinates of the cursor. Then edit the name and coordinates to those that you wish as described in this subsection.

A typical Waypoint screen is shown in figure 4-17. This screen shows how a waypoint is entered into

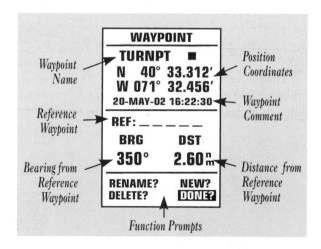

FIGURE 4-17. *The Waypoint Screen. Waypoints are entered, edited, and reviewed using this page. Waypoints are the bread and butter of navigation. Waypoints that you designate in your GPS receiver by their coordinates allow you to navigate from point to point. The Waypoint screen is the vehicle for entering or editing the parameters associated with your selected waypoints. The waypoint can be named. Symbols that appear on the Map screen can be selected to characterize each waypoint. Its coordinates can be entered or edited. The waypoint can be referenced to another waypoint, say the next waypoint in a route. If it is referenced to another waypoint, the bearing and distance to that waypoint is indicated.*

the GPS receiver. When this screen is brought up for a new waypoint, the name field is filled with a number selected by the GPS unit. If this field is not highlighted, highlight it by moving the cursor over the field and pressing "Enter." Figure 4-18 demonstrates the method for entering or editing the waypoint name. The GPS is not unlike many electronic devices such as a VCR when it comes to programming. The process of menus, submenus, and highlighting are common to both devices, as well as others. Once you are satisfied with the waypoint name, press "Enter" to accept your selection and return the highlight to the entire name. You now can use the cursor to select the next field to edit. You can edit the symbol that will appear on the Map screen for this waypoint, or you can enter the coordinates.

Tip: *Consider using an alphanumeric waypoint-naming scheme that is meaningful to you.* You will want to indicate aids to navigation as waypoints so you can recognize them on a chart. Since aids are numbered, and these numbers are repeated in different locales, you can use a letter to distinguish specific areas and the number to indicate the specific aid.

Most GPS receivers will permit six or more characters for a waypoint name. These characters can be any alphabetic, numeric, or standard keyboard symbol. Use a name that reflects the waypoint such as "SP12R" for the red buoy number "12" near Smith Point, or "SP1RCK" for one group of rocks in the same locale. In addition, your GPS unit typically allows you to select a symbol that will be plotted on the Map screen. For example, danger can be marked by a skull and crossbones.

The waypoint coordinates are en-

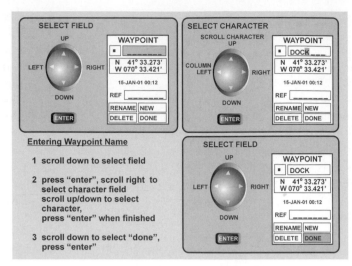

FIGURE 4-18. *Entering Waypoint Names. While on the Waypoint screen, you can scroll to the name field. Pressing "Enter" moves the highlight to the first individual character field within the name field. This is your signal to scroll up or down to change the character value, or scroll right or left to select another character for editing. When you're done with the field, press "Enter," and the full name field will be highlighted. From here you can scroll to edit another field or press "Quit" to exit this screen.*

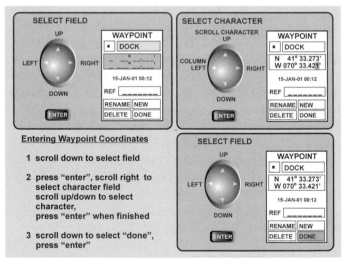

FIGURE 4-19. *Entering Waypoint Coordinates. After editing the name field, you may choose to enter or edit waypoints. By scrolling over the coordinates field, the entire block is highlighted. Pressing "Enter" moves the highlight to the first character, which is the N or S designation for latitude. Scrolling up or down alters the selection of N or S. Scrolling right enables you to change the numeric value of the first latitude field. After you enter the latitude, scrolling right moves to the longitude field, where you select E or W and then the numeric values. Once complete, pressing "Enter" highlights the entire coordinates field again. From here, you can scroll over another field to alter its value, or press "Quit" to leave the Waypoint screen.*

tered in a similar fashion, as shown in figure 4-19. After scrolling down, notice that the entire coordinates field is highlighted until you press "Enter," after which only the first character is highlighted. First, you enter N or S by scrolling up or down (these are the only options offered). Then, you enter the numerical value for the latitude, character by character. Once the latitude is entered, scrolling right will take you to the second row over the longitude. Select E or W and the numerical value for the longitude. Once complete, pressing "Enter" will highlight the entire field. Now you can move on to other tasks. Make sure that the values for latitude and longitude are correct!

The Waypoint screen permits the entry of a reference waypoint from your list of installed waypoints. This is a useful technique for relating waypoints to each other, such as in a string of waypoints. As soon as the reference waypoint is entered, the GPS unit computes the bearing and distance from the waypoint on your page to that reference. The screen includes a comment field that may be used to fill in additional information. On most models, the GPS unit automatically indicates when the waypoint was created in this field; however, you can edit the information and create your own reference. Prompts permit the waypoint to be renamed, deleted, or accepted (done), or you can press "New" to enter another waypoint. Alternatively, other GPS models with a "Menu" button may give you additional choices, such as showing the waypoint on the Map screen, or averaging the waypoint. With the GPS receiver fixed in location, averaging the waypoint will cause the receiver to continue to monitor the location and average the readings for as long as you wish. This technique can overcome some of the errors inherent in GPS navigation, especially if averaging is done over an extended period of time. Usually, this technique is not very useful for boating unless you want a more precise position of your dock or other fixed position.

Where do you find the coordinates to enter a waypoint? Typically, waypoint coordinates are scaled from our charts while planning our routes or searching out points of interest. The coordinates are read using dividers and the appropriate latitude or longitude scale in degrees, minutes, and tenths of minutes.

Some newer commercial charts show the coordinates of buoys, aids to navigation, and other points of interest. Books with waypoint lists also are available. Waypoint coordinates can also be found on the Internet. Always double-check waypoint coordinates from independent sources to make sure they are accurate. This approach is useful for planning a trip, or planning the next leg of a trip while underway, using charts. Entering data into the Waypoint screen is tedious, but it can be accomplished accurately with a bit of patience.

Appendix 3 gives a sample exercise for entering a series of waypoints and subsequently entering a route. This may be a good time to begin the exercise by entering some waypoints into your GPS receiver.

Mark

While underway, you can "Mark" a waypoint while passing over a point of interest. Simply press the "Mark" button (if you have one) on your GPS unit and the Waypoint screen will come up. The GPS receiver will automatically determine the position and record the waypoint's coordinates. The waypoint name will be a number assigned by the GPS unit. You need only accept or change that name and press "Save" or "Done." Henceforth, this waypoint is stored within your unit. Individual GPS units have different ways to access the "Mark" function. Some units have a "Mark" button. This brings up the Waypoint screen directly. Others have the "Mark" function combined with another such as "Enter/Mark." With those GPS receivers, pressing the button twice will bring up the Waypoint screen.

Marking waypoints is by far the easiest method for entering waypoints. It is also the most convenient, because you can enter waypoints for objects not shown on your charts, such as interior harbor buoys, fishing holes, unmarked rocks, etc. You need to be aware that the accuracy of the waypoint corresponds to the accuracy of the GPS unit at the time that you marked it. It is good advice to go back and recheck important waypoints from time to time.

Tip: *Generally, it is easier to mark waypoints during your cruise and let the GPS unit number them.* You can either record the numbers on a piece of paper or identify them on the Map screen afterward.

Then you can edit them and give them names for future reference.

Scrolling

On the Map screen, you can use the cursor to scroll to a point of interest and press "Mark." This will bring up the Waypoint screen with the coordinates. The same process is used, as described under "Mark," to adjust the name and save the coordinates as a waypoint. Scrolling on the Map screen can be done off-line in the Simulator mode to plan a trip, or while underway. Scrolling is implemented using the cursor. Once depressed, you enter the scroll mode and the crosshairs reflect the cursor position, which you control. Scrolling is a convenient technique while underway.

Tip: *Most GPS sets display a window on the Map screen when you scroll using the cursor.* The coordinates of the cursor are displayed within the window. Using this window, you can scroll to a predetermined set of coordinates and press "Mark." Many find this easier than the manual method of entering the numbers individually.

This mode also can be used to temporarily evaluate a point that you may not choose to add as a waypoint. By scrolling the cursor to the desired spot, the GPS receiver will compute the course and distance to that point as if it were a waypoint.

The cursor is a convenient way to look around on adjacent map areas not shown from your current position. Using the cursor in this manner does not alter any ongoing course until you press "GoTo," followed by "Enter." When you are finished using the cursor and wish to return to the current location, that is, to undo the scroll mode, simply press "Quit" or "Esc" depending upon your unit.

Computer

Using a computer with the GPS unit is presented in chapters 8 and 9. At this point, let it suffice to say that using a computer is by far the easiest way to plan waypoints and routes. Once planned, it is an easy task to upload that data into your GPS receiver. This technique also permits archiving waypoints for future reference, or sharing the same waypoints between multiple GPS units.

Editing a Waypoint

Pressing "Enter" on a highlighted waypoint in the waypoint list will bring up the Waypoint screen. This is the same screen that is used to enter the waypoint data. However, using this screen, you can also edit the waypoint name, coordinates, or reference data. If you scroll over the "Save" icon and press "Enter," the updated waypoint information will be stored.

Selecting a Waypoint for Navigation

Once waypoints are stored in your GPS receiver, it is easy to access them. There are several ways to do that.

- *use "GoTo":* press "GoTo," select the desired waypoint from the list, and press "Enter"

- *scroll over a waypoint:* scroll to the desired point on the Map screen, press "GoTo," and press "Enter"

- *use a route:* select the desired route, which is made up of multiple waypoints (see the Selecting a Route for Navigation section, page 58)

Using "GoTo"

The quickest way to access the waypoint list is to press the "GoTo" button. This brings up the entire list of waypoints that you have entered into the GPS receiver. Scroll down to highlight the waypoint that you wish to select and press "Enter." The receiver will set a course from your current location to that waypoint. *Note:* Many GPS models will display the waypoint screen for the selected waypoint; pressing "Enter" again will activate navigation. The GPS will also draw a line on the Map screen from your current location to that waypoint and create a corresponding highway on the Highway screen.

Generally, the waypoints on the waypoint list appear sorted by number first and then alphabetically. In most recent models, you can enter up to 500 waypoints, while the very latest units can hold several thousand. If the number of waypoints that you have recorded is large, it could be a bit cumbersome to find the one that you want. Many GPS units offer ways to speed up this process, such as presenting the most recent or nearest waypoints first, or by permitting you to enter part of the name by scrolling over the first character or two. The Spell and Find mode will bring you to the waypoint name and comment field, so you can scroll through the characters to find the one that you want.

Tip: *To get maximum utility from your GPS unit, you will want to enter many waypoints.* However, with a large number of waypoints, it becomes useful to select a naming convention. The GPS receiver lets you conduct a search by name, and having a naming convention will make such a search infinitely easier. It is recommended that the first character or two reflect a region, such as "SH" for Sandy Hook or "F" for Falmouth. In this way, all of the relevant waypoints will be in the same general area of the waypoint list. When using the Find function, you highlight the waypoint name and press "Enter." Now when you scroll up or down, you are presented with the recorded waypoint names that use that character. If you start from the left and enter the location characters, then the distinguishing mark characters, you will home in on the waypoint of choice.

Another technique is to assign characters such as W, X, Y, or Z (letters at the end of the alphabet) for those waypoints that you use frequently. These can be accessed quickly by scrolling up on the waypoint list. This will cause the list to roll over to the end of the alphabet. This is preferred over waypoints beginning with "A" because you must scroll through all of the numeric waypoints before you get to the beginning of the alphabet. A GPS unit assigns three-digit numbers to new waypoints that you otherwise have not named, so scrolling through the numeric waypoints could prove tedious.

Scrolling over a Waypoint

You can scroll over and select an established waypoint on the Map screen. Once you have scrolled onto a waypoint, the label will be highlighted to indicate that it has been selected. As soon as you press "GoTo," the GPS unit will compute the course from your current location to the selected waypoint and commence navigation to that waypoint.

Alternatively, you can press "Enter" while scrolling over the waypoint to bring up the Waypoint screen to edit or check information regarding the waypoint. This screen also shows the bearing and distance from your current location to this waypoint. Accessing this screen does not cause the GPS receiver to enter this course, nor to interrupt another course that may be in process. At this point, you can edit the waypoint if you so choose, or press "Quit" to go back. You can also press "GoTo" to begin navigation, or move the cursor to highlight another waypoint.

Common Errors with Waypoints

Figures 4-14 and 4-15 demonstrated how easy it is to make an error in transferring the GPS coordinates to a chart. So it is with entering waypoints into the GPS unit. The greatest source of error in navigating with a GPS receiver is incorrect waypoint coordinates. Since the coordinates are simply two strings of numbers, it is easy to transpose the numbers while entering the waypoints into the receiver. *It is essential that you double-check the entered waypoints before using them to navigate.* This can be done by remeasuring the coordinates on the chart and comparing the results with the coordinates recorded in the GPS unit. A better way to double-check is to compare on a chart the range and bearing of each waypoint to a reference object. Select one of your waypoints and locate it on the chart. Next, set the present position in the GPS unit to that waypoint in the Simulator mode. Now scroll through your stored waypoints, one at a time. Each Waypoint screen will give you a range and bearing from the present position. Using your chart, see if these values agree.

A second common error in using a GPS receiver is accidentally selecting the wrong waypoint. The waypoint list is simply an alphabetic list of waypoints. The waypoint on your list directly above or below the one that you want is likely to be some distance away. It is very easy to select one of these by mistake. While at sea, the motion of the boat makes pressing the buttons a bit of a challenge. Once the waypoint is selected, you need to make sure that its bearing and range seem reasonable. Take a quick look at your chart just to make sure.

Navigating with Waypoints

Once you select a waypoint, the GPS unit computes the bearing and distance from your current position to that waypoint. This is illustrated in figure 4-20. On the Map screen, the GPS unit draws a line from your current location to the selected waypoint, and on the Highway screen, the unit creates a highway. In this example, you are navigating to a destination waypoint that is 5.0 nm distant on a true course of 0°at a speed of 10.0 knots.

As you navigate, the GPS receiver continually updates the bearing and distance to the selected waypoint. The receiver also provides your course over ground and speed over ground. As noted earlier, these values may not correspond with your compass readings (even if you have the GPS receiver set on magnetic) or your boat's speedometer. Because the effects of current

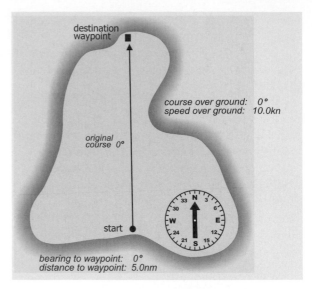

FIGURE 4-20. *Once a Waypoint Is Entered for Navigation, the GPS Receiver Computes Its Bearing and Distance. As soon as the waypoint is selected, the receiver draws a course line on the Map screen from your current location to the selected waypoint, and creates a highway on the Highway screen. This course line stays on the screen until another waypoint is selected. From the starting point, the bearing to the waypoint is the same as the course over ground for the boat. The distance to the waypoint is equal to the charted distance from the starting waypoint to the destination waypoint.*

and wind can cause your heading and speed over water to differ, a GPS receiver provides a more accurate position and direction relative to the chart.

Using Waypoints to Get Back On Course

If you get off course, as shown in figure 4-21, the GPS unit provides quite a bit of useful information. In this example, the boat maintained its original heading, so its compass course did not change. The GPS receiver does *not* provide information regarding the heading of the boat—this comes from the ship's compass. However, a strong wind and/or current pushed the boat off course to starboard. The GPS receiver provides course over ground (COG) and speed over ground (SOG), not the speed or direction over water. Since both the propulsion of the boat and the effects of wind and current are acting on the boat, the COG is 45° while the heading is 0°, and the resultant SOG is 14 knots at 45°. In this case, the boat is making headway at 10 knots through the water toward 0° but is

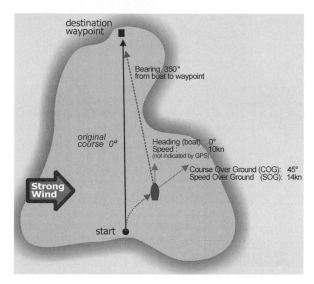

FIGURE 4-21. *Off Course. If you are off course, the GPS unit provides valuable cues. The GPS receiver continually computes and updates the bearing and distance to the waypoint. The track (TRK) or course over ground (COG) of the boat reflects its net motion, taking into account the propulsion of the boat plus all external effects. If a strong wind or current pushes the boat off course, the track reflects the net effect. In this case, the heading of the boat as indicated on the compass has not changed, but the boat no longer is on the original course line. The GPS receiver tells a different story. It is telling you what is happening over the ground. The course over ground is 45°, and the speed over ground is 14 knots. The boat actually is moving faster than its propulsion alone would indicate. This is the effect of the strong wind and current. The boat is still moving northward at 10 knots, but it is no longer on course. The new bearing to the waypoint is 350°.*

progressively moving farther away from the original course line. However, with constant updates from the GPS unit, it is known the bearing toward the destination waypoint is now 350°, representing a straight path from the current position. The course over ground and speed over ground are the result of the boat's motion through the water to the north and the motion to starboard caused by the current and wind.

What the GPS Unit *Doesn't* Do

The GPS unit has no way to check the straight-line path between your current position and the destination waypoint to make sure that it is safe. The GPS unit simply determines your 3-D position in space and compares this with the 3-D position of the way-

point. It has no knowledge of local features or hazards. If, as in figure 4-22, you have wandered farther off course, the direct path to the waypoint would take you across a spit of land. The bearing to the waypoint is now 340°. The Map screen would show

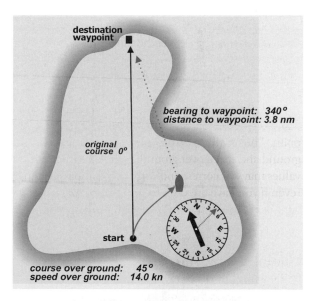

FIGURE 4-22. *Once Off Course, You May Not Be Able to Head Directly to Your Destination Waypoint. In this figure, you are off course with a hazardous path to your destination. You have drifted farther off course than in figure 4-21. The indicated bearing to the waypoint now reads 340° on your GPS. However, that bearing does not indicate if that path is safe. Whenever your boat veers away from its original clear course line, there may be hazards between the boat and the objective waypoint. One indication that you no longer are on the original course line is that the bearing to the waypoint has continually changed, from its original value of 0° to 340°. You must plot your current position on a chart to determine that a section of land prevents you from proceeding directly to the waypoint.*

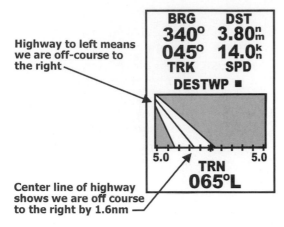

Highway to left means we are off-course to the right

BRG	DST
340°	3.80^n_m
045°	14.0^k_n
TRK	SPD

DESTWP ■

5.0   5.0

TRN
065°L

Center line of highway shows we are off course to the right by 1.6nm

FIGURE 4-23. The Highway Screen. Information useful to the boater can be found on the Highway screen. This Highway screen reflects your current position and heading from the previous figure. The highway shows that you are to the right (or starboard) of the center of the road (your original course line). The course deviation indicator scale shows that you are some 1.6 nautical miles to starboard. The Highway screen also shows that your track is well to the right of your intended waypoint objective. This means you are continuing to progress away from your intended objective. Notice that the highway shows no indication of the spit of land that blocks your path.

your location to be some distance to starboard from the original course line that still appears on the page. However, even the Map screen does not show the shoreline. On the Highway screen shown in figure 4-23, the GPS receiver indicates you are 1.6 miles to the right (starboard) of the center of the road (your original course line).

Plotting Your Position

It is very important that you plot on a chart your current position and the corresponding bearing line to the waypoint. Scanning along the plotted path on the chart will indicate whether it is safe to proceed. Clearly, it is not safe in the previous example. In many such situations, you may wish to return to the original course line as directly as possible, as illustrated in figure 4-24. You also need to check to ensure that this path is clear. In the example, you have turned to the left (port) to intersect with the original course line by the shortest reasonable route.

You can use the Highway screen effectively for navigation, but you need to understand what the dis-

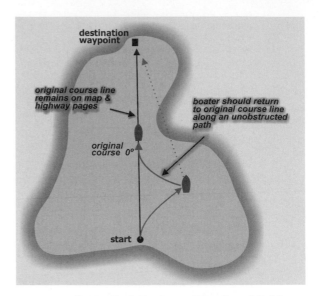

FIGURE 4-24. Getting Back On Course Directly and Safely. From your current position, you would be wise to return to the original course line as directly as possible. Even this path must be checked on a chart to ensure that it is safe to traverse.

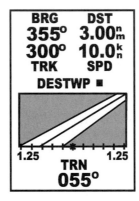

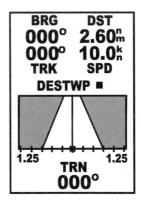

BRG	DST
355°	3.00^n_m
300°	10.0^k_n
TRK	SPD

DESTWP ■

1.25   1.25

TRN
055°

BRG	DST
000°	2.60^n_m
000°	10.0^k_n
TRK	SPD

DESTWP ■

1.25   1.25

TRN
000°

FIGURE 4-25. The Highway Screen Tells You When You Are Back On Course. You have turned toward the course line shown in figure 4-24. The corresponding Highway screen (left) provides graphical insights. Next, you have returned to the center of the highway (right) and are headed toward the waypoint. You should endeavor to maintain this picture on the display by adjusting the steering of the boat into the wind or current. By carefully tuning the boat's heading, you can stay in the center of the highway with the destination waypoint straight ahead. This means that the boat is proceeding on the intended course line. The TRK (or COG) will not match the compass reading if there is a crosswind or crosscurrent. The boat heading will not point toward the destination, but toward the wind; however, the boat's motion will be in the proper direction.

play is telling you. The Highway screen corresponding to an intermediate point after you turned back toward the original course line is shown in figure 4-25 on the left. The highway appears to be crossing your path, but still some distance away. This is what you would see if driving a car back to a highway from a field off to its right. The destination waypoint now is off to your right indicating that you are intersecting the highway at some midpoint. Once you have returned to the original course line and are properly aligned to the waypoint (fig. 4-25, right), the Highway screen shows you in the center of the highway and heading in the proper direction.

Tip: *You can use the Highway screen to stay on course.* If the wind or current were pushing the boat off course, you would need to turn the boat into the wind to stay on course. The Highway screen can be used to tell you when you are traveling in the correct direction. Simply adjust the heading of the boat into the wind until you find an angle that maintains your position in the center of the highway, heading directly toward the waypoint. That is, the highway should appear exactly like the graphic on the right in figure 4-25. The compass will tell you that the heading of the boat is different. However, don't worry about the compass: steer to the highway.

Beware of the Hooked Course

A common problem shared by boaters steering toward a mark or waypoint is the *hooked course.* If for any reason you drift from your course line, the natural tendency is to correct your course to head directly for the waypoint. However, whatever caused you to drift is still affecting the boat, so you will drift farther off course. You will find that you must readjust your course a short time later, as the bearing to the waypoint has continued to change. By steering directly to the waypoint, you will continue to readjust your course until you reach the waypoint—from the side, not the front, as figure 4-26 demonstrates. The track of the boat has taken a wide curve rather than a straight line. Unfortunately, if as in this example there are hazards to starboard of the original course line, you would probably hit them. This can be a common occurrence when sailing in a channel and steering visually from buoy to buoy. It is rather easy to drift out of

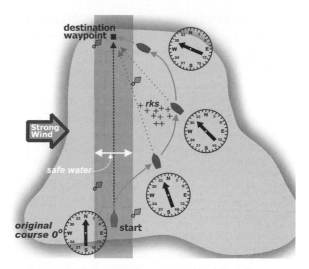

FIGURE 4-26. *Steering to the Waypoint Can Get You into Trouble. The process of steering directly toward the waypoint under conditions of a crosswind or crosscurrent may result in a path that takes you far afield of the original course line and into danger. All the while you are adjusting your course to point toward the waypoint. In reality, you must overcompensate to stay on the course line to your destination.*

the channel while all the while believing you are on course steering toward the destination buoy.

How do you prevent the hooked course? Following the previous tip, using the GPS receiver's Highway screen, steer to stay in the middle of the highway. If your position drifts to the right side of the highway, steer a little left and repeat the adjustment until you stay in the center. At this point, your boat heading, as recorded by the compass, will be different from the course over ground (or track) shown on the GPS unit. In reality, your boat is pointing to the left of the waypoint, but it is moving on the course line. This is analogous to observing an airplane come in for a landing in a crosswind. The plane points in a different direction from its actual motion. This is often called *crabbing.* Your boat is doing the same thing in the water. Using the Highway screen and adjusting your heading to stay in the middle of the road automatically compensates for the crosscurrent effects.

Tip: *A note of caution for those who may be using an older GPS unit on a fast boat.* Each GPS receiver model recalculates information at a relatively uniform time interval. For a newer receiver model this is typically each second. In older models this interval may be somewhat longer due to the slower processor then available. Therefore, if you are traveling at 20 knots or more with an older unit, the GPS receiver's reported position and course may be 10 seconds or more behind. This means you could be steering a different course and have a reported position some 350 feet behind your present location. Keep this in mind near hazards. Also, most GPS models smooth the course direction over a number of sequential position calculations (equivalent to dampening with a compass). Each GPS model will exhibit a different rate of responsiveness to changes in boat direction. If you find it difficult to maintain a course using the GPS receiver because of this time delay, you may find it easier to steer using your compass. Nonetheless, monitoring your position relative to the centerline of the highway on the Highway screen will keep you on course.

Correlating Chart Data with Your GPS

In addition to determining where to go, an equal part of navigation is determining where *not* to go. The water masks a variety of hazards such as shallow water or rocks that must be avoided for safe passage. The chart provides this needed information. Therefore, it is imperative that you know your position on a chart at all times.

Correlating between the GPS receiver and the chart is not an easy and convenient task, especially on the water. The next four topics cover techniques you can use with your GPS that enhance your safety and enable you to get a better feel of where you are relative to the chart position.

Map Screen. The Map screen is one of the most useful GPS screens. Unfortunately, unless you have a chartplotter (addressed in chapter 7), the Map screen does not provide key information found on the chart. Figure 4-27 shows a typical Map screen on a GPS unit—it's not very satisfying. You need to transcribe the GPS position onto a chart before you have a sense of where you are, but there are ways to make the Map screen more useful.

GPS waypoints can be invaluable when they are added to the Map screen. The sample chart in figure 4-28 shows the same area as the Map screen in figure 4-27. Waypoints can be added to the GPS receiver's

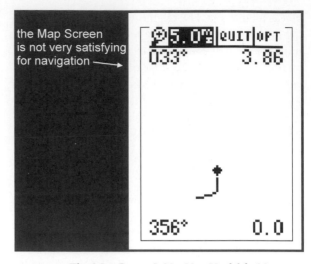

the Map Screen is not very satisfying for navigation ⟶

FIGURE 4-27. *This Map Screen Is Not Very Useful for Navigation. Without additional information, the Map screen is not as useful as the Highway screen for navigation. In this example, you have the boat, a line corresponding to its track, and little else. Clearly, you cannot use this limited information for safe navigation without frequent reference to the relevant chart.*

Map screen to mark the buoys shown on the chart. Waypoints can also be used to mark visible landmarks on the Map screen, even landmarks on land such as a church spire and danger in the water such as rocks. Most boaters use only a fraction of the available waypoints for course markings in their GPS units, so this leaves a number of waypoint locations for other uses. If you enter all the key features from your sample chart into the GPS receiver, the Map screen will display them, as shown in figure 4-29. Now the Map screen has significant meaning. Although the Map screen does not show features such as the shoreline and depth contours, it does show many of the aids to navigation and hazards that are of great importance to the navigator. A waypoint does not need to be a physical object. There are times when you might want to mark a spot to take some action or simply to use as a reference. This is true for your favorite fishing hole or for a convenient reference point outside of your harbor. The Map screen also shows the boat's course over ground (track) on the screen. If this same path has been taken in the past, old tracks may still be seen on the page to further assist the navigator to replicate a previous safe passage.

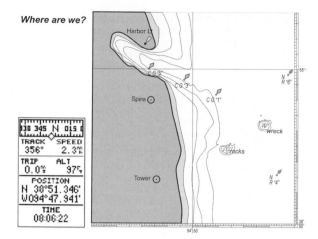

Where are we?

FIGURE 4-28. *The Chart for Your Area of Operation. This chart corresponds to the area of operation reflecting the screen in figure 4-24. There are hazards nearby that you must take into account. Plotting your GPS-indicated position frequently on this chart can be tedious and takes you away from your primary task in operating the boat.*

Nearest Waypoints Screen. Your GPS unit can provide relative position data while you are underway without interrupting an active course. The Nearest Waypoints screen can be accessed from the Main Menu. Once activated, Nearest Waypoints displays a screen with the stored waypoints that are closest to your current position. This is very handy if you are lost! It is also useful to get a sense of where you are relative to those objects that you entered into the GPS receiver. The Nearest Waypoints screen (see fig. 4-30) shows the bearing and range to each of the waypoints in our field of view—ranked from closest to farthest. Armed with this information, you can use your hand-bearing compass and binoculars to look for objects and cross-check your position. You can also see how far you are from hazards.

Proximity Waypoints. A special type of waypoint, often called a *proximity waypoint*, is available on most GPS receivers. Typically, memory is allocated for only 10 or so proximity waypoints, which are designed to mark danger. The user not only can select the center point of the hazard, but can also set a radius of danger around it. The user can also set an alarm to sound if the boat ventures within that radius. These are described in greater detail in chapter 6.

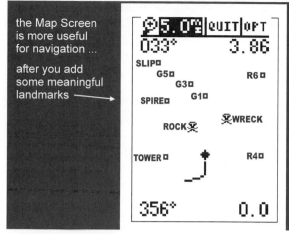

the Map Screen is more useful for navigation ...

after you add some meaningful landmarks ⟶

FIGURE 4-29. *Entering Chart Features into the GPS Receiver. You can add important chart features to the GPS receiver's Map screen. The coordinates are transcribed as waypoints for each object of interest from the chart to the GPS unit. Now, the Map screen shows relevant features. This screen alerts you to the nearby rocks and helps you to navigate to G1, the first waypoint in your route. Given that you have identified all of the key features along your path as waypoints, you can navigate safely using the GPS unit.*

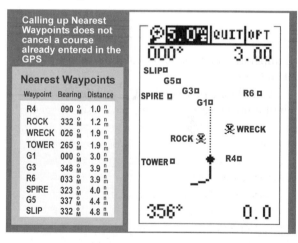

Calling up Nearest Waypoints does not cancel a course already entered in the GPS

Nearest Waypoints

Waypoint	Bearing	Distance
R4	090 °M	1.0 nm
ROCK	332 °M	1.2 nm
WRECK	026 °M	1.9 nm
TOWER	265 °M	1.9 nm
G1	000 °M	3.0 nm
G3	348 °M	3.9 nm
R6	033 °M	3.9 nm
SPIRE	323 °M	4.0 nm
G5	337 °M	4.4 nm
SLIP	332 °M	4.8 nm

FIGURE 4-30. *The Nearest Waypoints Screen. The Nearest Waypoints screen provides position data on all local waypoints. Going to the Main Menu and selecting "Nearest Waypoints" brings up this very useful screen. This Nearest Waypoints screen shows the closest points to your current position that have been stored in your GPS receiver ranked from closest on top. The data reflect the example in the previous three figures. Given this information, the helmsman can verify bearing and distance to each of these recorded waypoints, including buoys, rocks, and landmarks. Using a hand-bearing compass, the helmsman visually can verify position and avoid danger. Select "Quit" to return to the previous screen.*

When Not to Use the Bearing to a Selected Waypoint. As shown in the examples above and as was demonstrated more dramatically in figure 4-6, there are times when the direct path to a waypoint is not safe. In the example in figure 4-6, there is an is-

land between your current position and destination. In order to navigate safely around the island, you created a number of sequential waypoints, each representing a course change, as shown in figure 4-7. You can navigate these waypoints, one at a time, by manually entering the next waypoint as soon as you reach the current waypoint.

To make this type of multiple waypoint navigation more convenient, GPS receivers can automate the sequence as a *route*.

Routes

The GPS receiver can store a route.

> → *A route is a sequence of waypoints. It has a name, and it consists of a set of "legs."*
>
> → *Routes can be "activated," in either a forward or "inverted" direction, and they can be edited.*
>
> → *The Route screen shows the distances and bearings between waypoints and the distance for the entire route.*

Boating manually from waypoint to waypoint is simple enough in concept, but it can be tedious or even dangerous when actually at sea. Typically, a waypoint signifies a course change. So, there you are at sea, implementing a course change on a moving, rocking boat, and attempting to locate and activate the "GoTo" for the next waypoint. It is easy to activate the wrong waypoint accidentally under these conditions.

The alternative to this problematic scenario is called a *route*. A route is a programmed sequence of waypoints. Once created and activated, the route sequentially calls up the next appropriate waypoint automatically. This frees the helmsman to concentrate on the water and not on making waypoint changes in the GPS receiver.

Figure 4-31 shows the use of a route to go from one location to another. Waypoints are established at each point where an action is taken. The segments between waypoints are considered "legs" of the route. The leg that you are on is called the "active leg."

Preventing an Accidental Change in the Active Course

One fear many GPS users have is accidentally changing the active course they have set. As a result, these individuals are hesitant to press buttons while underway. But by not actively using the GPS unit while on the boat, they miss out on its many features that can assist with their navigation. The following is a brief summary of what you can do that will not interrupt the course in progress.

On most models, the active course (or route) being navigated within the GPS receiver will be changed only if you enter a new "GoTo" or "Nav" waypoint, or a new route. The operative term here is *enter*: until you press the "Enter" button, the active course will not change. You can access most functions within the GPS receiver for viewing and then return to the previous screen by pressing either the "Quit" or the "Page" button. Typically, the "Enter" button is the only button that causes the receiver to execute an action: *use it with care.* Generally, you can press "Enter" in association with almost any task other than "GoTo" or "Route" without altering the active course.

For example, you can press "Enter" to work your way through the menus or to edit a waypoint. You can bring up the Nearest Waypoints screen from the Main Menu by highlighting that option and pressing "Enter." Use "Quit" to return to the previous page you were using. You even can review and edit waypoints and routes as long as you don't attempt to make them active by using "GoTo" and "Enter."

There are times that you want to change the active course. Let's say you would like to update the course line from your current location to that same waypoint that you previously had entered. By pressing "GoTo" or "Nav," you usually are presented with the current active waypoint. By pressing "Enter," you reset the course line to display from your *current* location to the active waypoint. Alternatively, you can change your course to a new waypoint at any time by using "GoTo" and selecting the waypoint by pressing "Enter."

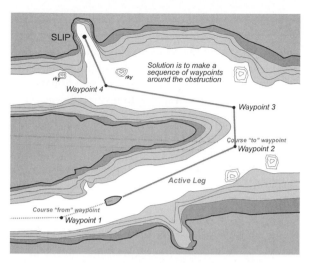

FIGURE 4-31. *Using a Route to Navigate the Waypoints Automatically. Many boaters will use the GPS receiver to navigate manually from waypoint to waypoint, one at a time. This requires the helmsman to work with the GPS unit at each turn, when his attention is needed most at the helm. Using a route automates this process. A route is simply a recorded sequence of waypoints. Selecting the route automatically activates one leg at a time. The current segment is called the "Active Leg," which ends as the "Active Waypoint" is approached. This permits the helmsman to engage one route instead of sequentially engaging each waypoint manually.*

Establishing a Route

The first step in establishing a route is planning. A route can be a special trip you have planned, or more simply, paths that you frequently take on local cruises. Route planning can be done on a chart table with chart, dividers, and paper to record the coordinates of the waypoints. Typically, key features of the route involve an analysis of the best courses and waypoints to select in order to safely navigate from one place to another. Waypoints, as previously mentioned, also mark the end points for legs of the trip. Each leg is a straight-line segment of the trip that is checked on the chart to assure safe water along the entire path. Since you are likely to travel the same waters and the same paths frequently, it is a good practice to lay out point-to-point legs on your chart and convert them to GPS route segments. As you enter the route segments, the GPS receiver will compute the course directions and distances for each leg, which you can annotate on the chart. This bridging

of chart and GPS unit builds a repertoire of paths that you can use to safely traverse your cruising waters. While underway, you simply decide on the preplanned routes that take you where you want to go. This also simplifies following along on your chart. This concept is demonstrated by the simulation exercise in appendix 3.

After planning a route, you must make sure that each waypoint's name and coordinates are entered into the GPS unit. As identified above, a waypoint should be established for each and every point along the planned route where an action should be taken. Besides changing course, you may wish to plan a stop, crew change, check for depth, or any number of other actions.

To begin entering a route, access the Route Menu from the Main Menu. This brings up the Route Definition screen, as shown in figure 4-32. The GPS receiver will display a name for the new route, such as "Empty-2." Below the name and route number is a set of blank fields listing waypoints and other information. By scrolling over the first empty field and

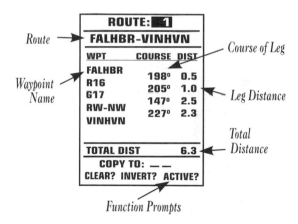

FIGURE 4-32. *The Route Definition Screen. The Route Definition screen is used to select waypoints sequentially and in order. The process of entering a route into the GPS unit entails scrolling and sequentially entering each waypoint in the order that you will follow in the route. The waypoints are drawn from the stored list within the GPS. Once completed, the Route screen indicates the course and distance for each leg between waypoints, and the total distance for the route. The route can be activated, inverted, or edited on this screen. Selecting "Active" starts the route navigation. The invert feature enables you to activate the same route in reverse order. Some GPS models require that you press "Menu" to access the list of options shown at the bottom of this screen.*

pressing "Enter," you will access the field for that way-point. By scrolling first the left character field, and then successively other fields to the right, you will bring up waypoint names stored in memory until you have displayed the name of the desired waypoint for this part of the route. This is a waypoint you have pre-viously planned and entered into the GPS unit. (You can see the advantage to selecting an alphanumeric character for a given region as the first character while entering waypoints. By so doing, you are able to access waypoints in that region quickly using that first character.)

To accept the displayed name as the desired way-point, press "Enter." Now the Route Definition screen will show the name of the first waypoint. The distance will appear as "0.00" since this is the starting point of the route.

Next scroll over the waypoint field immediately below the first one, and repeat the process. Select the second waypoint in the same manner. Once the sec-ond waypoint is entered, a leg is established, and the distance and course fields will have values that reflect the course and distance from the first waypoint to the second.

Repeat the process until the entire route is en-tered. The distance field will reflect the distances be-tween successive waypoints, and a total route distance will be displayed below. The route is now available for use. The route name will now reflect the first and last waypoint names of the route. On some GPS models you can edit the name to one of your own choosing.

Tip: *Break a lengthy route into segments of routes.* You are likely to have many parts of your various routes in common. You will save time and memory in the GPS unit by using these common route seg-ments, such as the dock to some common buoy as one route, and the various routes from that common point separately.

Appendix 3 lays out a sample route. Three way-points are entered first. At this point, it would be useful to follow along with the explanation of establishing a route to test your new skills with the exercise.

Selecting a Route for Navigation

Once a route is established within the GPS receiver, it can be activated by entering the Main Menu, se-lecting "Route," and selecting the desired route name. Pressing "Enter" moves you to the Route Definition screen that you used originally to enter the route. You can double-check your intended path and waypoints before proceeding. Depending upon your particular GPS model, either you will see function prompts on this screen, or you will need to press "Menu" to get the choices. These choices are "Act" or "Activate" to start the route at the first way-point, "Inv" or "Invert" to start the route in reverse order of waypoints, or options to delete (clear) or copy the route.

Tip: *You can use the Copy command to copy com-monly used route segments into longer routes and save the effort of repeatedly entering the same data.* You can also edit a route to add or delete waypoints. Many GPS models also allow you to edit routes on the Map screen.

Following a Route

Once activated, the route (or the inverse route) will start navigation to the first waypoint and display this in-formation on the screen that you were using prior to entering the Route Definition screen. Most GPS re-ceivers will permit you to enter a route at some inter-mediate point rather than at the first waypoint. To do this, activate the route and sail toward any leg of the route. Usually, the receiver will recognize that you are between waypoints, activate the appropriate leg, and provide you with instructions from your position.

Tracks

Track is a Map screen function. A track, or a record of your position history, is indicated usually as a dashed line on the Map screen. It is also recorded in the memory of your GPS receiver. On the Track Setup screen, as shown in figure 4-33, you have the option to use or not use the track function, and you can change how a track is recorded.

Tracks can be very useful for navigation, as they appear on the GPS unit as lines showing previous paths you have taken. These paths offer you a high degree of confidence in their safety, barring the ef-fects of tide. Using the Map screen, you can zoom in for a finer picture and simply follow the previous path. Understand that your new position could differ

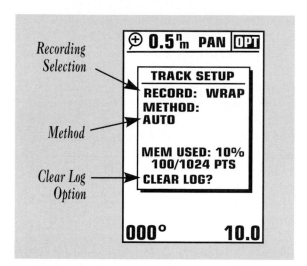

Recording Selection

Method

Clear Log Option

FIGURE 4-33. *User-Selectable Track Features. Tracks provide a historical record of where you have been. Their characteristics are selected using the Track Setup screen. You can turn the track feature off or select a one-time fill or wrap feature that continually fills in the most recent points. The track points can be selected automatically, by distance traveled, or by time increment.*

by as much as 100 feet (30.5 m) even though you may indicate being right on top of the previous track. The original track could be in error by 30 to 50 feet (9.15–15.25 m), and your new position is subject to a similar potential error. Generally, you will be reasonably close. In fog or other adverse conditions, it may be the best data that you have available, but proceed with caution.

By accessing the "Record" field on the Track Setup screen, you are given choices such as "Off," "Fill," or "Wrap."

- "Off" shuts down the track process.

- "Fill" records one track until the memory is used and stops until you clear the memory.

- "Wrap" records continuously, overwriting the older data when the memory is filled.

Usually, GPS units record 1,000 to 2,000 track points. This may be enough for an extended day of cruising. The "Method" or "Interval" field on the Track Setup screen allows you to choose how the GPS receiver records the waypoints. You may have a choice of automatic, time, or distance. Generally, au-

tomatic or distance is better than time, because with automatic or distance you do not use up points while stationary. You also may have the option to select the recording interval. The larger the interval, the fewer points required, but the recorded track will be less refined. It also is possible to erase old tracks from your screen once it becomes too cluttered by selecting "Clear."

Many GPS receivers also offer a Track Back mode. This feature allows you to use your historical track to return to your point of origin. Once entered, the receiver will compute a course and direct you in following approximately the same track back to your starting point. The GPS unit usually simplifies the path to fewer track points, so beware, the track back could take you over some hazards. Generally, Track Back is more useful to hikers than boaters.

Trip Computer

Many GPS models provide features that help you plan and monitor your trip. Features such as Fuel Planning and Trip Times are incorporated with the Route function. By entering your intended speed, fuel consumption per hour, and departure time, you will be presented with fuel use per leg and trip, time per leg and trip, and arrival time at each waypoint.

During your cruise, you can use the Trip Computer to provide such information as trip distance, total distance for the season, average and maximum speed, total operating time, trip time elapsed, moving time, stopped time, and trip average speed. These functions usually can be reset for the trip, or totaled. You can use the total counters to keep track of the season or total use for the boat.

Other GPS Functions

Tide Computer

A number of newer GPS models have incorporated a tide computational program. A large number of tide locations are offered. Once activated, the Tide Computer uses the current time and data received from the GPS satellites to provide a tide graph showing the current conditions as well as the times and heights of high and low tide. You can change the date to forecast the tide conditions at some time in the future or look back to the past.

The Tide Computer will often provide an indication of the distance and bearing from your current location to the location for the tide calculation. Obviously, tidal information is of high importance for traversing areas of low water or in planning an arrival at a harbor.

Celestial Data

Many GPS receivers provide celestial information, including sunrise and sunset times for your current location. Some also include the times of moonrise and moonset, and the current phase of the moon. A few newer models also show the present location of the sun and/or the moon from your current position. Some models also permit calculation of these same data for another location, such as a waypoint, distant city, or aid to navigation. These units usually permit performing these calculations for any date and time.

Alarms

Alarms were briefly discussed in chapter 3. Most GPS models offer a variety of alarms that can be set by the user. Typical alarms include a standard alarm clock function, anchor drag distance, off-course distance, arrival (predetermined time or distance from waypoint), depth, and battery voltage.

In addition to these user-selectable alarms, most GPS receivers also provide alarms when they lose lock with the satellites, or at other times when the navigation performance changes, such as losing the WAAS or DGPS signal. WAAS and DGPS are supplemental systems to improve GPS position accuracy and are described in chapter 10.

Fixed-mount GPS models have more user inputs and outputs than a typical handheld. Many of these also provide a connector for mounting an external alarm that can be heard throughout the boat.

Depth Sounder

Newer GPS models incorporate a greater number of input and output ports to share data. Many will accept input from a depth sounder using the NMEA protocol. An alarm can be sounded if the depth becomes to shallow, or too great. The latter can be used as an alternate indicator of anchor drag, or that you are venturing too far out to sea. Many depth sounders also provide a measure of water temperature. If temperature is reported by the depth sounder, the GPS receiver may be able to display the value, as well as displaying the depth.

Chapter 5

GPS Receiver Selection and Cost Considerations

By now you should have a good appreciation of how to use your GPS unit to navigate and how to use the buttons, screens, and menus to your advantage. This chapter presents some of the practical considerations of using your GPS receiver on board, including what additional equipment you may wish to use. The second part of the chapter presents those factors you should consider when purchasing a GPS unit and accessories.

Competition in the GPS receiver marketplace has driven a continuing array of offerings from a sizable number of companies. Prices range from as little as $100 to over $10,000 for GPS receivers. A wide range of hardware and software accessories is available to the customer. Where to start? Selection of the best GPS unit depends upon how you intend to use it. This chapter describes how to get the most from your investment, and then describes migration paths to the tailored ideal solution. A range of street prices are provided for relative reference; however, competitive pressures and product changes may affect the current prices for specific components.

The basic performance of a typical GPS unit far surpasses almost any other navigation instrument for a very nominal investment. However, it must be used properly. There are important considerations that affect a GPS receiver's performance as well as your ability to navigate safely using the receiver.

Most individuals start by purchasing a handheld GPS receiver. Handhelds offer the advantages of low to moderate cost and portability. Many handheld buyers believe they will use the receiver on the boat in the summer and in the car or hiking on other occasions. A handheld GPS unit can be a very wise investment, but it may not be the ultimate match for your boating needs.

The Handheld

The handheld GPS receiver provides great position accuracy. Certainly, this is of prime importance to your boating safety. However, handhelds do have some disadvantages. Handheld GPS units have small screens that are difficult to see, especially on a bouncing, moving boat. The buttons are small and similarly difficult to push while you, the GPS unit, and the boat are all moving. Therefore, your greatest challenge is positioning the handheld optimally. Holding it in your hand all the time is not very comfortable, practical, or safe, and the receiver must always have a clear view of the sky to receive the satellite signals.

Since the antenna is integral with the GPS unit, where you locate the unit is of prime importance. You should consider a bracket to hold the GPS receiver near the helm station. In order to function properly, the receiver must be nearly vertical so that the antenna is properly positioned. A handheld lying on its back does not cover the entire sky, so some available satellites will be lost and performance will suffer. The antenna also must have a clear view of the sky almost from horizon to horizon. Obstructions, particularly metallic ones, will degrade the signal. Wood and fiberglass also degrade the signal, especially if they're wet. If you mount the GPS unit for optimum sky coverage, you may not be able to read the screen. The best place to put the GPS receiver mount is as high as possible at the helm.

Since the antenna location is important, use your GPS receiver to help you determine where to put it. Compare the signal levels on the Satellite screen from various locations on your boat. The height of each reception bar provides you with a reasonable indication. If the signal levels drop as you move to the helm station, you should consider an external antenna, if your model accepts one. Garmin, as well as other manufacturers, offers an external marine antenna for a little over $100. The external antenna removes concern over GPS receiver placement so that you can place the unit where it is easiest to see and use. Typically, external antennas can be mounted on a guardrail, atop the windshield, or on a hardtop if the boat is so equipped. The antenna is attached to the GPS unit by a cable and derives its power from the unit.

The next consideration is power. Handheld GPS receivers use batteries. Make sure you have a spare set of batteries—or several sets—aboard. In addition, most handheld models can operate from external power using a 12-volt cigarette lighter adapter. If your boat does not have a suitable 12-volt socket, consider installing one. Alternatively, you can hardwire the cord into your electrical system. If you do this, a switch and fuse would be a good idea.

The last consideration is environment. Many handheld GPS receivers are water *resistant*, not water*proof*. Place the receiver in a location where it is protected from the environment. Salt spray can seep into a GPS unit and destroy it. Consider placing a zippered plastic freezer bag or waterproof transparent pouch over the handheld under adverse conditions to protect it from direct exposure to water.

As already mentioned, handheld GPS units must be used in conjunction with charts to assure safe passage. The small screens are not amenable to presenting charts, so paper charts are required. On a small to midsize boat, finding a place to work with charts is a challenge. The best alternative is to have routes and waypoints preplotted on your charts corresponding to those in the GPS receiver, and have the charts folded so that you can observe the areas in which you are boating, much like the AAA trip map for highway travel. Label your charts with the same waypoint names that you have stored in your receiver. Some of the commercial chart books are especially suited for this purpose.

The Chartplotter

Alternatively, consider the ideal solution for small to midsize boats—the chartplotter. These devices are described in more detail in chapter 7. A chartplotter is a device that displays the GPS Map screen information superimposed over a digital chart. The digital chart reflects the same character and detail you typically find on the paper charts from which the digital chart was derived. The GPS receiver is usually, but not always, integrated into the chartplotter, as explained in chapters 7 and 9. Contrary to some opinions, chartplotters are not used only on larger boats; they are very useful aboard the average runabout or fishing boat where space is at a premium. A chartplotter with a 5-inch (127 mm) screen and current chart chips offers a safer, less error-prone solution to boating. The chartplotter is fixed and usually is equipped with an external antenna. Now you can place the GPS unit where it is most convenient and still get good coverage. Chartplotter buttons are larger and more plentiful, so operating the unit is easier than operating a handheld GPS unit. Waypoints are indicated on the electronic chart, so you're less likely to select the wrong one erroneously. But don't throw out that handheld or the paper charts, if you have these: take them along as backups.

This next section addresses the selection process for a GPS receiver. Many of these points apply to selecting any GPS unit. For the most part, GPS receivers have similar performance. Most offer 12 channels, each capable of receiving a separate satel-

Ergonomic Considerations

When buying a GPS receiver, consider the motion caused by the wind and sea. You may be in less than an ideal lighting situation and confronting spray or swells. Under these conditions you'll need display screens that are easy to see and interpret and buttons that are easy to select and press.

lite's signals. The newer units are WAAS enabled, which is a distinct plus. Most units will work with DGPS, but this requires another receiver and antenna on your boat. WAAS and DGPS are described in chapter 10. The major considerations are the environment and your ability to see and control the GPS unit under boating conditions.

Selecting a GPS Receiver

First of all, it is a wise decision to own at least one handheld GPS unit if you plan to use GPS for marine navigation. Consequently, part 1 of this book is heavily oriented toward the handheld GPS receiver even though the same functions are also available on fixed-mount units. This chapter discusses considerations in selecting a GPS receiver. These same considerations generally apply to handheld and fixed-mount units alike, including chartplotters.

A number of questions follow, along with some of the alternatives you should factor into your decision-making process.

What's Your Budget?

One could ask in response, "how much is your life worth?" You can purchase a GPS receiver for as little as $100 that will provide very accurate position information. However, a more practical budget range would be $200 to $250 for a handheld unit and $500 to $1,000 for a fixed-mount unit. More will be presented about features versus cost below.

Will the GPS Receiver Be for Marine Use Only, or for Use on Land as Well?

The marine user should consider a unit with a marine database. This database will include buoys and aids to navigation. Handheld examples include the Garmin GPS 76 model, the Magellan 330M, and the Meridian Mariner. Typically, fixed-mount units will be used only on a boat, so you should select one that includes chartplotting. If you purchase a chartplotter for the boat and want a handheld as well, you can save some money by purchasing a basic unit such as the Garmin GPS 12. The basic units typically offer the same GPS position performance in a price range around $140.

What Is the Likely Operating Environment?

Will the unit be operated on deck exposed to sea and rain? If so, make sure the unit is sufficiently waterproof for this type of use. As noted earlier, you can save some money by using a waterproof transparent pouch designed for marine applications to protect a GPS receiver as an alternative to high-performance waterproofing.

Will the Unit Be Operated in Direct Sunlight?

Make sure the screen can be read in sunlight. Try a friend's unit, or ask for an outside demo at the store. Earlier color units were particularly susceptible to washout in full sunlight, but quality transflective color screens, which reflect available light back to you, making the screens even brighter in direct sunlight, are now available on most models. These displays add about 20 to 70 percent to the price over units with gray-scale screens, but they offer much better visual cuing to important information. More expensive fixed-mount units use high brightness active matrix displays and special optical filters to reduce the effects of the sun. These color displays may add to the price of the unit over a receiver with a gray-scale display and draw more power, but they offer optimum presentation in any lighting condition. Within a few years, almost all of the displays on fixed-mount units will be color, and most will be sunlight readable.

Will the Unit Be Operated at Night?

Make sure the unit has backlighting that is bright enough for screen viewing at night. Most new units have backlighting. The backlight on handheld GPS models usually is designed to stay on for a brief period of time to save the batteries. If you will use your handheld GPS unit at night, you should use a 12-volt power adapter and set the handheld's backlight to stay on continuously. This is accomplished in the System Setup Menu. Most fixed-mount units are designed with ample illumination modes.

Will the Unit Be Operated on a Small Boat in Choppy Seas?

Make sure that the screen is large enough to read, preferably without glasses, in a chop. The screen should have a good resolution, and the characters should be bold enough to read under adverse conditions. Also make sure that you will be able to operate the buttons while both you and the GPS receiver are bouncing in the boat. Many boaters with a 16- to 26-foot (5–8 m) boat may consider a handheld to be suitable. However, smaller boats react to the chop even more than larger boats. A 5-inch (127 mm), waterproof, color chartplotter may be the ideal small-craft unit for ease of use, visibility, and safety. In addition, the limited space on small boats makes it difficult to open paper charts, so the chart on the screen is an important safety advantage.

Will the GPS Receiver Have a Clear View of the Sky?

The GPS receiver relies on good signals from well-dispersed satellites. A hardtop, particularly one with a good deal of metal, may obscure parts of the sky or attenuate the signal. If so, make sure the GPS receiver can be connected to an external antenna.

Try to position the GPS unit so that nearby consoles and other obstructions don't block the internal antenna. There are generally two kinds of antennas available on handheld GPS units: the internal patch antenna and the removable quadrifilar-helix. The internal patch antenna is located inside the top of the unit just above the screen. The receiver needs to be in an upright position with the top clear of obstructions. The quadrifilar-helix antenna can be swiveled. It looks like a ½-inch-diameter (12.7 mm) rod. The antenna should be pointed upward and clear of obstructions. The quadrifilar-helix is considered to be of slightly higher performance; however, the internal patch is more convenient. Either unit will provide quality fixes if in clear view of the sky.

Regardless of the antenna used, use the signal level bars on your Satellite screen to tell you which location is optimal.

Will You Operate the GPS on Internal Batteries?

Screens, backlighting, large memories, and processors take power. Make sure that your supply of batteries is consistent with the length of your journey. Also consider the expense. A good alternative is to operate the unit on board through a cigarette lighter adapter. Make sure this is possible with the unit you purchase. Even if you have such an adapter, make sure you have a backup supply of batteries on board.

What Degree of Accuracy Do You Require?

The basic performance of the majority of GPS units is suitable for most maritime use. Most GPS units have twelve receiver channels. Most specifications suggest the unit can be accurate within 50 feet (15.25 m). Thirty-three feet (10 m) is typical.

Should you plan to use your GPS to navigate within constrained waterways under adverse conditions, you will need greater accuracy. The U.S. Coast Guard's DGPS (Differential GPS) system provides accuracy of 10 to 16 feet (3–5 m) 95 percent of the time. DGPS requires an additional receiver and antenna. Most GPS units are differential ready so they can be connected to the appropriate equipment. As noted earlier, DGPS is available along coastal regions and some inland waterways.

Most of the latest GPS units are WAAS enabled. Basically, WAAS (Wide Area Augmentation System) is a DGPS-type system for aircraft but works well for boats. The FAA developed and implemented the system. WAAS transmits corrections to be applied to each received satellite to improve position accuracy. The corrections are relayed to the user via geosynchronous satellites on the GPS L1 frequency. Geosynchronous (or geostationary) satellites are placed directly over the equator at an altitude of some 22,000 miles. At that distance they orbit the Earth in 24 hours, so they appear stationary to users on the ground. The GPS unit uses one of its existing channels to receive the corrections. WAAS satellites are postioned over the Atlantic and Pacific Oceans. You must have a clear view of either one to receive the updates. The accuracy is better than DGPS (typically better than 10 feet/3 meters). More on DGPS and WAAS can be found in chapter 10.

What Accessories Should You Consider?

Most GPS receivers are self-contained and need few, if any, accessories. The top accessories to consider for handheld GPS receivers are

- power cords or adapters
- computer connection cables
- protective cases
- mounting brackets
- external antennas
- chart chips
- uploadable software and data on CD-ROMs

For fixed-mount units, the major accessories are chart chips and extra computer connection cables. Fixed-mount units typically come with brackets, cables, and an external antenna.

The power cord adapter allows you to connect the GPS receiver to a cigarette lighter for auxiliary power. Alternative power cords enable direct connection to the boat's electrical system. These cords typically cost $25 to $35. Computer cables allow you to connect the GPS unit to a computer for uploading and downloading information. For the most part, these cables and the software, described more fully in chapters 8 and 9, are designed to work on PCs; however, there are a limited number of programs that are Mac compatible. These cables are in the same price range as power cords, and most manufacturers offer a cable that both powers and uploads-downloads for slightly more money.

Protective cases can be used to further waterproof the GPS unit. Some of these cases enable the user to view the screen and press buttons while the unit is in operation. These cases sell for $20 to $40.

Since the orientation of the GPS receiver is important, it makes sense to have a bracket to hold it

in place. A variety of brackets, priced $30 and up, are available from the receiver manufacturers and third-party companies. The primary considerations are antenna and screen visibility and access to buttons on the receiver. If you have a fixed-mount unit, you can purchase additional brackets to mount your GPS on another boat or to a piece of wood for use at home. Twelve-volt DC power adapters for AC also are available from GPS receiver dealers or electronic suppliers such as RadioShack. You can purchase an extra power cord to connect to the DC power source.

Most handheld users don't need an external antenna unless the GPS unit's internal antenna is blocked from satellites when the unit is positioned where you need it. When required, these antennas do provide excellent performance at a price. Most external antennas suitable for marine use cost over $100 and come with a 20- to 30-foot (6–9 m) cable. Most fixed-mount units use external antennas; however, a few are available with antennas mounted on the unit. Use the same considerations described above for properly positioning the unit on the boat.

Most chartplotter fixed-mount units use chips for the charts (see chapter 7). Alternatively, many of the newer GPS units boast maps or charts that can be updated from a CD-ROM. Most of these maps are based on land-based rather than nautical features, although "waterways" CD-ROMs offer buoys and lights. These features are discussed in greater detail in chapters 8 and 9. Chart chips generally cost between $100 and $300. The CD-ROMs typically cost from $60 to $200, depending upon the expanse of territory covered. Accessing a CD-ROM requires the GPS receiver to be connected to a computer. Many GPS receivers designed to allow the updating of maps from software come with a computer cable. Otherwise, the cable must be purchased separately.

What Brands Should You Consider?

Most GPS receivers provide similar performance with respect to position accuracy. Consequently, selecting a receiver is influenced primarily by company reputation, support, warranty, and operating features. An other relevant consideration is *installed base*, that is, the number of a particular company's products in the marketplace. Those with a larger installed base generally have more sources for support. Also, third parties have sprung up to provide accessories, software, and additional technical data.

Garmin currently has the largest installed base of handheld GPS units, followed by Magellan. Lowrance/Eagle have quality handheld units incorporating a map feature. Standard Horizon also has introduced a handheld GPS unit. Most of these companies maintain websites offering owner's manuals and firmware updates (the program that operates the GPS unit), which can be downloaded to a computer and then uploaded into the GPS receiver. There are other manufacturers with quality models, particularly for a user who wants to use only basic GPS functions for navigating.

Fixed-mount units, including chartplotters, are available from a host of companies. The resources section in the back of the book lists these companies along with their websites. Moderately priced units are available in the nominal 5-inch size from Standard Horizon, Navman, Garmin, Lowrance/Eagle, and others. More expensive units for use on larger boats are available from Furuno, Raymarine, Si-Tex, Simrad, Standard Horizon, Northstar, and Garmin. Most of these manufacturers also offer other marine products that will integrate with the GPS unit, such as depth sounders, fish finders, radars, and autopilots. A key consideration in selecting a chartplotter is the source for the chip—each model accepts only one type (see chapter 7).

What Features Do You Need?

Chapter 4 covers most of the navigation features offered on GPS units. The major difference is the means of accessing them. It makes sense to try various receivers in the store to make sure you are comfortable with how easily you can access the functions that you will use the most. The fixed-mount units offer these features and more. A fixed-mount GPS receiver or chartplotter typically provides a larger display and more buttons than a handheld unit. Using more buttons enables these manufacturers to simplify the menus so you can directly access important functions that could be buried under submenus on a handheld unit.

As noted in chapter 4, newer GPS receivers offer additional useful ancillary features, such as a Tide Computer and data for celestial bodies. These newer units also offer larger memories for data and waypoints.

One of the major considerations is the additional map feature offered on higher-priced units. These maps generally are land based; however, Garmin offers a Waterways and Lights CD-ROM with data on aids to navigation and BlueChart CD-ROM with navigation charts. Chartplotters, which overlay GPS position data on a navigation chart, are described in chapter 7. Generally, chartplotters are larger, fixed-mount GPS units and displays. The typical cost of a handheld GPS receiver goes up $100 to $150 with the addition of the map feature, not including the cost of the maps. This feature is more important if it is used for land-based navigation, although the shoreline features are useful for boaters. If your principal intended application is boating, you may be well advised to move up to a fixed-mount chartplotter rather than purchase a handheld GPS receiver with a map feature.

Part 2

Advanced GPS Techniques

Part 2 explains practical techniques to help you navigate safely. Chapter 6 builds on techniques using waypoints, routes, and tracks and provides a better understanding of how the information in those other data fields can be used to safely navigate your boat. Although these techniques facilitate the process of overlaying GPS data on a chart and verifying your position with visual observations, you ultimately may want to consider a chartplotter, as described in detail in chapter 7.

Chapters 8 and 9 walk you through connecting a GPS receiver to a computer to access software, and to other devices for either off-line planning or on-line navigation. Chapter 10 describes enhancements available for more precise navigation using DGPS and WAAS.

Advanced Simulation Techniques

In part 1, you learned how to set up the GPS receiver in the Simulator mode. Now, armed with an understanding of navigation using a GPS unit, you'll learn how to simulate that navigation using the Simulator mode available on most GPS receivers.

GPS models differ as to where and how you enter the simulation parameters, but the manufacturer's users manuals don't always explain how to do this.

Simulating navigation requires that you enter three pieces of information: starting position, course, and speed.

For the Garmin GPS 12, you set up the simulation on the Position screen after first putting the unit into the Simulator mode, as described in appendix 1. On the Position screen, you can enter all three pieces of information. On the Garmin GPS 76, "New Location" is set using the "Menu" button while on the Satellite screen, but speed can be set on the Highway screen, and course over ground can be adjusted on the Compass screen. Detailed screens for simulating navigation with the GPS 76 are shown in appendix 3. A few GPS units do not permit manual setting of the current position in the Simulator mode. Usually, when you start the Simulator mode, if you have not otherwise set the starting position, you will be placed at the last position for which the receiver had a live fix.

On the GPS 12, speed is adjusted by highlighting the appropriate speed field and pressing "Enter" to highlight the individual numeric fields. The actual speed can be entered by scrolling the fields up or down to the desired value and again pressing "Enter" to activate. Some GPS units, such as the GPS 76, permit changing speed in 10-knot increments using the Highway screen by pressing the cursor up or down.

Most units will present a choice for course over ground. The course can be selected as "Auto Track" or "User Track." With Auto Track set, the GPS receiver will position you directly on the active course or route that you have selected. Alternatively, you can manually select the course track to be followed. Some units also permit setting altitude, which you probably will not find very useful on the water.

The navigation simulation is dependent upon speed. You can adjust speed as you proceed. If you wish to pause, set speed to zero. Similarly, you can investigate off-course conditions and observe their effects on the various screens and data fields. Doing this as practice is an invaluable way to become familiar and comfortable with what your GPS receiver is telling you on the water. Simply place the course into the User Track mode and adjust the navigated course to suit your needs. With models like the GPS 76, you simply go to the Compass screen and use the left-right cursor to adjust your course.

6

Using Your GPS Receiver to Navigate with Charts and Local Observations

As we learned in part 1, a GPS receiver provides data; it has no knowledge of your surroundings or the waters in which you sail. Your GPS unit provides very accurate position information, but relating the latitude and longitude data it provides to the real world, which is crucial for safe navigation, can be a challenge. As mariners, there are four important navigation questions that you must have answered in the context of the real world around you.

This chapter demonstrates techniques to match up the GPS receiver with the real world around you. As demonstrated in chapter 4, it can be a somewhat tedious and error-prone task to transfer the latitude and longitude coordinates from the receiver onto a paper chart. However, you must do this to determine

if there are hazards in your path. This chapter demonstrates techniques that make the transfer of GPS information to the chart easier and more accurate, and therefore safer. This chapter also shows you a number of practical techniques to combine quickly what the GPS receiver tells you with charts and your personal observations to navigate safely.

Relating GPS to the Real World

The Four Dimensions of GPS Navigation
→ *Where You* Are
  • *latitude and longitude (not intuitive)*
→ *Where You* Want *to Go*
  • *waypoints and routes*
→ *Where You* Don't Want *to Go*
  • *proximity waypoints and avoidance techniques*
→ *Where You* Have Been
  • *track of prior path*

Where You Are (Current Position)

Although the primary GPS contribution to navigation is its ability to tell you where you are with great precision, there are two major sources of potential error. The first is a mistake in not accurately transcribing the coordinates from the GPS receiver to your chart. These errors are too easy to make, as was demonstrated in chapter 4. The second is some malady affecting the accuracy of the GPS receiver. This could be due to an equipment failure or from the obscuration of satellites. You need to double-check and cross-check your perceived position with objects around you, especially if you are near hazards.

"It won't happen to me," you say! Let's ask the former captain of the *Royal Majesty*. This 568-foot (173 m) cruise ship with state-of-the-art navigation equipment on board ran hard aground on Rose and Crown Shoal in June 1995, some 10 miles east of

Massachusetts's Nantucket Island. The sky was clear, the seas calm. The captain purportedly boasted to passengers just hours before the accident about the sophisticated navigation equipment, including GPS receivers, that assured their safety. What happened? Well, while the crew of the *Royal Majesty* were so confident in the GPS unit, they failed to exercise the traditional practice of using two independent sources of position information. The GPS receiver they were using for navigation had its antenna connection severed. The GPS continued to navigate using dead reckoning based on the last good data, not on current position. The result: the *Royal Majesty* ran aground some 17 miles west of its intended course. The official National Transportation and Safety Board findings cited the crew's overreliance on the electronic navigation equipment. This could have been prevented by better situational awareness.

Where You Want to Go

Navigation is inherently the process of going somewhere—usually to a specific destination. Using electronic navigation, just as in traditional navigation, this involves using the techniques of waypoints and routes as described in chapter 4.

Waypoints and Routes

Apart from telling you where you are, your GPS receiver supports the extremely important task of showing you how to get to where you want to go. The use of waypoints is a fundamental feature. As discussed in chapter 4, a waypoint, once entered into your GPS unit, provides the bearing and distance from your current location to the selected waypoint. In addition, most receivers will draw a line on the Map screen indicating a straight line from your current location to that waypoint. Beyond that, given that you are making way, most GPS units provide other relevant information such as the estimated time of arrival, the course to steer to reach the waypoint, and/or the estimated time en route.

GPS navigation is ideally suited to the mariner since a straight line between points is frequently sought as the most efficient path. On land, we seldom have that luxury. However, that straight-line path on the water may be fraught with peril.

Where You Don't Want to Go

Unlike land navigation, which may involve locating and following specific roads or paths, marine navigation has vast expanses of apparently open water. The mariner may choose to reach a destination any number of ways, so long as it is safe to do so. This consideration of where you do not want to go adds a major dimension to navigation for the mariner. The GPS receiver has no knowledge of the local conditions, but it has features that facilitate safe navigation.

Proximity Waypoints and Avoidance Techniques

On the water, you are as concerned about where *not* to go as you are where to go. Locations that you want to avoid may represent great danger to the boat and crew, or perhaps just discomfort and delay from running aground in the mud. Your GPS unit performs an important role in helping you avoid the unwanted—if you know how to use it. Just as you recorded waypoints as places you wish to go, you can use waypoints to mark danger. Using a special kind of waypoint called a *proximity waypoint*, you can set an alarm to warn you of an unwanted spot or area. The following sections also explain a number of other avoidance techniques.

Where You Have Been

Mariners, like other navigators, may have reason to want to know were they have been. This may be for navigation purposes to follow the same path again, to create a log, or to use in planning future cruises.

Track of Prior Path

Your GPS unit can record a track of where you have been. Within the constraints of memory and settings that you provide, the unit records your specific location as a set of coordinates at regular intervals. This information can help you find your way back, rerun a previous track, use your historical track to prepare routes for future reference, or simply record a log of where you have been and when.

GPS Navigation Techniques

Navigation is the process of safely getting to where you want to go. Inherent in this process is the knowledge of where you are. As introduced in chapter 4, the fundamental means of navigating to a destination is the creation of one or more waypoints linked by straight lines representing your intended path. However, with a GPS receiver you can use waypoints for additional purposes, including waypoint techniques that help you relate the GPS data to the real world. This is an essential part of situational awareness. Even if you use a chartplotter (see chapter 7), which shows your position on a chart, you need to double-check your position from time to time using other observations.

Waypoint Techniques

→ *Present a Picture (Map screen)*
  • *Mark Buoys, Landmarks, and Danger (Proximity)*
→ *Provide Relative Position*
  • *Nearest Waypoints Screen*
  • *Range and Bearing to Waypoints*
→ *Provide a Course*
  • *Bearing and Range to Waypoints*
  • *Verify the Safety of the Path on a Chart*

As has been demonstrated, the numerical translation of coordinates provided by the GPS receiver to your charts can lead to errors. At a minimum, it can be time consuming and cumbersome in a moving boat. What you need are ways to easily relate the GPS data to the real world so that you can rapidly ascertain your position vis-à-vis where you want to be, or more importantly, where you do not want to be.

Up to this point waypoints have been used primarily to mark a point to which you wish to navigate and have been grouped together in a sequence to define a route. But waypoints can be used for much more than that.

Present a Picture (Map Screen)

In chapter 4, a view of a Map screen was presented in the absence of many waypoints (fig. 4-27). Waypoints could be used to bring meaning to that display, as was shown in figure 4-29. The number of waypoints that can be entered into your GPS receiver is extensive—generally far more than you will ever need for point-to-point navigation. Typical GPS models offer storage for some 500 waypoints. Some of the newer receivers offer storage for 3,000 or more. You should use these waypoint positions to mark any and all chart features (such as buoys, aids to navigation, landmarks, shoreline features, docks, shallow water, and, most importantly, danger) that impact your navigation. You can facilitate this task using a computer off-line, as is described in chapter 8. Should you exhaust your available waypoint memory, you can save groups of waypoint positions by region on your computer and freely upload the appropriate group as you sail into new waters. One important note: Even by using waypoints liberally to mark objects, the Map screen does not replace a chart. It still does not show water depths, shorelines, or other pertinent navigation information.

Provide Relative Position

Once waypoints are entered into your GPS receiver, they can serve as reference points from which you can compare your position. One of the features built into your GPS unit is its ability to present the "Nearest Waypoints" relative to your current position. Accessing this screen *does not* interfere with ongoing navigation. This enables you to view information that can be very useful to relating your position physically to all stored nearby objects while continuing to navigate your course. Most GPS receivers present the ten nearest waypoints in order from closest to farthest. However, if you record danger objects as waypoints, they will appear at or near the top of the list if they are sufficiently close to be of concern. This page also provides bearing and distance to each of the nearest waypoints. You can use this information to check your position or to take action. The Nearest Waypoints screen is accessed from the Main Menu on most GPS units.

Provide a Course

Once a waypoint is accessed for navigation via a "GoTo" or other technique, a course line is drawn on the Map screen and a highway is created on the Highway screen. The reference course, from your location at the time you selected the waypoint for navigation to the waypoint, remains on the screen and serves as the reference highway. The GPS bearing and distance to the waypoint is updated continually to reflect that information from your current location. The course line and highway provide tools with which you can check your progress to ensure that you stay on the original course. Given that you checked that course at the outset, you can be reasonably assured of safe passage by staying on that course (to the extent the original chart data are accurate).

Relating the GPS Receiver to the Real World and to Charts

The techniques and features outlined in this section make it easier for you to relate your GPS data to the real world around you and to your charts.

Data Fields

In addition to basic position, a GPS unit provides a great deal of computed information through data fields. These data fields can be very useful for navigation and avoiding danger. Chapter 3 describes data fields in detail.

Figure 6-1 illustrates the definitions of the data fields, as well as the relationships between the various data fields available on a GPS receiver. Course, bearing, and track are referenced to north. As discussed in chapter 4, a GPS receiver user can select either true or magnetic north for navigation. *Course* refers to the intended direction. *Bearing* refers to the actual direction to the destination waypoint from your current location. *Track*, or *course over ground* (COG), refers to the actual direction in which you currently are moving over ground. *Turn* displays the amount by which

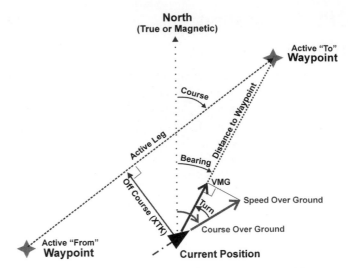

FIGURE 6-1. *Definition of GPS Data Fields. The GPS receiver provides a great deal of data regarding your position, your course, and information relating to your selected waypoints and course line. This figure represents graphically what each of these fields means to the navigator.*

the current track must be modified to move directly toward the destination waypoint. There are two distances displayed: the distance to the destination waypoint and the distance that you are *off course*, also called *crosstrack error* (XTK). Speed is shown in two values. *Speed over ground* (SOG) displays the motion over ground that the boat is making in the COG direction. The effective velocity component in the direction of the destination waypoint is called *velocity made good* (VMG).

The other optional data fields relate to planning and information of interest. For example, a GPS unit provides a Trip Computer function that gives you distance since it was last reset, trip timer, average speed, or maximum speed. A GPS receiver also offers data such as estimated time en route (ETE) and estimated time of arrival (ETA). This information can be very useful for planning or arranging a rendezvous with others at your destination.

Navigating with Waypoints Using Data Fields

Now, let's expand on the Navigating with Waypoints section of chapter 4. Once a waypoint is selected, the GPS receiver computes the bearing and distance from your current position to that waypoint, as well as

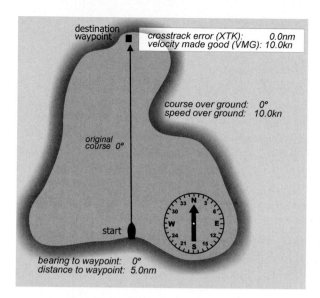

FIGURE 6-2. *Data Fields Add Information to Waypoint Navigation. Two new data fields, crosstrack error (XTK) and velocity made good (VMG), have been added to the diagram from figure 4-20. In the example, you are on course (the XTK is zero and the VMG equals your speed over ground).*

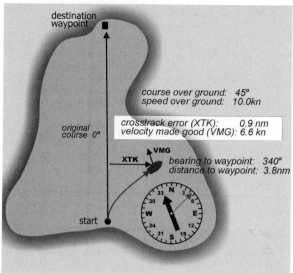

FIGURE 6-3. *XTK Indicates When You Are Off Course. In this example, the helmsman has been inattentive to the original course and has wandered to starboard. The XTK data field reflects this departure showing a 0.9 nautical mile deviation from the course line. Although the boat is moving at 10 knots through the water, the VMG has fallen to 6.6 knots, reflecting that you are no longer heading directly toward the waypoint.*

other data. Figure 6-2 illustrates this process. The receiver draws a line on the Map screen from your current location to the selected waypoint. The receiver also creates a highway on the Highway screen. As in the earlier example in chapter 4 (fig. 4-20), you are navigating to a destination waypoint that is 5.0 miles distant on a true course of 0° at a speed of 10.0 knots. At this point, XTK is zero, because you are on course. The VMG is the same as the speed over ground since you are on course.

As you navigate, the GPS unit continually updates the XTK and VMG, in addition to bearing and distance information to the selected waypoint. The unit also continually provides your course over ground and speed over ground.

If you get off course, as shown in figure 6-3, the XTK and VMG vectors are shown relative to the boat. XTK indicates the distance from your current location to the closest point in the original course line. In this case, you are 0.9 mile off course. The VMG indicates the effective speed toward the waypoint is 6.6 knots, as opposed to the 10.0 knots of the boat motion. In this example, the captain simply steered the boat in the wrong direction. The figure

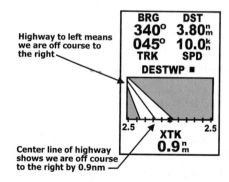

FIGURE 6-4. *The Highway Screen Also Shows When You Are Off Course (and Off Bearing). From your position in figure 6-3, the Highway screen shows that you are well to the right of the highway and heading even farther away. The crosstrack error (XTE) shows you to be off course by 0.9 nm. The bearing to the waypoint is indicated as 340°, but the GPS does not indicate if that path is clear.*

demonstrates that the course over ground (COG) is 45° and the speed over ground (SOG) is 10.0 knots (no wind or current are assumed). Figure 6-4 shows the corresponding Highway screen.

Before simply changing course directly toward the

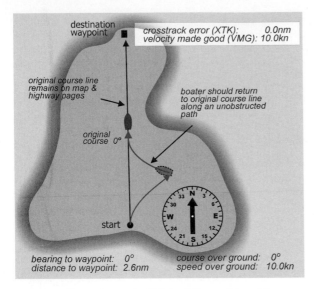

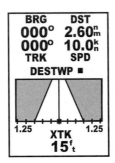

FIGURE 6-5. *Returning to the Original Course Line. After you have returned to the original course line, the XTK is again zero, and the VMG is equivalent to the speed over ground. You can use XTK in conjunction with a number of screens to stay on course.*

FIGURE 6-6. *XTK on the Highway Screen Helps You Stay On Course. Chapter 4 introduced using the High-way screen to stay on course. Displaying the crosstrack error field makes this task even easier, and you can set an alarm to alert you when you stray off course.*

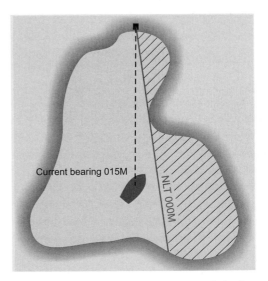

waypoint, it is very important that you plot your current position and the bearing line to the waypoint on a chart to ensure the safety of this path (fig. 6-5). Clearly, it is no longer safe to follow a straight course to your destination in the current example. In many such situations, you may wish to return to the original course line as efficiently as possible, provided this path is clear. When you return to the original course line and get your boat properly aligned toward your destination, the Highway screen now shows you on the center of the highway and heading in the proper direction, as shown in figure 6-6. The XTK data field shows that you are only 15 feet (4.6 m) from the course centerline. Therefore, the Highway screen

can be used to keep you on course by making sure that you are lined up, as shown in the figure.

Danger Bearing: A Useful Technique

A useful technique for assuring that you do not hit that spit of land (or other hazards) is to plot a *danger bearing* from a waypoint across the near side of the hazard, as shown in figure 6-7. Using a protractor or parallel rule with the compass rose, you ascertain that in this case the bearing to the waypoint across the hazard, the danger bearing, is 000° Magnetic. Now all you need do is monitor, on the GPS receiver, the bearing to the waypoint from your current position. If, while you move around, that bearing never falls below 000° Magnetic, you will never encounter the "danger," in this example the spit of land. In other words, the safe bearing will be not less than (NLT) the value of 000° M.

For example, if you were fishing in this body of water and wanted to make sure that you didn't hit the

FIGURE 6-7. *Danger Bearing. A danger bearing helps keep you away from hazards. Many navigators will draw a danger bearing on their chart from a known point across a hazard or shoreline. In this example, the area marked with diagonal lines is to be avoided. This ensures that you cannot run aground on the point of land. The danger bearing line in this case corresponds to 0° Magnetic. If the bearing to the destination waypoint shown on the GPS unit never falls below the danger bearing of 0°, you cannot be in the crosshatched area. The helmsman simply monitors the bearing to the known point.*

spit of land, establishing a danger bearing would provide you with an instant check that you are clear. Danger bearings can be used for entering harbors and for avoiding rocks or other hazards. You can plot a number of danger bearings on your chart using any landmark. Once you enter the coordinates of the landmark into your GPS receiver, you can monitor the bearings to the selected landmarks (as entered waypoints) on the Nearest Waypoints screen to make sure you don't venture into dangerous areas.

Other Tricks with Waypoints

Situational awareness is an important part of boating, especially if you are near any hazards. Under these circumstances, you will want to know precisely where you are on the chart that marks these hazards. At a minimum, you will want to maintain a good visual feel for your position. Here are some tricks to make this easier by using your GPS receiver.

Often, in areas where there is a danger concern such as rocks or wrecks, you are within sight of visual landmarks. Even if the rocks are not marked, you can gain a good feel of your location relative to the danger spots by visually referencing your position with respect to those landmarks. Alternatively, there are ways to mark your location quickly and easily on a chart with data provided by the GPS receiver, data which are more intuitive and less likely to produce an error.

Techniques Using Nearest Waypoints

Your GPS receiver provides a quick way to get information on your position relative to other nearby objects. It typically is called the Nearest Waypoints function. When this function is selected, the GPS receiver typically displays the ten waypoints nearest to your current location (the actual number depends upon the GPS model), as shown in figure 6-8. The receiver displays this list of waypoints with the nearest to your current location listed first. The Nearest Waypoints screen can

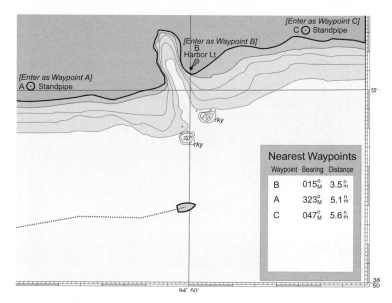

FIGURE 6-8. *The Nearest Waypoints Page Helps Provide Situational Awareness. Situational awareness involves having a physical relationship with your environment. It is imperative that you relate the GPS-provided position coordinates to the world around you. This ensures that the GPS receiver is neither misinterpreted or in a failure mode. Using the Nearest Waypoints screen (as shown in the lower right corner), the helmsman can use the relationship of fixed landmarks on the chart to cross-check position.*

be useful in many situations and provides you with a quick sense of your current location.

Range and bearing from your current location to each waypoint are also displayed and updated instantaneously as you move. You can access this page without interfering with ongoing navigation tasks that you are performing with your GPS receiver. Once you have the information that you need, simply press "Quit" to go back to the previous function and screen.

In this example, you are using visible objects to cross-check your GPS position and to plot your position quickly on the chart. Three waypoints have been entered: the two standpipes and the Harbor Light. They are labeled A, C, and B, respectively. The Nearest Waypoints screen shows the waypoint name, followed by the bearing and the distance. The parameters for bearing (true or magnetic) and the range (miles or nautical miles) depend upon how you set up your GPS receiver. In this example, magnetic north and nautical miles are used.

Figures 6-9 and 6-10 show two relatively quick techniques for plotting your position. In figure 6-9,

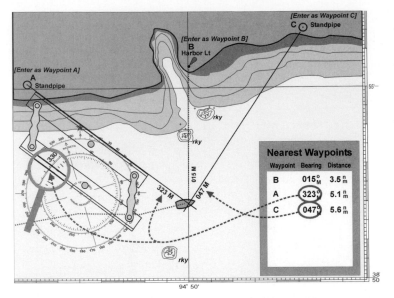

FIGURE 6-9 (left). *Drawing Bearings for Position Information. Drawing bearings to nearby waypoints quickly provides your location on a chart. Using the bearing data to two of the nearest waypoints (taken from the list on the Nearest Waypoints screen), the navigator can quickly plot position. Using a parallel rule, the bearing lines can be drawn using magnetic bearings and the inner compass rose on the chart. This is far easier and less error prone than plotting latitude and longitude, and it also provides a meaningful relationship with the physical environment. You also can quickly verify that the GPS is working properly by using a hand-bearing compass to sight on the same waypoints and comparing the visual bearings with the GPS bearings.*

FIGURE 6-10 (right). *Using Distances to Waypoints for Position Information. Distances from nearby waypoints can help determine your position on a chart. By drawing swing arcs the precise distances from each of two landmarks (noted on the Nearest Waypoints screen), you can plot your position at the spot where the arcs meet. In the example, you used a drawing compass set to a distance of 5.1 nm and drew an arc from waypoint A, followed by setting a 5.6 nm distance and drawing an arc from waypoint C.*

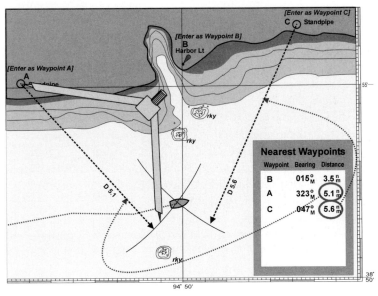

bearings were plotted to the two standpipes. In this case, magnetic bearings were used, so the inner rose on the chart reflecting magnetic headings must be used. After plotting the two bearing lines, you can see that your boat is located at their intersection. You used the two standpipes since they provide a wider angle (and therefore a better fix) than would be afforded by using the beacon. This technique is quicker, easier, and less prone to error than plotting latitude and longitude from your GPS data. It also en-

ables you to use physical objects in your environment as the reference. The technique shown in figure 6-10 may be even faster and easier. Using a drawing compass or pair of dividers, you scale off the respective distances from each of the two standpipes and draw corresponding arcs centered on the standpipes. Your location is at the intersection of the arcs.

The two techniques described above use two or more objects to help you locate your position. The first of these techniques also allows you to check your GPS

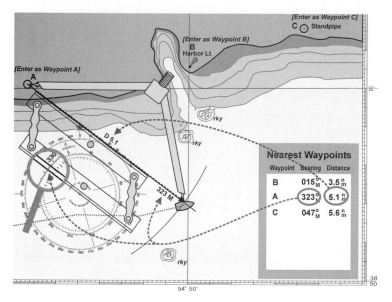

FIGURE 6-11. Using Bearing and Distance from a Single Waypoint for Position Information. Using a parallel rule, a magnetic bearing line is drawn. Using dividers and the latitude scale, the distance from the waypoint is marked on the bearing line. This locates your position quickly and easily with only a single waypoint.

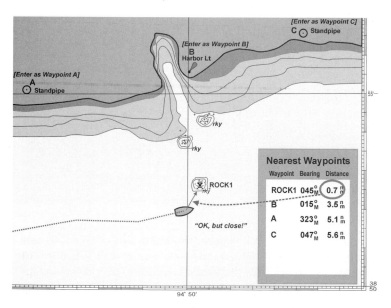

FIGURE 6-12. Adding Hazards as Waypoints. By adding nearby hazards to your GPS receiver as waypoints, you can tell where they are located relative to the boat. The cluster of rocks ("ROCK1") shown has been marked as a waypoint. Using the Nearest Waypoints screen enables the helmsman to monitor distance and bearing to the rocks. But unless the rocks are visible, the helmsman will need to use other viewable landmarks to cross-check position.

data using visible fixed objects and comparing the bearings reported by the GPS receiver with sightings on your hand-bearing compass. Both techniques show you how to quickly plot your position on a chart using two or more objects. A third technique is even faster and requires only one object. Any recorded waypoint within view can be used. As shown in figure 6-11, you plot both the distance and bearing, as reported by the GPS receiver, to waypoint A. Using your parallel rule you can draw the bearing, and using your dividers on the latitude scale you can set the distance along that line from the waypoint to quickly pinpoint your position on the chart. Typically, the accuracy of this technique is enhanced using waypoints that are reasonably close to your current position. This third technique can also be used with your destination waypoint—if it is close enough. Not only does this technique help you plot your position, but it provides a line on the chart that you can check to see if the path is clear to steer that course.

Using an additional method, you could have marked and named the rocks as waypoints. Then the range and bearing would tell you directly where you are relative to the rocks and enable you to take evasive action, if necessary. This is especially useful when you are closer to the rocks, as shown in figure 6-12.

Since you're quite close to rocks, it is extremely important that you know precisely where you are on the chart. The figure has been modified by adding rocks. These rocks have been added to the recorded waypoints as "ROCK1." Now, the Nearest Waypoints screen shows the rocks as the closest object. Note that the screen displays the bearing and distance to the rocks. Given that

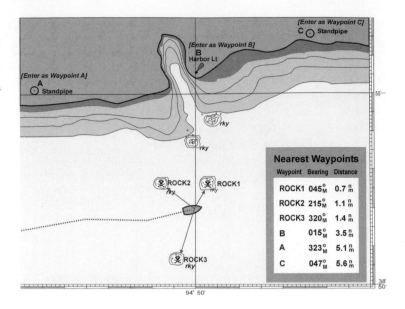

FIGURE 6-13. *Adding Multiple Hazards as Waypoints. In traversing areas with multiple hazards, you can track all of them as waypoints. The Nearest Waypoints screen provides continuous indication of your position with respect to the three hazards, which were entered as waypoints. However, assuming these hazards aren't visible, they don't provide visual cuing afforded by A, B, and C.*

Nearest Waypoints

Waypoint	Bearing	Distance
ROCK1	045_M°	$0.7\,_m^n$
ROCK2	215_M°	$1.1\,_m^n$
ROCK3	320_M°	$1.4\,_m^n$
B	015_M°	$3.5\,_m^n$
A	323_M°	$5.1\,_m^n$
C	047_M°	$5.6\,_m^n$

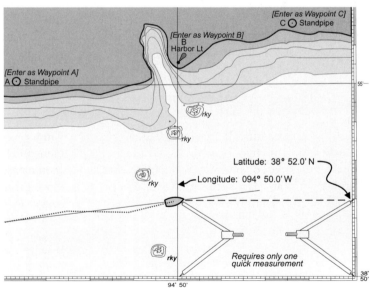

FIGURE 6-14. *Using Grid Lines for Position Information. By taking readings from the GPS receiver while crossing a grid line, you need only measure one coordinate with your dividers to determine where you are on the chart. This easy method can be used to verify proper GPS receiver operation from time to time.*

Latitude: 38° 52.0' N
Longitude: 094° 50.0' W

Requires only one quick measurement

you would like to stay over ½ mile away from the rocks, it would be prudent to watch carefully. The combination of the displayed bearing and distance makes it easy for you to look out and identify the rocks, provided they are visible above the surface. Every opportunity should be taken to cross-check your position on a chart under these circumstances.

The chart in figure 6-13 has been modified to add more rocks. If all of these rocks were entered into the GPS receiver as waypoints, the Nearest Waypoints screen would appear as shown. The nearest rocks are listed first, followed by ROCK2 and ROCK3. You can quickly see that rocks 2 and 3 are behind you and no longer present a threat, but the rocks at position 1 are a concern. Marking and tracking the rocks will assist in avoiding them, but visible landmarks help you perform a quick position plot and give you a visual feel for your location.

If you wish to mark position by using latitude and longitude coordinates, you can facilitate the process by taking GPS readings while crossing one of the grid lines on your chart. This enables you to use the chart grid line as a plotting reference, as shown in figure 6-14, where you are crossing the 94°50′ W meridian. By watching the GPS receiver and recording only the latitude at this crossing, you need to make only one measurement to plot your position on the chart. This technique can be used on either meridians of longitude or parallels of latitude.

So far, you have used waypoints to mark points to which you intend to navigate, and used waypoints to indicate a myriad of other features of interest on the chart. You can make use of some 500 waypoints (or even more on the most recent models). This provides plenty of positions for a localized boating area. Should you use all of the available waypoint slots, you may wish to *partition waypoints* by region as explained in the tip on page 58. This is more likely to occur when you cruise to distant locales. Under these circumstances, you can load the waypoints of interest for the intended cruise. The process of entering waypoints and exchanging waypoints is made far easier by using a computer, as is described later. As previously described, another function of waypoints is to use them in sequence to form routes. Additional navigation issues in using routes are described in the next section.

Route Techniques

As described in chapter 4, a route is a programmed sequence of waypoints. Entering and using a route offers a number of advantages in navigation. Once a route has been activated it is displayed as a sequence of direct line segments from waypoint to waypoint on the Map screen. An excellent example for a route is shown in figure 6-15. You anticipate taking this route back to your slip frequently during the boating season. In this example, there are no evident aids to navigation. This is not unusual in inland channels, and

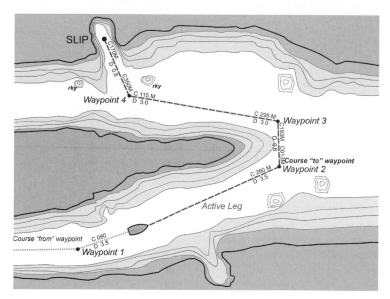

FIGURE 6-15. *Example of a Practical Route. Route segments, or legs, should be preplanned on charts in advance to bypass obstructions and hazards, then transferred to the GPS receiver. You can safely traverse these route segments by monitoring your position on the receiver and staying close to the plotted course lines. When planning on charts, note the course angles and the distance between waypoints. Label the reciprocal course values at each end of the leg. Magnetic bearings are commonly used. Many chart kits provide preplotted legs for channels and popular routes.*

you have determined this route to be the most efficient and safe course for your return to the slip. You then measured the coordinates of turning points along this path using dividers and the latitude and longitude scales on the chart, and then entered them into the GPS receiver. You then opened the Route screen and defined the sequence as waypoint 1, waypoint 2, etc., as described in chapter 4.

Finally, on the water, you activate the route. The route is displayed on the GPS receiver as a series of course segments on the Map screen and highway segments on the Highway screen. The amount of the total route displayed depends upon the zoom scale. The receiver will provide the bearing and distance to the first waypoint on the active leg of the route. As each waypoint is achieved, the receiver shows the bearing and distance to the next waypoint. However, there is more to navigating the route than just following the displayed bearings. Often, wind and currents drive you away from your intended route and into danger.

At any time, you can determine your position relative to the intended route by comparing your position with the centerline of the route. In some cases, the route was selected to avoid obstacles. Under these circumstances, it will be important to stay close to the course line during the active route segment. Having the line indicated on the GPS receiver's Map screen is very important, since the bearing and range to the next waypoint alone will not prevent you from straying off course and venturing into dangerous conditions. The bearing may be correct to reach your next waypoint; however, if you are off to port or starboard from the intended track, you could encounter obstacles. In this situation, you will want to recover to the route centerline before proceeding to the intended waypoint.

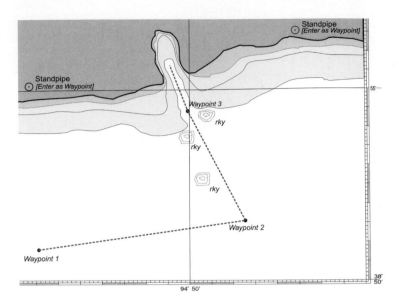

FIGURE 6-16. *Routes Are Useful for Frequently Used Courses. Route segments are particularly useful for planning your way in and around harbors. Given the tighter conditions in channels, these routes should be prepared with care to make sure they are centered. Determine the channel widths to evaluate your degree of risk using a GPS receiver with typical error limits.*

The Highway screen is another display that illustrates the value of using a route. On this screen, each leg of the route, depending upon the scale selected, is illustrated at each waypoint as bends or turns in the road. This presents a 3-D view of your intended route.

In addition to providing a route map and graphical guide on your GPS receiver's Map and Highway screens, selecting a route facilitates navigation at sea when you need to execute complex maneuvers, or when it may not be convenient to divert your attention from other duties to sequentially enter successive waypoints manually. However, there can be problems when using routes to navigate under tight situations.

Figure 6-16 shows a route into a tricky harbor: you must maneuver between rocks to enter the harbor. Any lateral deviation from the route centerline could put you in danger. Under these circumstances, you must be aware of a practical programming issue with GPS receivers. The receiver may indicate that you have "realized" an intermediate waypoint (waypoint 2 in the diagram) before you actually reach it. For practical reasons, a GPS unit is programmed to recognize a waypoint when you approach it. It is not practical

nor safe to assume you will cross directly over a waypoint before the receiver believes that you have reached it. Once the receiver believes you have achieved the desired waypoint, it indicates a new course to steer to the next waypoint (in this case waypoint 3). In this example, which continues in figure 6-17, you may be told to steer a course of 330° as soon as you have reached the edge of the waypoint arrival radius, as shown in the figure. Clearly, you don't want to execute this maneuver at this location or you will steer directly over the rocks. In Avoidance Techniques, the next section, you'll learn how to handle situations of this nature.

Avoidance Techniques

→ *proximity waypoints: set alarm if too close to danger*
→ *relate to visible objects: monitor danger bearings and distance off*
→ *crosstrack error (XTK): set alarm if too far off course*

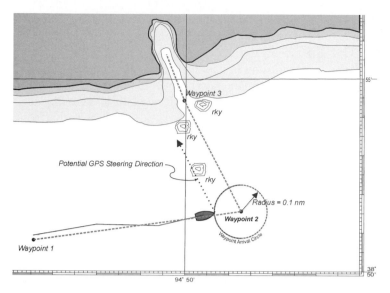

FIGURE 6-17. *A Potential Problem with GPS Route Navigation. Navigating into a harbor using a GPS-indicated route may result in a dangerous steering command. Beware: the GPS receiver recognizes that you have achieved waypoint 2 before you actually reach it. As soon as the receiver recognizes the waypoint, it provides a new steering direction for your course. If you immediately execute a turn, you could be venturing into danger, as shown. (The size of the Waypoint Arrival Circle is enlarged to illustrate the point.)*

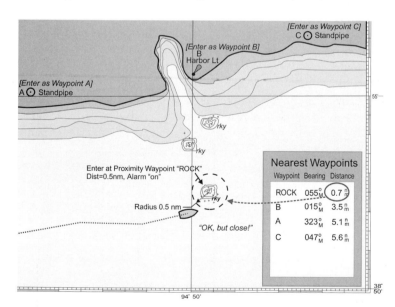

FIGURE 6-18. *Using Proximity Waypoints to Avoid Danger. This form of waypoint sounds an alarm if you get too close to a waypoint, such as the rocks here. You can set the radius for the alarm using the Alarms Setup Menu under Setup. Most GPS models with this feature offer only a limited number of proximity waypoints. Alternatively, you can use a standard waypoint to do the same thing, but you must monitor the distance yourself without the alarm feature.*

Much of navigating on the water involves avoiding submerged objects, as well as objects above the surface that may not always be visible. Also, there are areas to avoid, such as those that are restricted for one reason or another. Usually, this information is available on charts, but correlating this information with the current position as reported by the GPS receiver is a constant plotting task. Using the following techniques, you can use the GPS unit to help avoid obstacles and regions of concern.

In planning any course or route, it is incumbent upon the mariner to examine your intended path to identify points or areas of concern. Given wind, current, or instrument error, it is easy to deviate from the intended path, so the navigator must examine risks not just along, but near, the intended track. Once these risks are identified, you can employ one or more of the techniques below to enhance the safety of your cruise.

Proximity Waypoints

Most GPS receivers offer a special type of waypoint, usually called *proximity*, or *avoidance, waypoints*. You enter these waypoints in much the same way as conventional waypoints, but you also make an entry for distance. The *distance value* sets a radius around the waypoint. If you enter within that radius, an alarm sounds to let you know that you may be in danger.

Figure 6-18 provides an example of a proximity waypoint. In this example, your concern is a group of rocks. You determine that you do not want to be anywhere within 0.5 nautical mile of the center of these rocks, so that is the value you set for the alarm radius. In this case, you were concerned about a region of rocks, so you selected center-point coordinates and a radius that would encompass all of the hazard area. This information is obtained by using a compass on the chart and experimenting with various center points and radii until you arrive at a reasonable compromise that encompasses the hazards.

Tip: *Most GPS receivers that offer the proximity waypoints feature provide for a limited number of proximity waypoints—typically ten.* These can be reallocated and renamed as you cruise in different areas. Alternatively, you can use normal waypoints to mark danger areas; however, you will not have the alarm feature available. In this case, you need to set these danger waypoints to mark the near side of the hazard rather than its center. This is analogous to how buoys are set to mark hazards by the local authorities or U.S. Coast Guard. It is perfectly reasonable for you to create "artificial danger buoy" waypoints on your GPS even though they don't exist on the water. Be sure to label these danger buoys accordingly. Also, the Waypoint screen enables the selection of a symbol to reflect the waypoint. This symbol is displayed on the Map screen. For example, danger can be depicted by the skull and crossbones, typically offered as one of the choices. The choice of name should also reflect danger—for example, "RCKS2" or "WRK4."

Once set, proximity waypoints will sound an internal alarm when your boat enters the alarm radius no matter what page you are viewing on the GPS. If you use ordinary waypoints to mark danger, you will need to use either the Map screen, which will show these waypoints with respect to your current location, or the Highway screen. In the latter case, the simulated 3-D display will show your danger waypoints in relationship to your current position looking forward.

Distance Off

Another technique for avoiding danger or restricted areas is to determine a preset distance from a fixed landmark on the chart. You can do this using a draw-ing compass by setting the center on the fixed landmark (or buoy) and drawing an arc of sufficient size to encompass the danger. Next, determine on the chart what radius in nautical miles is set on the compass. The landmark must be entered into the GPS receiver as a waypoint (or proximity waypoint). At no time, to remain safe, do you want to be any closer to that landmark than this predetermined distance. The radius of the arc is considered a *danger circle*, and its radius is noted on the chart.

You can monitor the distance by periodically accessing the Nearest Waypoints screen. Whenever you access this list, the GPS unit will present a list of those waypoints closest to you, with the closest listed first. The page displays the waypoint names and their respective ranges and bearings, continuously updated. As long as the distance to your selected waypoint does not fall below the predetermined value or distance, you are clear of the identified danger. This is demonstrated in figure 6-19.

Tip: *The use of Nearest Waypoints offers a significant advantage.* This page provides you with useful data but does not interrupt any navigation process

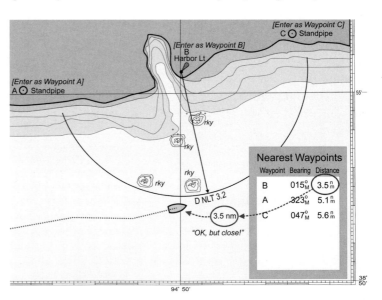

FIGURE 6-19. *Distance Off. Distance off, or distance not-less-than (D NLT), can be used to avoid danger. A variant of the danger bearing, distance off uses distance from a reference point to keep you safe. Using your chart, determine the radius from a fixed object that assures safe passage around one or more hazards. By using the Nearest Waypoints Page to make certain that you don't venture closer than this predetermined distance, you'll remain safe.*

that was set into the GPS receiver. For example, you can access Nearest Waypoints while executing a route without disrupting the ongoing route. As soon as you press "Quit," you will be returned to the route in process.

Crosstrack Error

Crosstrack error (abbreviated as XTK or XTE depending upon the brand of your GPS receiver) provides a measure of just how far to port or starboard you are away from the intended track or course line. This is the line established in your GPS unit at the time you engaged the current active waypoint. This course line stays on the Map screen. It also shows up as the highway centerline on the Highway screen.

Often, it is important that you stay close to the center of the course. Danger may lurk to either side. If you rely solely upon steering a course using your compass, wind or the current can push you away from your intended course. Also, inattention at the helm can cause the same result. Once off course, if you use the bearing to the waypoint as your steering direction, your path could take you into danger, as demonstrated in figure 6-20. You can use the crosstrack error feature to make certain you stay close to the intended course line.

Tip: *You can usually get to the crosstrack error data field option using the Menu button on the selected screen.* You select this option by moving the highlight over the data field that you want to change and then by pressing "Enter." This produces a list of alternative data fields. Select the field appropriate for your unit (e.g., XTK, XTE, or "Off Course") by scrolling up or down with the cursor and then pressing "Enter" again. This displays the data field, but

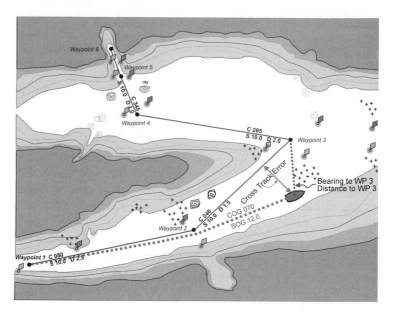

FIGURE 6-20. *Following the Bearing to the Waypoint Can Result in Danger. Failure to monitor drift away from the course line can lead to trouble. Monitor crosstrack error as a means of staying on course.*

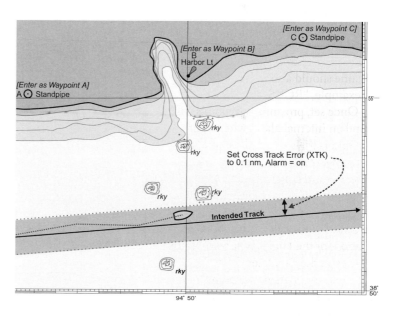

FIGURE 6-21. *Crosstrack Alarm. A crosstrack alarm helps you navigate between hazards. By preplotting course segments on a chart, you can determine a centerline and maximum deviation from center that can be navigated safely. Take into account the potential error in hazard location on the chart and the GPS error to make sure the limits are far enough away from hazards. You can preset an alarm for the maximum crosstrack error using the Alarms Setup Menu under Setup. Setting the alarm for crosstrack error can be used to help negotiate a narrow channel.*

does not allow you to set the alarm. To set the alarm, go to the Alarms Setup Menu, usually under Setup. Here, you move the cursor over the appropriate field and set the alarm to "on," and then move the cursor over the distance field to enter the distance off in nautical miles above which the alarm will sound. "Quit" this page, and you have armed your crosstrack alarm. Now, you will be alerted if your path takes you beyond the selected distance away from the course line. *Note:* it isn't necessary to display crosstrack error in order to use the alarm feature.

Using crosstrack error and setting the alarm is particularly useful if you must navigate through waters where danger exists on either or both sides of a clear channel. The course line is selected to be the clear path down the middle, as demonstrated in figure 6-21.

Using Special Techniques to Navigate a Route Safely

A GPS receiver recognizes that you have achieved, or reached, a waypoint when you get within a predetermined distance from that waypoint. This is called *arrival radius*. In most sets, this is a value determined by the manufacturer of your GPS model and may not be adjustable. Arrival radius is a compromise for the GPS designer. If it is set too close to the waypoint, it may not be recognized as you sail near the spot, and the route will not switch to the next leg. If it is set too far from the waypoint, you may turn too soon. Generally, you can expect the arrival radius to be somewhere on the order of 0.10 nautical mile.

Tip: *You can set your own arrival radius notice as you approach a waypoint.* Many GPS units enable you to set an alarm for a preset distance from a waypoint, which will sound when you are within that radius. Usually, the alarm is accompanied by a message on the screen that you are approaching the waypoint.

Tip: *When setting waypoints to use in your route, make sure that they are*

separated by more than a few tenths of a nautical mile. If they are too close, they will have overlapping arrival radii, potentially confusing the GPS receiver. This may result in unpredictable steering directions.

The automatic arrival radius has an impact when you are executing a route. As soon as your GPS determines you have arrived at the current waypoint, it presents the course and distance to the next waypoint. Under normal circumstances, this automatic switch to the next waypoint is just fine. As the skipper, you adjust your course accordingly and move toward your next waypoint along the route. However, there are situations under which this could be a problem. Figure 6-17 is just one example. In that case you need to make a tricky turn between rocks to head for your harbor. The arrival radius has caused the GPS unit to indicate the new course too early. You have not yet reached the appropriate turning point, and the new course will run you across rocks. The example illustrates two issues: you should not put blind faith in what the GPS unit tells you to do; and you need to know some techniques to cross-

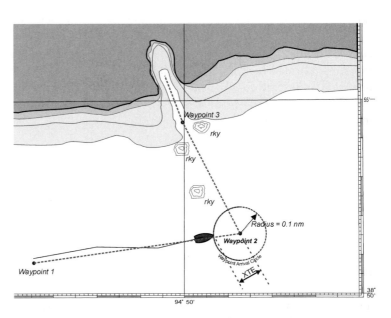

FIGURE 6-22. *Using XTE or XTK to Tell You When to Turn. Monitoring crosstrack error can be used to resolve the problem of early waypoint recognition, demonstrated in figure 6-17. When the GPS switches to the new course leg, crosstrack error indicates the deviation from the new course centerline. Since you want to be on that centerline, simply stay on the old course until the XTK reaches zero, and then turn.*

check what it says to ensure that you are doing the right thing.

There are two ways to make sure you turn at the appropriate time. The first technique uses crosstrack error. As soon as the GPS receiver indicates the new course to steer, as would be the case when crossing the circumference of the waypoint arrival circle shown in figure 6-22, you look at the crosstrack error data field. If you have not yet reached the actual turning point, the crosstrack error data field will indicate your distance away from the new course line segment. Using this technique, you continue on your original course until the crosstrack error reads zero, or nearly so. At this point, you are on the center of the new course line, and you can safely execute the turn to the new bearing.

The second technique to assure that you turn at the appropriate time also uses a waypoint. By drawing a straight line on your chart extending down the middle of the channel, you can determine the course that directs you safely through the hazards. Now all you need is a reference point, preferably some distance away on land. Note the compass angle for this intended course and enter the reference point as a waypoint. Now, you can monitor the bearing to that waypoint on the Nearest Waypoints screen. When the bearing equals the intended course direction, you turn. To stay in the channel, simply make sure that the course continues to equal that bearing until you are clear of the obstructions. Also, you can use the Highway screen to facilitate staying in the center of the channel (within the tolerances of the GPS receiver's position accuracy). If, as in figure 6-23, the reference point (the standpipe) is visible, you have the additional advantage of using a hand-bearing compass to site the object and double-check your position. However, any set of coordinates can represent a waypoint in a GPS unit, so if there is no prominent object on the course line, create an artificial one. This is true of waypoints 1, 2, and 3 in figure 6-23, since no aids to navigation or other fixed

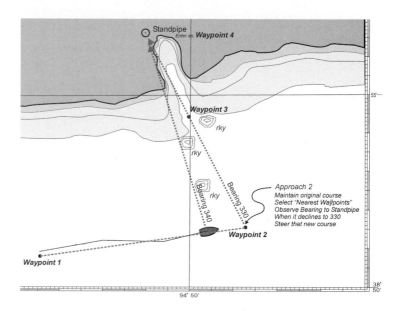

FIGURE 6-23. *Monitoring the Bearing to a Waypoint to Tell You When to Turn. Alternatively, you can preplot a bearing to a waypoint to judge when to turn for a safe entry into your tricky harbor. Don't turn until the desired bearing to the waypoint is indicated. A visible object is preferred since you can verify your course with a hand-bearing compass.*

objects are indicated in the diagram. When you lose the ability to correlate your position visually using fixed objects, you should use other techniques to cross-check your position. Remember the *Royal Majesty!*

Using GPS for Sailing or Powering in Rough Seas

A GPS receiver is an ideal navigation instrument for sailors. Since the sailboat often cannot go directly toward its end objective due to wind direction, the sailor must tack. Knowing the optimum time to tack is of paramount importance to making headway. Those in powerboats often encounter the same situation in heavy seas where it may not be possible to head directly toward the waypoint. There are a number of GPS receiver data fields that can be useful. Obviously, the bearing to the destination waypoint is very useful, as is the course line and distance. The direct path, displayed from the starting point to the destination point, is called the *rhumb line*, as shown in figure 6-24; it is drawn as the course line on the GPS receiver's Map screen.

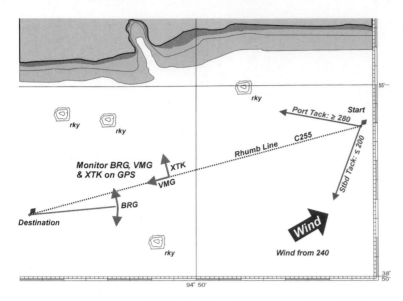

FIGURE 6-24. *Definitions of Navigation Terms for Sailing and Powerboating across Waves. Sailors and powerboaters in heavy seas often can't proceed directly to the destination waypoint. They must predetermine port and starboard tacks to suit conditions. Monitoring crosstrack error (XTK), velocity made good (VMG), and bearings (BRG) helps ensure a safe arrival at their destination.*

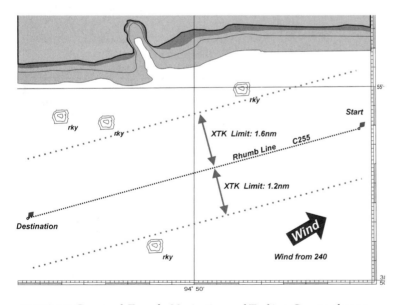

FIGURE 6-25. *Crosstrack Error for Navigation and Tacking. Crosstrack error (port or starboard) can be used to navigate safely and indicate when to tack. By preplotting a maximum crosstrack error, you can ensure clearing hazards and maintaining a reasonably compact track. The XTK can be different for port and starboard tacks, as in this figure, but you can set only one value for the alarm. Simply monitor the XTK against your predetermined limit for each tack.*

Given a prevailing wind direction, the sailor computes ideal port and starboard tack directions using the pointing characteristics of his sailboat as the criteria. The sailor then chooses the appropriate tack direction to sail. The GPS unit provides the boat track, or course over ground. This is the true motion of the boat with respect to the wind, which is an important value in determining how "high" the boat can point into the wind.

You can use the crosstrack error data field to assure that you tack no farther than a preselected distance from the rhumb line, as shown in figure 6-25. The XTK value can be set on alarm to facilitate this turn. It is not necessary that you tack at the same value of XTK on both port and starboard tacks; however, the alarm can be set at only one value. Therefore, it may make more sense to not set the alarm and instead visually monitor XTK against the preselected values you have recorded on your chart or log.

Also, you can monitor the VMG (velocity made good) data field. To do this, you need to know how your particular GPS model computes VMG. Some units present true VMG. This is the most valuable presentation of VMG, as it tells you continually what your effective rate of closure is in the direction of your objective. Under these circumstances, VMG constantly changes along your tack as the angle between the waypoint and your current tack changes. This presentation is very useful for letting you know when to tack. VMG calculated this way gives you the real effective rate of closure with the destination—the higher this value, the faster you reach your destination.

On GPS receivers that present true VMG, VMG will be highest when you commence your new tack and decline continuously as you progress. If you ever reach a point on the tack where the bearing to the waypoint is 90° (abeam) from your tack, the VMG will be zero. If you continue, the VMG will be negative, reflecting that you are moving farther away from your objective. The key is determining what level of decline from its highest value constitutes the best time to tack. An example of this effect is shown in figure 6-26. In this example, you decided to tack when the VMG dropped about 10 to 20 percent. The starboard tack is slower than the port tack due to the direction of the wind. You probably wouldn't want to stay on this tack too long, as shown in figure 6-27, where your VMG has dropped over 60 percent (from 4.2 down to 1.6 kn). Tacking earlier, as shown in figure 6-28, immediately increased the VMG on the port tack (now 5.7 kn).

Some GPS models compute VMG differently. These units consider only the angular difference between the course and the rhumb line (original course line) to compute the effective speed. In this case, VMG is constant as long as you are on the same tack. Therefore, you cannot use VMG to aid in tacking decisions with these GPS receivers.

Tip: *There is a way to find out how your GPS receiver performs the VMG calculation.* Put the receiver in the Simulator mode. Select a route that you have stored, but set the simulated COG to manual and select an angle somewhat different from the bearing— say 45°different. Set the SOG to move the boat and monitor VMG. If it remains constant at about 0.7 percent of the SOG, you cannot use the true VMG tacking technique described

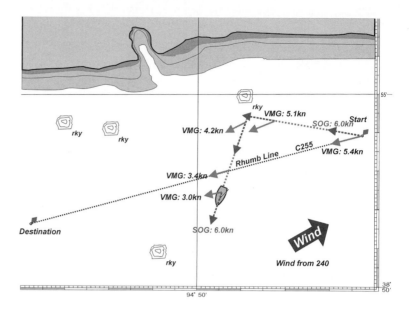

FIGURE 6-26. *VMG Changes Continually Along Each Tack. Velocity made good indicates your rate of progress toward your end objective independent of your current course. Its value changes based on your course and position relative to the destination waypoint. It can help tell you when to tack.*

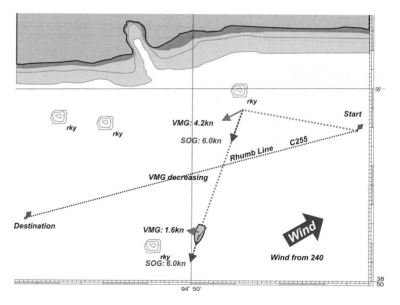

FIGURE 6-27. *VMG Drops if You Venture Too Far on a Given Course. In this example, you have waited too long to tack. Your VMG has fallen to a very low value (1.6 kn), indicating little progress toward your objective. To reach the destination waypoint efficiently and safely, you would need to tack earlier.*

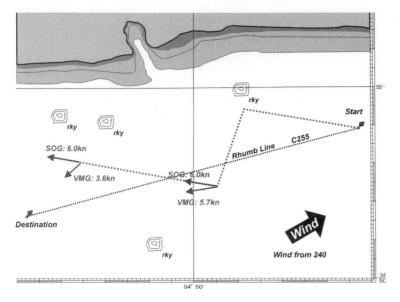

FIGURE 6-28. *Deciding When to Tack Is Key. Tacking earlier results in an immediate improvement in VMG (5.7 kn) and progress toward your objective. However, VMG continues to decline as you stay on this new tack. This close to the destination (mark) it may not make sense to tack again, so you need to know when to turn in order to reach your destination.*

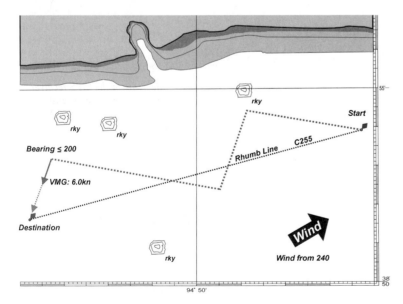

FIGURE 6-29. *Using Bearing to Make the Mark. In sailing, you must clear the mark (destination). By predetermining the closest bearing that clears the mark, you can use the GPS receiver to tell you when to tack. In this case, as soon as your bearing to the waypoint is less than or equal to 200, you make your final tack.*

above. If it changes constantly, declining over time, you can use this very effective technique.

Another tacking technique is to use the bearing to the waypoint. As shown in figure 6-29, using bearing is a way to determine when to make the final tack directly toward your destination. In this case, in order to reach the destination, you want the bearing to be less than or equal to your precalculated starboard tack angle (200°), as shown in figure 6-24. When you are heading directly toward the destination, VMG equals boat speed over ground (SOG), because you are steering directly toward the waypoint.

Using Tracks

Chapter 4 introduced the subject of tracks. They provide a historical record of where you have been. On the water, they represent a path that you can follow with reasonable confidence, knowing that you traveled this path before. Over a period of time, you'll find that you build up a number of tracks in and out of your harbor. Often, it is safe to navigate the center of the displayed tracks. Similarly, you can repeat a path to another destination, or use the track as a means to return. Using the Wrap feature in the Track Setup Menu means that the data constantly are being refreshed. If the buoys drift, or that sandbar shifts midseason, your newer tracks will reflect the changes. Tracks can provide you with a near real-time constant update. They come in handy when the fog rolls in or a squall hits.

Many people also keep a record of their tracks as a log of cruises on their boat. This record retains points where the boat has been and the time that it was there. These tracks can be plotted on electronic charts, as shown in figure

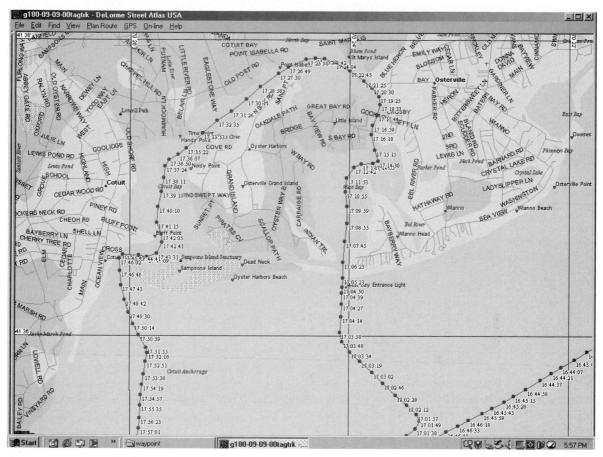

FIGURE 6-30. *A Track Plotted on an Electronic Chart Using a Computer and Software. Tracks recorded within the GPS receiver can be downloaded and plotted on an electronic chart to show where you have been. This is useful for planning routes and waypoints, or as a log of your travels. This example also shows time at each recorded point. The program used is Delorme Street Atlas, which is a map program for roads, not marine, but it is useful for plotting since it is supported by a number of the GPS download programs described in chapter 8.*

6-30, by connecting the GPS receiver to a computer and using software, as is described in chapters 8 and 9. The tracks can be invaluable in planning routes and determining where to place waypoints for frequently traveled routes. Some GPS models also permit uploading of tracks from your computer into the unit. For those without a chartplotter, you even can download coastline profiles and upload them into your GPS receiver as a track. Then when you view your Map screen, you will see the coastline as well as your waypoints. This may be interesting, but it's probably not very practical. If you're interested in learning more, go to the NOAA coastline extractor website listed in the resources section.

What You *Really* Want Is Some Way to Merge GPS and Chart Data Automatically

Transcribing the GPS coordinates onto a chart is tedious and error prone. Ideally, you would like to have that done for you. There are various ways to do this. The simplest was demonstrated in chapter 4 by naming all features of interest as waypoints. Since these waypoints show up on the Map screen, you have, in effect, a quasi-chartplotter. This approach lacks important features but helps you to safely navigate. The next three chapters describe various ways of achieving the objective of overlaying GPS information on a real chart.

Chapter 7

Chartplotting

Ultimately, as a boater, you'll at least consider owning a chartplotter. Once you have used a chartplotter with digital charts, you will wonder how you navigated without one. While the chartplotter does not replace the need for conventional navigation and paper charts, it quickly will become your primary means of navigation. The handheld GPS receiver provides you with accurate position information and useful navigation functions; however, its small screen is hard to read. Its small buttons are hard to push while you're on the water, and the handheld needs to be posi-

tioned with the antenna pointing upward in order to function. A typical chartplotter, shown in figure 7-1, features a larger display, more and bigger buttons, and a remote antenna.

> ## GPS and Chart Data on a Single Display
> → *shoreline features*
> → *depth contours*
> → *landmarks, waypoints*
> → *aids to navigation*
>
> ## Three Ways to Get There
> → *integrated chartplotter*
> → *chartplotter display and GPS receiver*
> → *GPS receiver connected to a computer*

A chartplotter is a device that overlays GPS data directly onto an electronic navigation chart. The chartplotter reduces the possibility of transcription error in plotting GPS coordinates onto a paper chart. At the same time, the combined GPS receiver and chart provides powerful tools for the navigator. Now, not only is position plotted, but landmasses, shoreline features, relevant landmarks, harbors, aids to navigation, hazards, depth contours, and relevant navigation information are also available. Effectively, a chartplotter could replace paper charts and conventional navigation if it were not for the need to have them as a safety backup.

There are several ways to achieve the functionality of a chartplotter. The most direct way is to purchase an integrated chartplotter, which includes the GPS receiver, chartplotter display, and processor in a single unit with a separate, remote antenna. An integrated chartplotter has the advantage of simplicity and usually lower final cost. Alternatively, an existing or separate GPS receiver can be integrated with a chartplotter display and processor. Often this approach is used with larger integrated systems wherein a number of devices such as a GPS receiver, radar, and a gyrocompass or fluxgate compass are integrated into a single chartplotter display and processor unit.

FIGURE 7-1. *A Typical Chartplotter. The chartplotter overlays the GPS receiver's Map screen on an electronic chart for the area. A chart chip provides the cartography, which is developed from paper charts. The chartplotter eliminates the toil of plotting coordinates onto a paper chart. The controls on the chartplotter are basically the same as those on a handheld GPS receiver. The screen is larger and has higher resolution. The buttons also are larger and, with more space on the unit, a chartplotter can accommodate more buttons.* (GARMIN)

This approach can integrate and display combinations of information derived from these various devices. The third option uses a computer with navigation software to provide the chartplotting function. Chapter 8 explains how to connect your GPS receiver to a computer off the boat for planning. Chapter 9 takes the computer to sea and offers powerful navigation solutions with some superb navigation software.

All fixed-mount GPS receivers are not chartplotters, but most chartplotters are fixed mount. Today, there are few fixed-mount GPS units that don't include chartplotting capability. The cost differential is so small that you should consider only those that include the chartplotter function, even if for budgetary reasons you don't buy the *chart chips* immediately. Conversely, there are a few chartplotters that are handheld. These are units that take the same chips as their larger cousins. Most of these have faded from the market because they cost about the same as a fixed-mount unit that has more features. If you have a handheld GPS receiver, keep it as a spare. Load the same routes and waypoints so you can press it into service if your fixed-mount unit fails.

The larger chartplotter provides room and capability for a much greater range of features than can be found on a handheld unit. The major difference is within the processing and display portions of the system. Chartplotter displays are larger with higher resolution. This permits the display of more detailed information on a single screen. Where a handheld would have one or two data fields, the fixed-mount unit may have six to eight at once. Alternatively, you can have fewer data fields displaying larger numbers, so you can read the data from some distance. The larger displays also enable the use of finer-scale cartography. The chart data can be more detailed for a given level of zoom. Symbols can be presented as they appear on charts, as opposed to as circles and squares. Also, a chartplotter typically has a higher-speed processor with greater memory than a handheld. This enables the unit to display information more quickly and perform faster screen redraws. The chartplotters are also designed to work with other equipment on the boat. As a result, they have multiple inputs and outputs for connection to a variety of devices. Often, these units can display information from radar, heading sensors, depth sounders, and wind sensors. Chartplotters integrate the data from these other devices to aid in safe navigation and to optimize sailing performance.

No matter which system you have, the chartplotter must be provided with chart information. The charts are digital and may be in one of two basic forms: raster or vector. A number of companies either digitize or scan chart data. The integrated chartplotters and systems tend to use the digitized vector charts, while many of the computer-based navigation systems use raster charts. There are advantages and disadvantages to each of the various alternatives for chartplotters, and for each type of chart presented in this section. The subject of digital charts is presented at the end of this chapter.

Chartplotters offer a dual function. When used off-line, in Charting Mode, they become effective planning tools. You can plan and lay out your cruise much as you would using charts. This offers a distinct advantage—you can enter waypoints and routes directly into the unit at the touch of a button. When used on-line, you are operating in Navigation Mode, wherein the chartplotter actively plots your position directly on the chart along with the attendant waypoints and routes.

Integrated Chartplotters

The *integrated chartplotter* is likely the least expensive approach to chartplotting. The GPS receiver and chartplotter are integrated into a single unit. Processing power, memory, and the display are shared. To present the chart data effectively, the chartplotter needs a larger, higher-resolution display than handheld GPS receivers. Typically the displays are 5 to 10 inches (130–250 mm) across.

The basic integrated chartplotter offers the ideal navigation solution for the small to midsize boat. Typically, space is limited on these boats, so working with charts can be difficult. It is not at all uncommon for these boaters to go some distance offshore, or to sail in adverse conditions requiring close attention to navigation. The chartplotter screen is large enough for the helmsman to view easily. The ease of electronic navigation makes setting bearings and looking for hazards far easier. Having the unit fixed on the boat makes it easier to operate. The key feature, above all else, is the presentation of the GPS-established position on a chart.

Figure 7-2 shows a typical section of a paper chart with the same information displayed in figure 7-3 on a basic integrated chartplotter. In addition to aids to navigation and hazards, some of which we entered into our handheld units, the chartplotter shows shoreline features and depth contours. Aids to navigation are annotated with additional information that can be obtained by moving the cursor over the spot on the screen. Moderately priced integrated chartplotters (those in the range of $400 to $1,000) typically have gray-scale (as opposed to monochrome) displays similar to the handheld GPS units, only larger. The chart may appear to lose something in the translation from color to gray scale. However, the critical information is preserved in a meaningful way. Experience has shown that, in a relatively short period of time, the operator can relate to the gray-scale charts. However, that said, the differential in cost between chartplotters with gray-scale and color screens is shrinking, and a color screen is better, since it provides quicker visual cuing to important features.

The newer color displays are sunlight readable and present a clearer picture than their gray-scale cousins. The latest transflective displays rely upon reflected sunlight to brighten the display. Many units use backlighting and reflective screens to provide a more uniform illumination under all lighting conditions, including darkness. At one time, color more than doubled the price of a chartplotter, and the earlier color displays were difficult to see. Not so today. Color now adds as little as 20 to 30 percent to the chartplotter price, but 50 to 70 percent is more typical. Eventually, the cost difference will shrink to a point that gray scale goes the way of the black-and-white television.

The controls for the chartplotter fundamentally are the same as those found on handheld GPS units. Figure 7-4 shows a typical chartplotter. With the increased space on the larger unit, manufacturers have room for additional buttons such as "MOB" (man overboard) and "Mark" that make entering waypoints easier. The buttons are larger and spaced farther

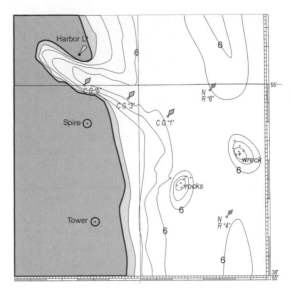

FIGURE 7-2. *A Sample Chart with Depth Contours. This is the same chart region shown on the integrated chartplotter screen in figure 7-3.*

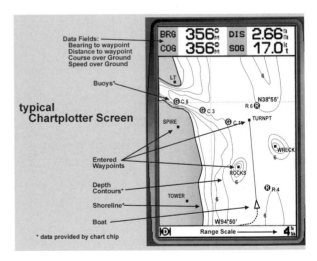

FIGURE 7-3. *A Chartplotter with Digital Charts Shows the Same Information. The key features from the chart in figure 7-2 are presented on the chartplotter screen. In this case, you need only add uncharted features as waypoints. Depth contours, coastlines, and key navigation features are all incorporated from a vector digital chart chip. The GPS receiver adds the current position of the boat, a track of where you have been, and an active course line to the selected waypoint, designated as "TURNPT." Data fields are presented with key navigation information. In this case, the current course over ground (COG) and speed over ground (SOG) for the boat are shown, as well as the bearing (BRG) and distance (DIS) to the active waypoint.*

apart, making them easier to use at sea. Beyond the Chart screen, the screens are quite similar to those on a handheld. Given the greater display size, finer resolution is offered on the Highway and Compass screens. Because the data fields are larger they're easier to read while you're at the helm. More data fields can be inserted and tailored to suit the user. But, fundamentally, if you understand how to use your handheld GPS receiver, you will have little difficulty performing the same functions on the integrated chartplotter. The differences in screens and controls from one manufacturer to another are minor. The major differences are in the choice of cartography, display, processor speed, number of inputs and outputs, and the packaging for the environment. These units are designed to be integrated with other electronic devices on the boat, which is described in detail in chapter 9.

A variety of basic integrated chartplotters are available in the moderate $400 to $1,000 price range, some with color displays. These chartplotters generally offer screens of 5 to 7 inches (130–180 mm) that are ideal for small- to medium-sized boats. Some examples are shown in figures 7-5a, 7-5b, and 7-5c. Chart chips typically cost an additional $100 to $300 each, depending upon the size of the region covered.

FIGURE 7-4. Chartplotter Buttons Are Similar to Those on a Handheld. A basic chartplotter is a powerful tool. This unit is a Garmin GPSMAP 180, recently replaced by the model 182. The buttons on an integrated chartplotter are similar to those on a handheld unit, only larger. The screen has sufficient size and resolution to display the chart. The compartment for the digital chart chip is located at the lower right of the unit. (CARTOGRAPHY BY GARMIN)

FIGURE 7-5A. Standard Horizon Chartplotters. Standard Horizon offers chartplotters with 5- and 6-inch (130–150 mm) screens in gray scale or color, both of which are sunlight readable and waterproof. Both models use C-Map NT vector chart chips. The chartplotter with the 6-inch screen (model CP-170C) communicates with a DSC-equipped VHS to display the location of nearby distress calls on the screen. (STANDARD HORIZON)

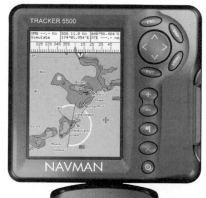

FIGURE 7-5B. Navman Chartplotters. Navman chartplotters have 5- and 6.4-inch (130–163 mm) sunlight-readable displays. They use C-Map NT vector chart chips. Both models are offered with either internal or external antennas. The Tracker 5500 is shown here. (NAVMAN)

FIGURE 7-5C. Garmin Portable Chartplotter. This 4-inch (100 mm) GPSMAP176 chartplotter has a built-in antenna and is available with a gray-scale or color screen. This unit is functionally similar to the GPSMAP 76 handheld unit but adds the capability of using BlueChart MapSource vector chart chips in addition to CD-ROMs for cartography. (GARMIN)

FIGURE 7-6A. *High-End Chartplotters Offer More Features. This Northstar GPS receiver is among the highest quality chartplotters available. Often used by professionals, the Northstar offers a larger screen, faster processing, and "hot buttons." Instead of submenus, the hot buttons have screen labels that indicate their function. The functions change depending upon the screen. This unit is easier to use than most handhelds and offers far more processing. The basic GPS performance is quite similar to the handheld. This unit also offers a keypad much like a telephone to ease the data-entry process. Vector cartography for Northstar is provided by Navionics with chips similar to those from C-Map.* (NORTHSTAR)

FIGURE 7-6C. *Raymarine Chartplotters. Raymarine chartplotters operate as central display systems. Units are offered with 7- and 10-inch (180 and 255 mm) gray-scale and color sunlight-readable screens. Both units offer the ability to display Raymarine radar and depth sounder screens as well. The model shown with the 10-inch color screen also permits overlaying the radar images directly on top of the chartplotter screen. This enables the operator to distinguish between fixed objects and other boats. All units permit arraying multiple pages and use C-Map NT vector chips. Raymarine uses an external GPS that is housed with the antenna, which isn't included with the chartplotter display.* (RAYMARINE)

Each chip incorporates the data from a number of paper charts. The type of cartography used depends upon the chartplotter manufacturer. Most chartplotters will accept only one type of chip, so check the cost, format, and availability of cartography for your application before deciding on a chartplotter. A few less-expensive chartplotters use cartography downloaded from a computer via a CD-ROM. These chartplotters can work quite well for a limited region of operation. If you venture beyond this area, you will need to download new chart data overlaying what is stored because the unit's memory is limited.

FIGURE 7-6B. *Simrad Chartplotter. This chartplotter offers a 6-inch (150 mm) sunlight-viewable color display and a keypad for data entry, and uses a C-Map NT vector chip.* (SIMRAD)

FIGURE 7-6D. *High-End Garmin Chartplotters. The 6- and 10-inch (150 and 255 mm) units from Garmin are offered with gray-scale and sunlight-readable color screens. They use an external antenna and GPS sensor, which are provided with the chartplotter. The chartplotter has keypads for data entry and integral hot buttons. These chartplotters use BlueChart vector chart chips. Shown is a model 2010 10-inch color chartplotter.* (GARMIN)

High-End Integrated Chartplotters

A high-end integrated chartplotter is designed for greater integration with other instruments on the boat. It offers larger displays, typically 7 to 10 inches (180–255 mm), and greater processing power. These units include the GPS receiver within the chartplotter. Some manufacturers of high-end units opt to use a separate GPS receiver housed with the antenna. Many of these are described in the next section. These chartplotters use the identical vector chart chips as those used in the basic chartplotters described above. Display size and the other features differentiate these units. As with the basic chartplotters, the choice of chart chip brand is determined by the manufacturer for each model. Consider the quality of the chip data and the ease of updates and support before finalizing your choice of chartplotter model. High-end chartplotters further expand upon the buttons available to ease control of the GPS unit when underway. Given the larger displays, manufacturers have elected to offer *hot buttons* to make operation a great deal easier. These buttons are located next to the screen. Their functions change, and the functions are labeled accordingly on each screen. These buttons replace the more cumbersome menus used on the handheld GPS units. Some chartplotter units also provide keypads, much like a telephone keypad, to facilitate the entry of numeric data. The high-end chartplotters typically integrate with other onboard devices. Often, the chartplotter display becomes the primary display on board for charts, radar, depth sounder, temperature, wind, and other data. High-end chartplotters offer faster processing, higher screen resolutions, and a host of features similar to the Electronic Charting Display and Information Systems (ECDIS) found on the bridges of large ships. All of these features come with a price. A typical high-end chartplotter costs $2,000 to $4,000, including a GPS receiver. Examples of several of these units are shown in figures 7-6a, 7-6b, 7-6c, and 7-6d.

Chartplotter Pages

Since chartplotter displays have a higher resolution than those on handheld GPS units, a chartplotter has better presentation on all screens. Screen formats may be similar to those on a handheld, but more data and display options are offered. The Map screen is replaced with a real chart. The chart uses information provided by a chip(s) inserted into a designated slot(s) on the chartplotter. Each chip covers a designated region, so you will need chips for each area in which you sail. The chip formats (generally vector) are unique to the supplier of the chip.

Figure 7-7 shows sample Chart and Highway screens for a basic chartplotter. The data fields are considerably larger and easier to read. The displays have higher resolution, enabling more-defined features to be presented. The larger display space and finer resolution permit additional data fields, providing more useful information to the helmsman, or fewer data fields with larger numbers that can be read from a distance. The Chart screen (right side of fig. 7-7) shows latitude and longitude grid lines, depth contours, waypoints, and aids to navigation. Numeric fields are shown at the top of the display providing waypoint bearing and distance, as well as course over ground (COG) and speed over ground (SOG) of the boat. The scale of the display coverage distance is shown at the bottom right. The Highway screen (left side of fig. 7-7) offers the same numeric data plus a graphic compass band similar to a mechanical compass presentation. Two user-selectable data fields are shown below the highway. In this example, crosstrack error (XTK) and velocity made good (VMG) are displayed. A steering vector is also provided, indicating the direction to steer to achieve the desired waypoint. The highway presentation has a higher resolution than a handheld and includes multiple legs of the selected route in addition to displaying flags for the waypoints that lie within the coverage window. Each specific chartplotter may have different presentations of data; however, most of the features and functions are similar.

Figures 7-8a and 7-8b show a chartplotter Chart screen and the paper chart for the same area. The chartplotter presentation is less populated with detailed information and is easier to read at this scale level. When you zoom in, greater detail is presented.

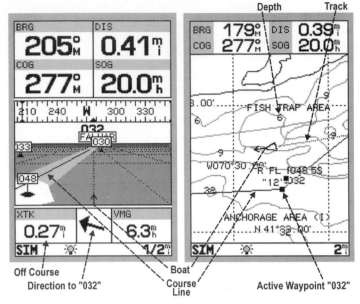

Depth **Track**

Off Course
Direction to "032"

Boat
Course
Line

Active Waypoint "032"

FIGURE 7-7. *Chartplotter Displays. Chartplotter displays provide a great deal of useful information. Even the basic chartplotter is quite powerful. These images come from a 5-inch (130 mm) screen. The image on the left shows a Highway screen with a ½-mile spacing between the dotted grid lines. This display has considerably more detail than handheld units. The screen indicates that the boat is off course to the right (starboard) of the course line and is headed toward waypoint 30 ("030") instead of the active waypoint 32. There are multiple data fields providing significant information. The example shows that you are 0.41 nm from waypoint 32 lying on a bearing of 205° while your current COG is 277°. This same information is shown graphically on the compass display. XTK and VMG displays are shown at the bottom. The arrow at the bottom is a cue to turn left to the active waypoint. Other waypoints are shown on the Highway screen. On the right is a comparable Map screen for a short time later. The Map screen in this case displays the same data field at the top, and provides a sense of the boat's position relative to the depth contours and the route "Course Line." The boat direction and track are shown. Chart grid lines are shown that facilitate comparing this display with an actual chart. The shoreline is shown at the top. This display is set for a 2-mile range top to bottom.*

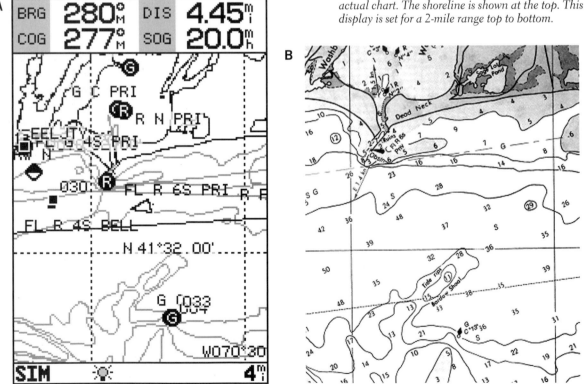

FIGURES 7-8A *and* 7-8B. *Comparison of the Same Area on a Chartplotter and a Paper Chart. The chartplotter screen in figure 7-8a is not as detailed as the chart in figure 7-8b, but the key information is there. In fact, the key navigation aids clearly are more prominent on the chartplotter display than the equivalent chart.*

Selecting a Chartplotter

Chartplotters range in price from about $500 to over $10,000. Your chartplotter's intended use will help you decide what features you need. If it will be at the helm and exposed to weather and direct sunlight, the display and housing are key factors. A color display adds to the price. Insist on sunlight viewability and waterproofing. The display size also affects price. Choose the display that presents information to you in a size you can see from the helm without squinting or using glasses. Newer units offer the option of displaying oversize numbers to make viewing easier, even from a distance. It is advantageous to have critical information displayed in a somewhat uncluttered manner to aid the helmsman and crew. You always can switch display formats to get other information on demand.

The area of intended operation of the boat and the performance and cost of the charts should also be considered before purchasing a chartplotter. The chartplotter manufacturer designs the unit to work with a particular type of vector chart chip. The major suppliers of these chips are C-Map, Navionics, and Garmin. Typical chart chips cost between $100 and $300. You won't be able to use a chip from one chartplotter model in another unless they use the same format. C-Map chips are used in chartplotters from Raymarine, Standard Horizon, Simrad, Navman, Furuno, Si-Tex, JRC, Interphase, and others. Navionics chips are used in Northstar, Lowrance, ICOM, some Furuno and Raymarine products, and others. Generally, these chips are interchangeable from one chartplotter to another using the same chip brand and format. Garmin chips are used only in Garmin models; Garmin chartplotters accept only Garmin chips. As previously identified, most chartplotters employ chart chips in vector format. With larger memory capacity in smart media cards driven by the computer and digital camera markets, you can expect to see chips in raster format as well in the future. Until recently, the Garmin chart data were provided by Navionics; however, Garmin has developed a new cartography format, called BlueChart, for its latest models, using cartography supplied by Transas. A very important consideration in selecting a chartplotter and its attendant chart chips is the support and ease of updating these chips. Gener-

ally, such services are available from the supplier of the chips. Companies like C-Map offer a subscription service enabling you to return a chip each year for reprogramming. Some companies require you to buy a new chip. Other cartography is available on CD-ROMs for use on a computer and can be uploaded into some GPS receivers. More on chart formats is presented later in this chapter.

Other considerations in selecting a chartplotter are the unit's performance and features. Most chartplotters provide comparable basic GPS receiver performance. For the most part, the GPS receiver is an integrated circuit board. Originally, the receiver chips were expensive to develop and consequently were produced by a relatively small number of companies. It is far less expensive for GPS receiver manufacturers to use the same chips from these suppliers than to develop unique receivers. This explains why the basic GPS technical specifications, particularly within units from a given manufacturer, are virtually the same. A 12-channel, WAAS-enabled, DGPS-ready receiver is the norm. The major chartplotter differences are in displays and processors.

Displays differ by size, color, resolution, and brightness as discussed above. The proper display is very important to the boat operator. The best way to make a selection in this regard is to look at displays in stores; ask if they have a sunlamp or bright light so you can see to what degree the display will wash out at the helm. Once you've identified several models that interest you, ask around to find installed units on boats similar to ones that interest you. Ask the boatowner's opinion of the chartplotter on board and ask to look at it.

Processors are the computing part of the GPS chartplotter. The processor is essentially a special-purpose computer. Better units have larger memories and faster processors. The larger the memory, the more adaptable the unit. Since these units are firmware driven (software typically loaded into a read-only memory), most can be updated. Some can be updated by the user, such as downloading replacement firmware from the Garmin website. Others require a trip back to the manufacturer. Those with sufficient memory can be updated as the manufacturer releases new or improved features. The other consideration for processing is the speed with which the screen redraws when the field of view changes. Longer redraws are usually just an inconvenience, unless, of course, you need to take quick action.

Most integrated chartplotters use external antennas, which are supplied with the unit. Usually, these antennas are active, meaning that they amplify the signal at the antenna before it begins its path along the wire to the receiver. Antenna placement is an important consideration. Antennas should be placed relatively low in the boat, but in a location that is not obstructed from the sky. GPS receiver antennas mounted on the top of a sailboat mast, for example, though generally unobstructed, will experience considerable motion that does not reflect the actual motion of the boat itself, and can result in distorted information.

Chartplotters Used with GPS Sensors

Chartplotters that use external *GPS sensors* are also available. These chartplotters perform the same basic computing and display functions as integrated chartplotters; however, they differ in that they do not include the GPS unit within the chartplotter. The GPS receiver is sold as a separate component. These chartplotters derive the position data from the GPS sensor. Virtually any GPS receiver, including handheld units, can be used as the sensor; however, most installations use a special GPS sensor that combines the receiver with the antenna. These sensors are sealed against the environment and have no external controls.

It is well known to radio engineers that the longer the connecting cables, the greater the reduction in signal quality. For this reason, you want your GPS receiver as close to your antenna as possible. This is not a problem on most recreational boats. On larger boats, the cable run can be of considerable length, so skippers of big boats generally opt for an integrated GPS sensor. The GPS sensor looks very similar to an external antenna, though it is slightly larger. Typically, the sensor is mounted in a dome-shaped enclosure with the antenna on top and the receiver just below. It does not include all of the typical computing equipment that is found in handheld or integrated fixed-mount units. Typically, a multiwire cable connects the sensor to the chartplotter unit. The cable carries power to the sensor and contains NMEA 0183 wires to control the GPS receiver and send the GPS data to the chartplotter. This does not preclude the use of other GPS units from working with a separate chartplotter by employing the NMEA data interconnects. Some GPS sensors are integrated with a DGPS receiver. Most newer units offer WAAS capability. Chapter 10 describes both DGPS and WAAS. A typical GPS sensor costs $400 to $500. Loran-C, which provides position data, can be used as an alternative or supplement to the GPS sensor with the chartplotter display unit.

The stand-alone chartplotter units typically have larger displays than the average integrated chartplotter. Skippers in the target market for these units typically have larger boats and can afford and accommodate the larger unit. Stand-alone chartplotters start in the $600 price range (exclusive of the GPS sensor), but higher-end units typically cost $2,500 to $10,000, plus the sensor. This configuration is well suited to integrated electronic navigation installations that include radar and other instruments. This enables the boater to invest more in a quality display that can be used for multiple functions. This saves the cost of separate displays for radar, chartplotter, depth sounder, and autopilot. It also saves valuable space at the helm for mounting all of these separate displays. Several marine electronics manufacturers now offer radar displayed on the same page as the chartplotter. Raymarine (shown in figure 7-6c) overlays the radar data on the color chartplotter. This permits the helmsman to independently verify her position and helps to separate fixed objects on the radar display from potential moving hazards.

There is a clear trend toward totally integrated electronics on board. NMEA currently does not support transmission of the large amount of data to support remote displays of radar screens or electronic charts, so some manufacturers have developed their own proprietary connections. Raymarine has the Seatalk electronic communication bus and the HSB2 for High-Speed Bus to support these interconnections. Furuno has developed a bus around the commercially available high-speed Ethernet bus. With these interconnections, it is possible to have multiple displays of radar and/or charts at different locations aboard the boat. Unfortunately, this requires that all of the equipment come from the same manufacturer. Chapter 9 provides more information regarding NMEA and interconnection.

Chartplotting Using a GPS Receiver Connected to a Computer

The third approach to chartplotting uses a computer to perform the chartplotting function. Software is available that enables a computer to perform virtually the same charting and navigation functions as the stand-alone chartplotter—and much more. These installations can use a standard GPS receiver, integrated chartplotter GPS, or separate GPS sensor. You can upload waypoints and routes to the GPS receiver from the computer, and the two units will then share the same information. Computers generally are not designed for operation in direct sunlight or in a location exposed to the elements, so most installations are below deck or at the enclosed helm on a larger craft. The computer-based system, just as its integrated and stand-alone chartplotter cousins, operates in two distinct modes—Charting and Navigating. When used off-line, the chartplotter is considered to be in the Charting mode. Using a computer with larger display and feature-rich software makes planning even easier. Many boaters use both an integrated chartplotter at the helm and a computer below. Chapter 8 discusses the GPS unit working with a computer for off-line planning and data exchange. Chapter 9 addresses the GPS unit working with a computer and other onboard electronics for active navigation. Chapter 9 also describes navigation programs operating in both the Charting and Navigation modes.

Raster Versus Vector Charts

Chart data for chartplotters are available on two principal media—chart chips and CD-ROMs. The solid-state chart chips offer speed, are smaller, and require only a chip connector slot to be read. However, their storage capacity is limited compared to that of CD-ROMs. Consequently, chips favor the use of *vector* data that require less memory for a given chart area, because only relevant points are saved, along with text and symbols. Since chart symbols are used repeatedly, they are stored as objects and need only be stored once and called up as needed. *Raster* charts are scanned from actual charts and stored as a digital picture of the original master. They must save all of the information on each chart, even if much of it is nothing but white space—all of that takes memory. Raster charts generally are distributed on CD-ROMs due to the larger storage capacity (up to 700 megabytes or MB). While for a typical region, a set of raster charts may require more than 200 MB of memory, the same chart area in vector format may require less than 10 MB and provide more supporting information. The proliferation of smart media for use in computers, digital cameras, and other devices will migrate into the chart world. With larger memory capacities and even lower prices, raster charts will become available on chips in the future as well.

Whether to buy raster- or vector-based equipment depends upon what you want to do with your GPS. If you plan to use an integrated chartplotter, you inevitably will use vector chips. CD-ROMs are less expensive to manufacture but are slower to read, and they require a special drive to read them, which is not practical if mounted on a GPS chartplotter that is exposed to the elements. As a result, chartplotters almost exclusively use chip cartography (vector).

The selection of a particular chartplotter should be based largely on the chip cartography that it employs. Each supplier of chip cartography has certain features and advantages. C-Map has the largest database of cartography and is used on the most brands. Navionics is used on a number of chartplotter brands. C-Map has a philosophy that they generally will not display data at a scale level that does not correspond to the source cartography. Others may extrapolate to provide what appears to be a continuous display even if the source data do not support that resolution. Both philosophies are used on high-end chartplotters as well as emerging lower-cost units. Chips can be interchanged between different chartplotter units designed for that format. Both C-Map and Navionics continually update their cartography and offer update programs to reprogram your chips. Updates and new chips can be purchased directly from the cartography company or through marine retailers. Chips, which generally are not supplied with the GPS chartplotter, add a separate cost ranging from $100 to $300, depending upon the area of chart coverage. Charts are available for all of the U.S. and most of the world.

Garmin produces their own chips using cartography provided by others. Their now-outdated G-charts use Navionics data. Their new BlueChart cartography uses data from Transas. Garmin offers a rebate program for the purchase of updated chips. Garmin chips operate only in the appropriate Garmin units and can be purchased through Garmin or retail outlets. Garmin is moving toward higher-end chartplotters, and this customer base is setting industry standards, which will increasingly result in similar performance and customer support from all three suppliers. In deciding which cartography format to buy, make sure you have each demonstrated to you so that you can see the differences in the way each functions.

Currently, some manufacturers are providing vector charts on CD-ROMs for uploading into GPS chartplotter units that do not support chips, but have sufficient memory to store some chart data. These lower-cost units often have limited internal memory for chart data, so the user must upload and overwrite stored chart data as each new region is traversed.

Future integrated chartplotters may offer chips with raster data as smart card technology finds its way into chartplotters. This is not yet an option. One disadvantage of the chartplotter for viewing charts is its limited display size. You can see only a small window. Computers usually have a larger display, and for this reason they are better suited to planning.

Charts on a Computer-Based Planning or Navigation System

Many mariners prefer raster cartography since it has the look and characteristics of paper charts. If you also prefer raster, you should opt for a computer-based solution, either for off-line planning or onboard navigation. The cartography choice is determined by the navigation software you use. Most programs use raster charts on CD-ROM, although C-Map, Nobeltec, and

> ### Which Is Better?
>
> *Raster*
> → *Advantages*
> - *looks like paper charts*
> - *better land features*
> - *ability to add photos and photo chart data*
> - *easier to produce*
>
> → *Disadvantages*
> - *details about aids to navigation and labels shrink as you zoom out*
>
> *Vector*
> → *Advantages*
> - *better scalability, can read key info in zoom*
> - *quicker redraws*
> - *lower memory requirements*
> - *vivid colors*
> - *layers can provide additional information (pop-up fields appear when you scroll over an object)*
> - *ability to extract data such as depths; depth alarm based on look ahead*
>
> → *Disadvantages*
> - *mechanical look*
> - *do not look like paper charts*
> - *overzooming can lead to false perception of accuracy*

Garmin offer some vector charts on CD-ROM. Programs from Raymarine and C-Map allow you to use C-Map chart chips on your computer with a supplied chip reader that connects to the computer.

Raster Charts

Many mariners prefer raster charts because they look like traditional charts. They have better imagery and provide land features that generally are not reflected in the vector charts. If you're looking to take visual bearings to towers or other features typically printed on the raster chart, you may not find these objects

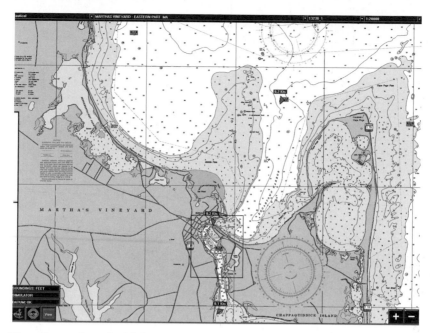

FIGURE 7-9A. *Raster Chart. Raster charts faithfully replicate NOAA charts in form and color. They look better than vector cartography, but these charts require more storage capacity. As a result, they primarily are delivered on CD-ROMs and used with computer-based navigation programs. When zoomed out, the labels are difficult to read. Zooming in corrects the readability, but narrows the area presented. This chart shows a segment of eastern Martha's Vineyard, Massachusetts. These digital charts are created by scanning actual masters from NOAA or other hydrographic offices.* (MAPTECH)

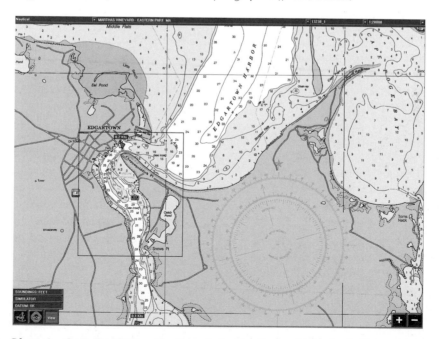

FIGURE 7-9B. *Raster Charts Are Quite Good When You Zoom in for Details. At a higher level of magnification, the raster chart is easier to read. The box around Edgartown harbor indicates that a larger-scale chart is available for that area. Many prefer the raster chart because its look is familiar and it offers many features.* (MAPTECH)

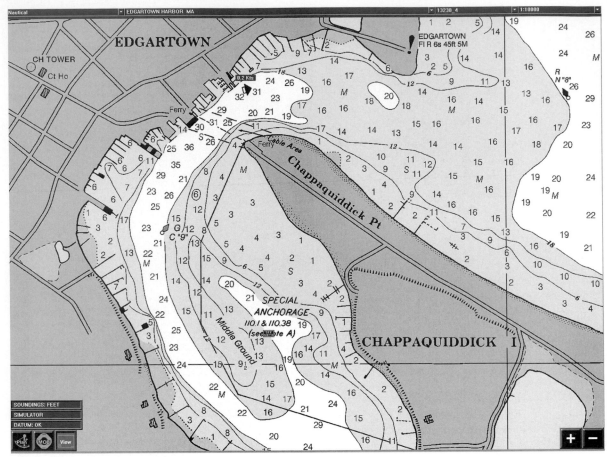

FIGURE 7-9C. *The Larger-Scale Edgartown Harbor Chart Shows Excellent Detail. This screen shows a section of the larger-scale chart indicated by the box in figure 7-9b. The raster chart provides extensive features on the water and the land. The GPS data can be overlaid on this electronic chart, typically with a computer-based navigation program. This display is presented with Maptech's Offshore Navigator.* (MAPTECH)

shown on the corresponding vector chart. In addition, a new form of cartography for marine charts is gaining popularity. Using satellite data, Maptech has created *photo charts* that can be presented on the screen next to traditional charts. This imagery, which requires a lot of memory to display, is naturally presented in a raster format and works well with most computer-based navigation programs. Ultimately, this same technology will be offered on chartplotters.

Digital raster charts have a disadvantage when displayed on a chartplotter or computer: When you zoom far out to see a larger section of the chart, the chart presentation may become cluttered and the data too small to read, as illustrated in figure 7-9a. When you zoom

in, the data become clearer, as shown in figures 7-9b and 7-9c. Zooming in further may magnify the picture, but not the detail. However, the cartography software includes detailed, larger-scale charts for some harbors and channels. Most popular programs automatically will shift to the more detailed chart when you scroll over that region using the cursor.

Vector Charts

Vector charts are faster to display and redraw on chartplotters with limited processing capabilities. They also provide more supporting data, and they scale well. Vector charts are created in layers, and as you zoom out, the labels and key aids to navigation

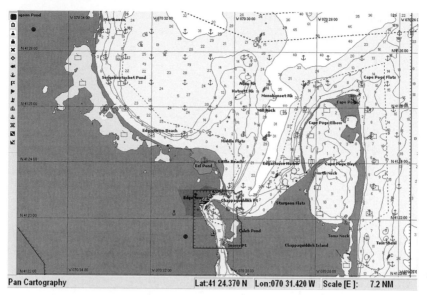

FIGURE 7-10A. *Vector Charts Are Commonly Used on Chartplotters. The vector chart is created from a raster chart by manually coding the features into a database. In vector format, the data can be compressed by a factor of 10 or more. This makes the vector chart more popular for chartplotters, since the data can be provided on a chart chip that can be inserted into the chartplotter. The vector presentation can also enhance labels and information to make it readable at all scale levels. This chart comes from a C-Map NT+ cartridge and is presented on their PC Planner software. Note the extensive navigation aids and water data, but limited land features. On the chartplotter screen, these data are quite readable even at the zoom level.* (C-MAP)

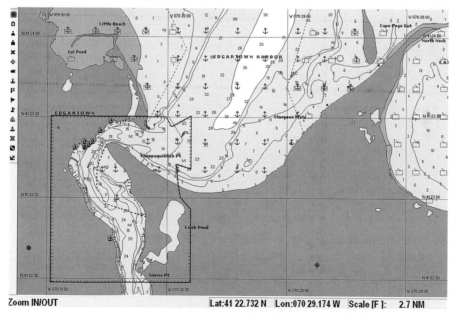

FIGURE 7-10B. *Zooming in on the Vector Chart Provides More Data. This chart presents a different level of digital zoom on a vector chart. Features unique to this zoom level are presented. Vector charts are created in layers, and the layers can be turned on or off to present more or less data. The data are clear and very useful for navigation. However, the presentation is considered by some to be too mechanical. The accuracy of the data is as good as the source information that comes from the NOAA charts. Some minor differences may be injected by the use of short straight-line segments to represent shorelines and alignment due to operator interpretation, but these vector charts are double-checked for accuracy.* (C-MAP)

Chartplotting **103**

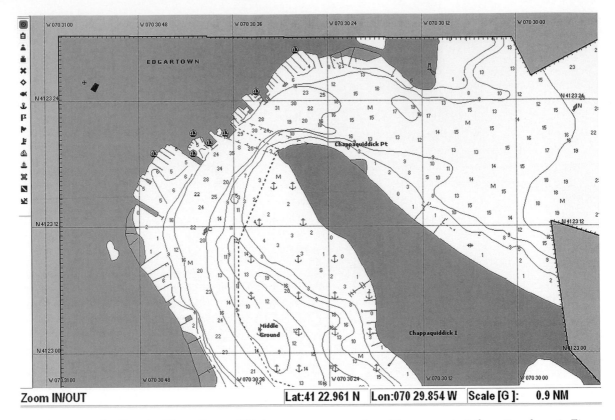

Zoom IN/OUT | Lat:41 22.961 N | Lon:070 29.854 W | Scale [G]: | 0.9 NM

FIGURE 7-10C. *Harbor Detail in Vector Format. This is a vector representation of the same raster information shown in Figure 7-9c. Key information is visible and clear; however, land features are missing. This display shows part of the limits for this harbor chart.* (C-MAP)

can be automatically sized to the display so you can read them. Zooming in for greater detail can be achieved by selectively turning on more layers, as shown in figures 7-10a and 7-10b. These charts are made from paper-chart masters, so they begin with the same information as the raster chart. However, the cartographers can add refined data from other sources, such as marinas, harbormasters, etc. It is possible to zoom in on a vector chart to a level where details, such as individual docks and slips, can be seen in a marina or harbor based on these supplemental data. Supporting information can be attached to individual objects, which can be displayed, as shown in figure 7-10c, by scrolling over the object or clicking a button. Other information for local services can be accessed in a similar manner. In addition, the digital format of the information allows navigation programs to access and use

the data, such as to plot a profile of depth in front of the vessel or to show a 3-D profile of depth. (The information on a raster chart is imbedded in the picture and cannot be retrieved for other uses.) The vector charts, whether on chips or CD-ROMs, are coming down in price. The producers of these charts need only update their databases to note changes and correct errors.

Although vector charts are easier to read, they appear to have a more mechanical look. The cost to digitize data from the source charts limits just how much is recorded. This is why many land features are omitted. Also the labels seen on vector charts may not display all of the same information as a raster chart unless you scroll over the object using the cursor to access a pop-up display. At sea, you may not wish to take the time to scroll over a buoy to get that information. This is another reason why it is advisable to carry and use the paper charts corresponding to the same area when navigating with a chartplotter.

Chart Accuracy

Both vector and raster charts are as accurate as the paper charts that have served mariners well. Those who have learned navigation using paper charts tend to favor the raster charts, while those who have learned to navigate on chartplotters tend to favor vector charts. In order to compete and win new customers, the makers of raster digital charts are improving their products with higher resolutions and enhanced features. The source data from the various hydrographic offices around the world are still provided primarily in raster format. Raster charts are quite good and will be around for a long time. The selection is largely one of personal taste for those using computer-based navigation programs. For those using integrated chartplotters, vector charts are the standard. Still, most of the popular navigation programs for the computer use raster charts, while only some accept vector charts.

Maintaining the data is an extremely important factor in using digital charts, just as it is with paper charts. The U.S. Coast Guard publishes *Local Notices to Mariners*, which provides regularly updated corrections to charts. This publication can be accessed online (see the resources section). Mariners are cautioned to annotate their paper charts on a regular basis from the *Local Notice to Mariners*. Many digital chart companies update their databases from these notices and a variety of other sources weekly. They publish updated charts at least several times per year. Usually, if you buy the cartography from the producer, you will have charts accurate almost up to the time of purchase. Unfortunately, unless you update your chips or CD-ROMs on a regular basis, you may miss important changes. These companies offer a variety of means to obtain updates, from replacement chips for a fraction of the original cost to on-line updated files. Some even offer subscription services that enable you to send back your chip to have it updated and then returned to you. For larger installations using computers, there are even on-line services to update the data directly. You should update your chips once per year—a good task for the off-season. At a minimum, it is recommended that you manually annotate your paper charts and refer to them regularly while navigating with your chartplotter.

Also, NOAA and other hydrographic agencies throughout the world update entire charts on a rotating basis. Cartography companies then digitize new charts. Considering the cost of purchasing paper charts, the digitized chart packages, which typically cover dozens to hundreds of paper charts, are a real bargain. Although you still should have paper charts for the waters you cruise, you are unlikely to purchase as many detailed, large-scale charts as may be found in a digital chart package.

The Future in Charts

Over time, the distinction between vector and raster charts will fade. The vector charts will incorporate more terrestrial data and features in order to address users' needs. By the same token, raster charts will increasingly use layers to provide supplemental data and overlays that enhance them. Charts increasingly will become available with a blend of both vector and raster features.

Traditionally, cartography has been provided in raster format from the hydrographic organizations that collect the data, such as NOAA. However, they are beginning to provide chart data for commercial shipping lanes in vector format. These new electronic navigation charts (ENC) are in response to new international standards developed by the International Hydrographic Organization that define the features needed for ECDIS (Electronic Charting Display and Information System) navigation. Under these new standards, known as S-57, commercial ships that carry ENC charts are no longer legally required to carry backup paper charts. Without ECDIS, commercial ships by law must manually annotate their paper charts with any changes listed in each new *Local Notice to Mariners* issue. Doing so is costly and time consuming.

The new standards require a significant improvement in detail that will enhance the source data used by all cartography companies. These standards, stipulated by NOAA and other government organizations, will be limited to areas of commercial traffic. Currently, samples of these charts are available on the

Web from NOAA, but they are not integrated or complete. The cartography companies will begin to package and enhance these data, and in turn, offer even more feature-rich products, as some of their costs of coding the digital charts will be borne by the hydrographic organizations. To maintain competitive position, these companies will incorporate greater amounts of proprietary information of significant use to mariners, such as harbor details, available services, local information, land features, and more. Look for companies to offer raster charts integrating these same vector data and to begin to offer hybrid products. Digital charts will continue to move in the direction of multiple layers of information that can be turned on at will, and in the direction of even more flexibility to add your own data to the charts.

An ongoing trend of importance to boaters is that cartography suppliers are providing increasingly larger regions of coverage at lower cost on fewer chips or CD-ROMs. Digital cartography is a real bargain. Many boaters purchase and use both chips and CD-ROMs. For example, many mariners use the raster data on a computer and upload the waypoints into a chartplotter using vector chips. Also, it is quite common for boaters to use both a chartplotter with vector cartography and a computer with raster cartography at the same time on the boat. They offer many complementary features that help the skipper ensure a safe passage.

8

Connecting Your GPS Receiver to a Computer

Most GPS units have a data port, so they can be connected to the serial port of a personal computer or other devices. This is relatively easy to do and provides considerable benefits. Almost every boater will want to use a computer for planning, to help manage waypoints and routes, and to upload or download them into the GPS receiver. Track data can also be downloaded from the GPS receiver and uploaded from the computer. Manually entering waypoints is tedious and prone to error. A variety of computer software is available, ranging in price from free to several hundred dollars, that will support communication between a GPS unit and a computer.

Planning off-line is highly recommended, especially if you own a small- to moderate-sized boat. Entering waypoints at sea can be hazardous, since it takes your attention away from the helm. It also leads to errors, as was demonstrated in chapter 4. To lay out safe routes, you need paper charts and plotted legs for the routes. You then need to measure the coordinates of the waypoints and manually enter them into the GPS receiver. All of this is difficult at sea, and smaller boats do not offer the space to do it properly by hand.

However, the computer is the perfect tool to do this almost automatically. The software available for this is superb. You can display a chart for your cruising area and construct routes and waypoints directly on the chart. You can look for obstacles on-screen, much as you would on a paper chart. Once you have laid out your route and waypoints, the software automates the task of transferring these to your GPS unit. This avoids transcription errors and speeds the process. You can also print out your routes and the charts on paper to keep as backups.

What Is Required?

All you need is a cable and appropriate software to connect a GPS receiver to a computer. Generally, cables are produced by the manufacturers of GPS receivers, and are available through dealers, on the Web, or from the manufacturer directly. These cables range in price from $20 to $50. At the computer end is a standard PC DB-9 (9-pin) serial port connector. Most GPS manufacturers and software suppliers offer cables and computer programs designed for the PC. Some suppliers that offer GPS-to-Macintosh cables, PC-to-Macintosh connector converters, and software written for the Macintosh. There also are some companies that supply serial port (DB-9) to USB adapters. The connector at the GPS end is based on the particular GPS unit. Figure 8-1 shows the wiring configuration for the connection. The particular pins designated for "data in," "data out," and "ground" on the GPS receiver can be found in the user's manual. Figure 8-2 shows a PC cable for a Garmin handheld GPS receiver. The pin designations are the same for any GPS. Not all GPS manufacturers offer cables for connection to a computer, and in many cases the cables that are available have bare wires that can be used for data output and input at the computer end. The interface standard between GPS units and other devices is defined by NMEA 0183, described in chapter 9. This standard also is compatible with the computer RS-232 standard common to computers using a standard serial port. For the PC, these leads must be connected via a DB-9 connector. For a Mac, these

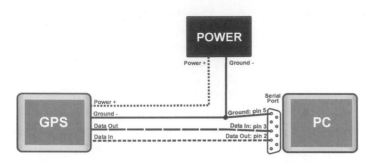

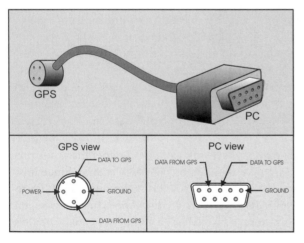

FIGURE 8-1. Connecting a GPS Unit to a Computer. A GPS unit can be connected to a computer with a simple cable. The diagram shows that three wires (within the cable) provide two-way communication between a GPS unit and a PC. The connection at the computer end is a common serial port 9-pin (DB-9) connector. The connector at the GPS end is unique to the model used. Usually, the manufacturers offer cables that interface with their units.

FIGURE 8-2. A GPS Receiver-to-Computer Cable. This cable connects a Garmin handheld GPS receiver to a PC. The connector at the GPS receiver end is unique to the brand. The computer connector is a standard serial port cable. Only three wires are connected: data in, data out, and ground.

leads will be connected via the 8-pin DIN connector used on Macintoshes. Since the vast majority of software and manufactured cables are offered for the PC, this section references the PC as an example.

There are only three wires that connect the GPS and the computer. They are identified as "ground," "data in," and "data out" at each end. Much like wiring your VCR to a TV, you need to make sure that the "data in" at the GPS end is connected to the "data out" at the computer and vice versa. The ma-

rine industry recognized early the need to connect GPS receivers and other electronics to a computer. As a result, they specified the interface for NMEA 0183, the standard, to be compatible with the standard computer serial port.

Most of the software will run on a moderate speed computer. Chapter 9 describes a number of these programs and their features. Some manufacturers, such as Garmin, have a unique protocol in addition to the NMEA interface. Using their special protocol, more flexibility is afforded for various transfers of data. For example, Garmin uses its special protocol to update the software in the GPS receiver directly from the computer, and the updates can be downloaded to the computer from their website. (See the resources section.)

Computer-based navigation programs generally support upload and download of waypoints and routes to most GPS receivers, in addition to active navigation. Mac software is available, but if you have a Windows-based machine, you will find far more software choices. Custom programs allow you to access features of a particular GPS model, even including screenshots for particular models. Though most GPS software for computers is distributed on CD-ROMs, the manufacturers of chart chips also offer software that uses their cartography to plan on a PC. C-Map offers a program called PC Planner that uses their chips in a custom reader. You plan on the same charts that your chartplotter uses to navigate. Garmin offers a separate PC program called MapSource BlueChart. The cartography is on CD along with the MapSource management program. Third-party shareware and freeware are available for some of the more popular GPS receivers, mainly handheld units. Generally, the more popular the brand, the more third-party software is available. Garmin leads this list, followed by Magellan, Eagle, Lowrance, and others. These programs are quite limited in what they do, but if uploading and downloading waypoints and routes is your mission, they may be the answer.

Computer Interface

Whenever you connect your GPS receiver to a computer, you will need to make sure that the interface mode set in the receiver corresponds with the software package that you are using. To check or change the interface mode in your GPS unit, you will need to access the Interface Setup Menu from the System Setup Menu. Check your software package to identify the data-transfer protocol required. In the Interface Setup Menu, scroll down to the primary field and press "Enter." A menu of choices will be displayed. Usually, two interfaces are identified, one for data in and one for data out. Most computer software for the GPS is capable of uploading data from the GPS receiver as well as downloading data to the GPS receiver. As a result, there are two connections for the GPS unit. Since the GPS can accept different protocols on the input line and output line, both must be set the same way for use with the software. If your software uses NMEA, select "NMEA/NMEA." If you have a Garmin GPS unit and software that uses the proprietary Garmin data-transfer protocol, select "GRMN/GRMN." Other choices reflect the GPS interfacing with other equipment and are presented in the next chapter.

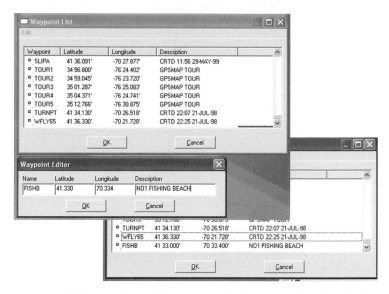

FIGURE 8-3. *Adding or Editing Waypoints on the Computer. A number of software programs permit the user to enter and edit waypoints, and upload them into one or more GPS units. This example uses the PC-based Waypoint+ freeware program.*

Software

A wide range of software that interfaces with a GPS unit is available. The simplest of this software permits uploading and downloading of data between the unit and the computer for editing or backup.

GPS Data-Transfer Software

Data-transfer software is widely available. It is somewhat limited in utility, since these programs may not include chart data. You use these programs strictly for entering, managing, and reviewing waypoints, routes, and tracks. Some of these programs will plot waypoints and routes, but without the chart data. However, many of these programs are offered as freeware or shareware and enable quick and easy manipulation of GPS data.

The obvious advantage to using data-transfer software with your GPS receiver is the ability to create or edit waypoints using a keyboard rather than the cumbersome buttons on a GPS unit (fig. 8-3). Since it is so easy to accomplish, every serious user of a GPS receiver should consider this method. In the figure, the waypoints installed in the receiver were downloaded into a PC freeware program called Waypoint+. This program is designed to work with Garmin receivers using the GRMN interface protocol. Using the Edit Menu, "New" waypoint was selected bringing up the Waypoint Editor screen. Data were entered into the Waypoint Editor screen using the computer keyboard. Once you press "OK," the new waypoint appears on the waypoint list. The resultant edited list can be uploaded back to the GPS unit.

There are many similar programs available (see chapter 9). Those that work with NMEA interface can be used with most other GPS brands. Many GPS manufacturers offer software for the PC to interface with their GPS. Also, most of the more sophisticated navigation software products can be used to upload and download GPS data.

Other waypoint tasks can be accomplished, such as downloading waypoints to the computer that were entered into the GPS receiver using the "Mark" feature. The receiver automatically assigned numbers to these waypoints as they were marked. You can download these waypoints and assign them new names or numbers off-line and then upload the newly named waypoints back into the GPS unit. In addition, prudent navigators who rely on GPS usually have more than one GPS receiver, usually a handheld and a fixed-mount unit. The data-transfer software provides an easy way to ensure that both GPS receivers share the same waypoints and other data. The same software usually permits downloading, editing, saving, and uploading routes and tracks, in addition to waypoints. The Waypoint+ program (as shown in fig. 8-4) has no chart data; however, the data can be plotted in a blank chart format with latitude and longitude references. These plots can be zoomed, printed, and used as a backup paper reference. The plots also enable the user to verify the coordinates of the waypoints. Alternatively, the same data can be presented and edited in a tabular format. These programs also permit sav-

ing the data in a variety of formats, with some readable by charting or map programs.

The primary purpose of the GPS interface software is the management, recording, uploading, and downloading of GPS data for off-line applications. Cruise planning and laying out routes in your regular boating area are excellent tasks performed off the boat or in the off-season. You can use charts, navigation programs, or GPS data from your prior boating to plan future navigation in that area. Software packages that permit you to plan your routes directly on a chart displayed on your computer and then to upload them into the GPS unit are described in the next section.

If you use a Garmin GPS, you can download Waypoint+ (see the Garmin contact information in the resources section). Waypoint+ permits uploading and downloading GPS routes, tracks, and waypoints between the GPS and the computer. Once loaded into Waypoint+, waypoints, routes, or tracks can be edited, or new ones added or old ones deleted. This program is quite intuitive and easy to use. It can save the GPS data for future reference in a number of different formats. It can export and import data to and from Delorme's Street Atlas mapping software (a popular street map program), and in a format for Map-Expert software. It can also save data in standard text format for printing or working in word processor or database programs.

Another excellent program is G7towin. This PC-based program supports upload and download of information with Garmin and Lowrance receivers. The program also permits copying screen displays of a number of GPS receivers to the computer. Like Waypoint+, G7towin will output for use with Delorme's

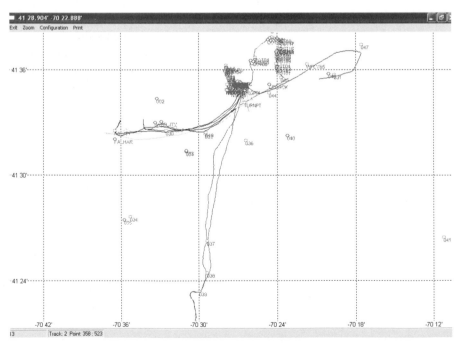

FIGURE 8-4. *Plot of Downloaded Waypoints and Tracks. Waypoint+ plots waypoints and tracks that have been downloaded from a Garmin GPS receiver.*

Street Atlas program. Although the Street Atlas program should not be used for marine navigation, it is a useful tool for displaying tracks, routes, and waypoints.

A number of data-transfer programs written for the Garmin GPS can be accessed through Peter Bennett's web page listed in the resources section. Most of these programs are shareware, and the author expects some nominal compensation for their use. One of the advantages to using a Garmin GPS is the large installed base of equipment and third-party enthusiasts who generate software, cables, reviews, and advice for their use. Peter Bennett's site includes links to software for Magellan, Furuno, Micrologic, Eagle, and Lowrance receivers. For example, GPS Utility is a PC-based freeware-shareware program that supports both Garmin and Magellan receivers.

The major shortcoming of these data-transfer programs is that they do not allow you to plan on an actual chart. This means you need to determine waypoint coordinates the old-fashioned way with dividers on paper charts, and plot routes with the appropriate chart tools. However, a number of programs, described in the next section, are available at moderate cost that enable you to do your planning directly on charts on your computer. In addition, should you be considering a navigation software package as described in chapter 9, these programs perform the same tasks but at a higher price.

Mapping and Charting Software

Marine charting programs are ideal for planning, uploading, downloading, printing, and recording data using a computer. These programs enable you to work directly on charts on the computer screen. This approach is intuitively easy as you plan, modify, edit, and save routes and waypoints. There are no rubber erasers involved, no plotting, and less chance for error. It avoids the potential for transcription errors in manually transferring waypoints from paper charts to the computer. The programs also provide bearings, distances, depths, hazards, ports, marinas, and a host of other information that makes your planning easier. They also enable you to make quick measurements from point to point. Several notable PC programs designed specifically for planning, uploading, and

downloading are C-Map's PC Planner, Maptech's ChartNavigator, Garmin's MapSource BlueChart, and Weems and Plath's Chartview Planner. These are programs usually costing between $100 and $150, as opposed to a somewhat higher price for navigation software. All except PC Planner use charts on CD-ROMs, usually at an extra cost. PC Planner uses the vector NT+ chips that you use in chartplotters. This saves the extra cost of a second set of cartography for those with chartplotters, and provides the same look and feel on the computer as on the chartplotter. The program comes with a two-slot chip reader that attaches to the computer. Usually a chart chip is installed in one of the slots. The second slot holds a memory chip that can be used to store information for transfer to and from the chartplotter. Nobeltec ships their GPS Visual Planner software with their Passport brand of vector chart CD-ROMs. Garmin offers a MapSource BlueChart CD-ROM. The charts are unlocked, usually for an additional fee, via contact with Garmin. The MapSource PC program enables uploading and downloading to Garmin GPS units with optional cables sold at a nominal cost. Chartview Planner uses raster charts on CD-ROM from Maptech, SoftChart, and others.

As with the data-transfer programs already described, these charting programs enable you to download data from the GPS unit, edit them, and return the edited data to the GPS. Even though these programs are only for off-line use, they overlay GPS data on a real chart, making waypoint and route management a great deal easier and safer. You can also print your planned routes overlaid on charts. Other programs offer both Charting and Navigation modes at significantly higher cost. These programs, designed for on-line navigation, are described in chapter 9.

If you simply want to display or print tracks for a record of your cruising or to make a visual log, there is an alternative. Since GPS has built a strong following among hikers and others who travel on land, there is GPS mapping software with a focus on land and roads. A leading supplier of such software is Delorme, whose top-selling Street Atlas software offers information on roads in great detail. This software can be useful for displaying tracks for near-coastal boating; however, this is not a marine charting program.

Navigating with GPS Receivers, Computers, and Other Equipment on Your Boat

The previous chapter explained how to use a computer with your GPS receiver for off-line planning. Chapter 7 described active navigation using chartplotters that overlay GPS data on an electronic chart. This chapter shows you how to use a computer with your receiver to perform the same functions and more on your boat. The key ingredient is navigation software that offers powerful features far beyond that available on a typical chartplotter. Moreover, the GPS unit and the computer can be connected with a host of other equipment to aid

with navigation and the operation of your boat. One of the principal advantages to the computer-based navigation approach is *incremental upgrade*. While chartplotters may become obsolete requiring a complete replacement to access new features, the computer-based system's hardware or software can be upgraded in parts as these new features emerge. Integrated chartplotters tend to undergo "block" upgrades in features, resulting in virtual obsolescence of the older unit in its entirety. Manufacturers often quickly lose interest in support and accessories for out-of-production units.

For most of us, the GPS receiver is the primary position sensor on our boats. It can be connected directly to other electronic equipment, such as DGPS receivers, chartplotters, radar, electronic compasses, depth sounders, autopilots, and more. Each of these devices has its strengths—using them together you can combine their contributions to obtain a clearer picture of the boat's environment. The process of connecting the GPS receiver to other equipment is a bit more complex than a simple connection to a computer. You can do it yourself, but you may prefer professional installation. In any event, knowing about the interconnection and performance issues will help you make informed decisions, appreciate the collective electronic navigation performance, and diagnose problems and effect repairs at sea.

If you install a computer-based system on your boat, you will find a host of excellent software available to assist with navigation. Closely related to software is associated cartography. With the computer approach, you can construct your own system tailored to your needs and desires. However, with such an array of choices, the process can appear intimidating. This chapter describes representative equipment, software, and cartography, along with their cost and the features that you should consider. The quality of the offerings is outstanding and getting better with each generation. Fortunately for the seagoing computer user, the new and improved software usually works on computers of nominal performance, giving your system a reasonable lifetime. To extend your computer's useful life even longer, you can upgrade parts without replacing the whole.

Using GPS with a Computer while Afloat

In chapter 8, we discussed the effectiveness of a computer connected to your GPS for planning and data management. This section takes the computer to sea with the GPS, which raises a number of considerations. First of all, where on the boat will you use the computer? Generally, a computer is more suitable below deck away from the sunlight, spray, and other rigors of the marine environment. If you plan to use the computer below deck, you can select from a wide range of computers and remotely connect it to the GPS receiver at the helm. On board, the computer with the right software becomes a valuable planning tool as well as a powerful navigation tool. Either a notebook or desktop computer can be used; however, many boaters moving into computer-based navigation will use a notebook computer. If you choose to use a desktop unit, you should purchase a unit designed for the marine environment. Notebook computers, on the other hand, can be easily carried off the boat and generally are designed for more rugged use.

Most helmsmen prefer to have access to data on the bridge. If the bridge is exposed to the elements, the computer will need to be protected. A number of notebook computers are designed specifically for rugged use, some even for use in wet environments, such as those available from Panasonic and Argonaut. Typical prices for laptops designed for marine use range from $2,500 to $6,000 depending upon display size, processor speed, and features. Unless you intend to use the computer unprotected on an exposed bridge, most standard notebook computers are reasonably suitable for the task. These units are susceptible to water, but they can be enclosed in a protective mount. The larger issue is the display. Commercial notebook computer screens generally are not sunlight readable, so steps must be taken to build a shroud around the display for viewing if located at the helm.

On most boats, a standard notebook will be just fine. However, shock can be a concern with planing-hull speedboats, which often take a pounding on the water. In these situations, a shock-mount or suitable foam padding will help protect the computer. The most vulnerable component usually is the hard disk drive, but today's designs have low mass and are quite resistant to shock. If your boat is exposed to high shock levels, consider a more rugged unit. Humidity is the larger concern for computers on a boat. At sea, you will encounter high humidity levels laden with salt. As long as the computer is powered-on you will have little problem. The heat keeps the moisture from condensing, but at night if the unit is powered down, a film of salt can be deposited inside your computer. Ultimately, the resultant corrosive effect may damage the unit. Notebook computers can be powered all the time while you are on the boat, and taken off with you when you leave. Built-in units require further consideration. A marine computer is recommended for such an installation.

A standard commercial desktop computer is not recommended for onboard use unless it has been marinized. A number of marinized computers are available at a reasonable price from companies such as Argonaut, Nauticomp, and Navigator PC Marine. Prices range from about $1,500 to $3,000 for capable units, more than for a similarly equipped standard desktop computer. The monitor drives the higher cost. Seagoing, waterproof, sunlight-readable displays currently start at $3,000, but these prices will come down as the technology matures.

For most recreational boaters, the computer will be used below deck connected to a GPS receiver or an integrated chartplotter located at the helm. The navigation software permits better planning and viewing of courses given the larger display on the computer and the many features of the navigation software. Most of this software will run satisfactorily on notebook computers of nominal performance running Windows 95 or higher. A smaller number of programs will run on Macs.

Another consideration in using a computer aboard is power. Many notebook computers can be powered directly from the available 12-volt connection on board. The fixed computer requires 110-volt AC, which can be provided by a power inverter. A modified sine-wave inverter will work with most notebook and desktop computers, but may not be suitable for older cathode ray tube (CRT) monitors. However, liquid-crystal displays are favored over CRTs for both notebooks and computers on board since they are smaller, draw less power, have lower weight, and are more tolerant to shock and vibration. Even with notebook computers, it may be desirable to use an inverter and the 110-volt power adapter that came with the computer. The power system on board your boat may generate electrical "noise" that could cause the computer not to work properly. Whether you chose a notebook or a desktop, a battery-backup un-interrupted power supply (UPS) should ensure steady, clean power, and provide an emergency backup to run your navigation program during a power outage. The preceding chapter described the wiring connection between a GPS receiver and a computer.

In the future, you can expect to see more custom computer systems designed specifically for boats. SeaRay has introduced an integrated onboard system powered by a computer system integrated by Maptech. This unit places a computer in a rugged housing with a color touch-screen display. Developed by Maptech, the software is designed for shipboard use with the touch screen. The on-screen buttons are large enough to use while underway in chop. The cartography is integrated into the system. The computer has external ports to interface with all of the other instrumentation on board. This is an example of the type of tailored, integrated design of hardware and software that you can expect to see from many boatbuilders in the future, and these systems will eventually become available to the general boating community for upgrade or retrofit.

As the computer industry migrates to new products such as handheld and portable computers for more applications, it will incorporate features that make them even more suitable for boats. Features such as ruggedization, sunlight-readable displays, waterproofing, and touch screens will be available at a moderate cost. As this occurs, look for a greater shift from custom chartplotters to computer-based systems for navigation. Due to the inherent flexibility of these devices for other applications as well as boating, owners of smaller boats increasingly will be attracted to this solution.

Although the computer-based navigation solution is not for everyone, those with boats of roughly 30 feet (9 m) or larger should consider the option, particularly those with an enclosed bridge. A computer system also provides a good complement to other onboard systems, including chartplotters. Also, look for more configurations that provide radar imagery on the computer beyond those offered by Raymarine and Nobeltec.

Navigation Software and Digital Charts

At the heart of the navigation system is the software and its associated cartography. The onboard computer becomes your central navigation processor. The software is your navigation control and interface, and the digital charts are your reference data. A host of features are available in computer-based navigation systems, and you can run multiple programs at the same time in the computer for complementary functions.

As noted in chapter 8, a number of very capable navigation programs are available for PCs and some for Macs. Perhaps the greatest challenge for a boater electing the computer-based navigation approach is the task of selecting all of the component parts, and then the software. This is the primary reason for the popularity of integrated chartplotters. It can be a challenge to compare and select the appropriate navigation software; however, most packages offer excellent features. These programs range in price from $100 for a relatively simple charting program to $5,000 or more for a professional package. They have an active Navigation mode using position data from the GPS unit, as well as the off-line Charting function described in the previous chapter. You can use the computer and navigation software for active navigation as your primary navigational computer rather than the GPS unit itself. Or, you can load the same routes and waypoints into both the computer and your GPS chartplotter, and use both simultaneously. While they usually share GPS position data, most of the displayed information will be computed independently. The chartplotter and the navigation computer each use their own cartography. Although this can be a relatively small additional cost, you gain an advantage because you can select each for particular features. Since the two processes are independent, there may be minor differences and some overlap in the data presented, but the redundancy can be valuable in a tight situation.

The charts on your computer system can be stored on your computer's hard disk, loaded directly from a chip reader such as the C-Map NT+ reader described in the previous chapter, or called up from a CD-ROM. If you have more than one set of cartography, make sure that the charts that you use for your primary navigation are the most current. If you use a chip reader, you will need to select which unit gets to use the chip, or have duplicates if you want to use both.

Computer software can provide a far greater range of cruise-related information such as tides, currents, weather, proximity to services, ship performance, optimum route generation, bottom profiles, 3-D presentations, photo cartography, thermal patterns, and much more. The key is determining which of these features are important to you, since they add to the price depending upon the selected package.

To illustrate the extensive features available, racing sailors can enter a "polar diagram," which represents the boat's wind and current performance, into some programs. They then download forecasts for wind and current, and the program optimizes their intended route for speed. Professional fishing-boat captains can plot their depth sounder data in a separate layer to search for and highlight favorable fishing areas, and then save the information for a future return. Programs can display a 3-D representation of the sea bottom with the ship indicated on the screen, or present a forward-looking depth profile based on current course and speed. Professional packages with these features are offered by MaxSea. RayTech also offers optional sail packages.

Computer software can perform some valuable manipulation of cartography. For example, Maptech offers photo cartography derived from satel-lite imagery and bathymetric data for bottom profiles. These images can be laid side by side to illustrate your position on a chart and a photo at the same time. The software can also provide a 3-D image of your boat over the bottom side by side with the chart. All the while, these split screens are tracking your current position. Nobeltec has taken this a step further with its professional navigation software, which allows you to overlay the photo imagery in a transparent mode over the chart. Figures 9-1a and 9-1b show examples of these displays. Today, these are some of the ultimate in navigation displays, but at a price. Many of these features will migrate into affordable packages for recreational boaters as demand increases.

Generally, computer-based navigation packages are better suited than chartplotters for planning and managing your cruise. You can review the day's cruise and plan the next day in the comfort of the cabin. Waypoints and routes can be uploaded to the integrated chartplotter for use at the helm. By the same token, the entire cruise can be preplanned on the computer at home and uploaded to the system on

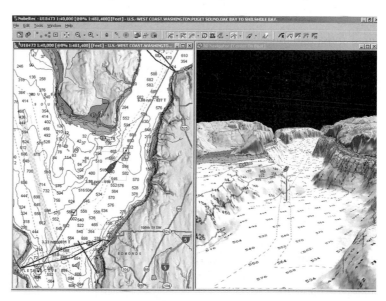

FIGURE 9-1A. *Displays of the Future Are Here Today. This display format shows an enhanced chart view on the left and a corresponding 3-D bathymetric view on the right. These Nobeltec Visual Navigation Suite screens enable safe passage through channels and aid in locating favorable conditions for fishing. The shaded relief for land and sea features enhances your ability to relate to the environment around you.* (NOBELTEC)

U11475 1:10,000 T@22% 1:45.435 (T@2 L UNITED STATES - EAST COAST FLORIDA, FORT PIERCE HARBOR

Vessel ▶
Goto Boat
Drop Mark
Objects ▶
Zoom ▶
Right Click
Next...
MOB

Vessel Position	Speed/Heading		✓ Menu
LAT: 27 28.314 N	SOG: 0 kts		✓ Info
LON: 80 17.353 W	COG: 83° T	HDG: 83° T	Tool

FIGURE 9-1B. Overlaying Displays. This example shows a photo chart set to "transparency" on top of vector chart data. This enables the navigator to correlate between real-world features and the chart, and adds realism to the vector charts. This feature currently is available only on high-end navigation software, such as this Admiral program, but look for this type of capability on packages for recreational boaters in the future. (NOBELTEC)

board. For these reasons, they are very popular with offshore navigators. They also do an excellent job of live navigation with many features that may not be available on the chartplotter. Many offshore sailors keep their radar and chartplotter displays below deck to protect them. Usually, under adverse conditions, one person mans the electronics while the helmsman deals with the outside environment. On larger boats with enclosed helm stations, the equipment generally is located near the helm station. Given their considerable capabilities, there are some very good reasons for favoring the computer-based solution over the chartplotter for active navigation. Those who have an integrated chartplotter and computer-based navigation software generally run both at the same time. Either unit, but not both, can drive an autopilot using NMEA 0183 commands. NMEA is further explained later in this chapter.

As a recreational boater, you may not need all of these features and may not want to pay the price for them unless you do extended cruising or fishing. An array of features tailored to your needs are offered in software packages generally in the $150 to $450 range.

Most of the recreational navigation programs perform similar functions. The high-end packages include more planning features and other features of utility to the boater such as information about weather, tides, and currents. Many of these same companies offer trimmed-down versions of the same software for about half the price. Recently, there has been a trend toward more features at a lower price bundled with some choice of regional charts.

Chart Considerations

Historically, navigation software has been sold without charts. Even if some come bundled, you will want to consider which chart types you want to use on your boat. This choice in cartography is not a feature available on chartplotters. It is important to check the software that you plan to use to see which chart types it accepts. Almost all of the navigation software packages accept raster charts. The leading suppliers of these charts are Maptech, which is licensed to produce NOAA charts, and SoftChart, which scans these same charts and adds their own enhancements. Internationally, the UK Hydrographic Office offers the Admiralty Raster Charting Service (ARCS). MapMedia raster charts are provided by the French company, Informatique et Mer, that also produces MaxSea navigation software. Euronav digitizes data from various hydrographic offices with excellent coverage in Europe, the Mediterranean, and the Caribbean.

Raster charts are offered with various forms of information. For example, in addition to its NOAA navigation charts, Maptech produces photo charts based on satellite imagery and Contour Professional 3-D software and charts showing profiles of the sea bottom. These charts are very helpful when tiled side by side with a navigation chart to help identify harbor and channel features. Several companies offer bathymetric charts showing depth contours of the region. These charts are offered in 2-D and 3-D formats for limited areas, but the coverage is expanding. Figures

9-1a and 9-1b show examples of these capabilities. Vector bathymetric data are also available.

A number of navigation software programs accept vector charts as well as raster. Some companies such as C-Map offer the same chart data in both chips (vector) and CD-ROM (vector) format. Nobeltec Visual Navigation Suite uses their own Passport CD vector cartography format, but also uses the raster charts.

Each cartography source has certain advantages over the others, usually dependent upon the region to be sailed. For most of us in the U.S., the NOAA charts form the reference for digital charts, but boaters in the Caribbean may favor British Admiralty Charts. The best package for you may be one that accepts the widest variety of digital charts. Computer-based navigation systems, unlike chartplotters, permit you to use a range of cartography from various sources. At its current cost, digital cartography is a bargain, and the trend is to offer more at even lower prices. It is not at all uncommon for boats to carry multiple navigation software packages and a range of overlapping cartography.

Advantages of Navigation Software that Includes Charts

→ Charts automatically are called up as you navigate into their coverage, and greatest detail charts are selected.

→ High-end programs "quilt" charts together to appear seamless.

→ Currents are shown on the chart for the selected time.

→ Tide stations are shown and can be accessed to provide tide information.

Most of the navigation software packages have the capability to select automatically the chart for the current region from those available in the computer, as well as the best scale and presentation detail for the chart. The better programs quilt the charts together so the presentation is seamless as you move across the page. On some programs, you appear to fall off the chart until another chart appears, often at a different scale. The quilted chart is ideal both for planning and navigating. The more expensive packages also show

currents and tide stations on the chart. You can access these features with a mouse click. Some of the programs will work with touch screens, a growing trend since operating any type of mouse at sea on a moving boat is a challenge. Those that are designed for touch screens offer a large-button feature to make locating these buttons easier.

Most programs offer the ability to tile different chart presentations side by side on the same page with your current position and course shown on both. You can observe a traditional chart on one page and an aerial photo chart of the same area on the other. In other cases, you may be able to present a raster chart on one page and the equivalent vector data on the other. Again, raster charts usually offer more land features and landmarks for visual bearings, while vector charts offer clearer navigation features, labels, and accessible supplementary information. Additionally, you can show a chart on one page and a 3-D depth profile for the same area on the other. One of the best applications is to show two different scales side by side so you can monitor your cruise progress on one and local conditions on the other.

Although slower to become popular on computers, vector-based computer cartography is emerging. Raster-based computer programs became popular and remain so because the electronic charts look exactly like the paper charts, and the CD-ROM format was a natural approach. They also can present features such as satellite photos that are inherently a raster format. However, the vector charts have the potential to offer features not available with a raster chart, such as scaling of features with level of zoom and the ability to utilize the data contained within the chart for other purposes. These differences can become quite pronounced near shore. It is here that the helmsman wants fine resolution. As more detailed data are added to the cartography for local harbors, marinas, and coastal areas, the vector charts offer the potential to offer a more refined picture and information. The potential is there, but, until the additional data are included, both chart formats coming from the same NOAA source data offer virtually the same marine detail. The raster charts generally offer more shoreline and land features, but vector charts are moving in this direction as well. The digital data can be extracted from the vector chart to set alarms. C-Map has a feature that scans the chart data in search of shallow water. If it finds a depth from the chart data that is below a preset threshold, an alarm is sounded. Although relying upon charted data is not foolproof, it can be more effective than a depth sounder, which cannot see very far ahead. C-Map also has a system to collect marina data and incorporate them into its cartography so you can see individual slips. For serious offshore sailors, a single CD-ROM can hold detailed vector charts for the entire world. Individual regions can be unlocked for a fee with a simple phone call.

Navigation Software

Chapter 8 described the most popular navigation programs for recreational boaters, such as Maptech's Offshore Navigator, Nautical Technologies' The Capn Voyager, NetSea's MaxSea Navigator, Nobeltec's Visual Navigation Suite, Raymarine's RayTech Navigator, and Weems and Plath's Chartview Professional. In addition to real-time tracking with the GPS position data, most of these programs offer

- an unlimited number of waypoints and routes

- seamless cartography

- choice of view (north up or course up)

- special night-view colors so as not to degrade night vision

- choice of true or magnetic north

- dead-reckoning modes

- the ability to upload data to the GPS receiver for off-line planning

- the ability to download to the autopilot

- tide and current data

- optional formats for presentation of charts and data

- customized toolbars

Additionally, RayTech Navigator illustrates a growing trend for equipment manufacturers to offer software compatible with their proprietary interconnects in addition to NMEA 0183. This program supports direct connection to the Raymarine SeaTalk bus that interconnects all of the instruments made by Raymarine. All the instrument data can be displayed on one computer screen. This program also accepts C-Map chips with a USB connection.

As noted earlier, many navigation software packages offer the ability to display depth data from onboard depth sounders, and to compare this with charted depth contours. Some software will present a 3-D view of the bottom, as well as land features. Magnetic heading can be read directly into the computer from a fluxgate compass or gyrocompass. Some of the navigation software packages offer a dead-reckoning mode that continues plotting using the last available data in the event that the GPS signal is interrupted. Other functions include integration of weather reports with the charts and route planning. There are some packages that automatically recommend alternate routing to avoid weather. The weather data generally are downloaded from satellites. Services are becoming widely available to access the Internet directly at sea. The more expensive navigation software programs also factor currents or winds into steering and estimated time of arrival.

One of the principal features of navigation software is the ease with which you can enter waypoints and routes by simple mouse clicks. Waypoints can be changed easily, and routes can be modified by simply adding or replotting intermediate waypoints. The distance for each leg and the route as a whole are readily presented. While navigating, you have sufficient screen space to present all your data fields rather than a select few. Planning and checking can be accomplished with mouse clicks to measure the distance and bearing between two points on the chart. Bearings to fixed objects can be charted quickly and compared with direct observations to cross-check position. Alarms can be set for a wide range of conditions and used to control other devices or to sound remote alarms. Most of the software programs will drive autopilots so you can automate your cruise. Many of the programs are compatible with touch screens, facilitating the entry of data while at sea under rough conditions.

Figure 9-2 shows sample plots in the Capn Voyager software from Nautical Technologies. The

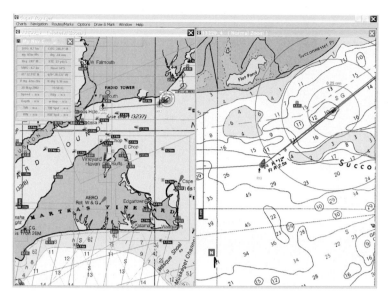

FIGURE 9-2. *Computer-Based Navigation Chart Display. The Capn Voyager program uses commercial raster charts to present a chartplotter display using real-time GPS data. The route is displayed with information for each leg. The program can display two side-by-side screens, such as the larger-scale chart on the left and a detailed presentation on the right in this figure. This dual approach overcomes most of the label-readability issues with raster displays.*

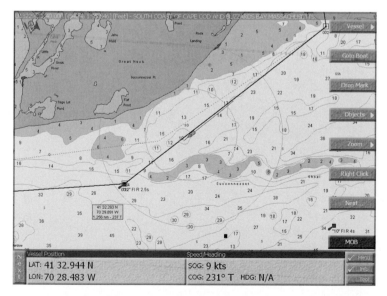

FIGURE 9-3. *The Same Route Using Vector Cartography. This Nobeltec Admiral program highlights the difference between raster and vector cartography. This easy-to-read display highlights key navigation features extremely well. Some users consider the display to be sparse in details, but there is no missing what you need to know. The display shows large buttons suitable for touch-screen operation of the program.*

screen presents two chart scales side by side. The detailed chart (right portion) shows range circles that facilitate gauging distance and comparing the presentation with the radar. The program identifies the particular raster chart source and displays a variety of data fields.

Figure 9-3 shows a similar sample plot for the same location using vector charts in Nobeltec Admiral. This presentation does not present as much in the way of land features, but the critical data needed for navigation are clearer and easy to read. Maptech offers an unusual display presentation, as shown in figure 9-4: they've wrapped the chart around a sphere. The display is very similar in character to the Highway screen on a handheld GPS receiver. The entire route is visible toward the horizon. The boxed areas indicate regions covered by higher-resolution charts. You can navigate with this presentation or place it side by side with a normal-view chart. Figure 9-5 shows navigation with a raster chart a short time later on the same cruise. This is the same region shown on the chartplotter screen in figure 7-8a. Figure 9-6 demonstrates on the MaxSea Yachting program the very refined data that are becoming available in S-57 vector cartography from NOAA. Fine details are available in a clear presentation. Floating toolbars facilitate using the features of the program while navigating. The chart even accurately locates the bridge supports using U.S. Army Corps of Engineers data. These charts will be prepared for all major shipping lanes, but you will likely need broader coverage for your charts. MaxSea will add value by incorporating their own separately compiled details for the areas in which we sail along with the S-57 data.

Recognizing that not all boaters are ready to pay $400 for software plus an additional $50 to $200 for charts, several of these same companies also offer less expensive packages costing around $200. Typically, these packages delete the tide and current capability and some of the alarm features. Maptech has a navigation program in this category called Offshore Navigator, which includes tides and currents. Global Navigation Software has a program called NavPak-Pro, which supports both raster and vector charts. Ultimately, most of these navigation programs will offer vector format as well as raster.

A program called Fugawi from Northport Systems enables the user to either use commercial BSB raster charts (Maptech) or scan his own charts. This program sells for under $100 and provides waypoint and route planning in addition to up/downloading to the GPS unit. Fugawi supports Garmin, Lowrance/Eagle, and Magellan GPS receivers. You should be cautious to ensure that charts you scan yourself are properly calibrated in the program. OziExplorer is a similar program that is offered as shareware. GPS Positioner Smart is a freeware program that uses charts scanned by the user. Anyone with a computer scanner can scan charts. After the chart is scanned and imported into the program, you need to identify a number of points and enter their coordinates, in addition to map projection and datum. GPS Positioner then automatically calibrates the chart. One disadvantage is that the scanned chart segments are relatively small. Most of these programs will switch to the needed chart segment automatically, but you lose continuity of your plot. You also run some risk of miscalibration. These programs provide an

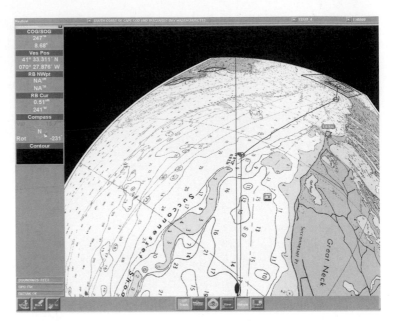

FIGURE 9-4. *Perspective Display Magnifies Close-In Navigation. This extraordinary display from Maptech Offshore Navigator lets you see nearby features and your entire route on the same page. This is much like using the Highway screen on a chartplotter, but with real chart data. The rectangles toward the horizon indicate areas covered by more-detailed small-scale charts. The somewhat squared-off shape at the edges represents the edges of the current chart.*

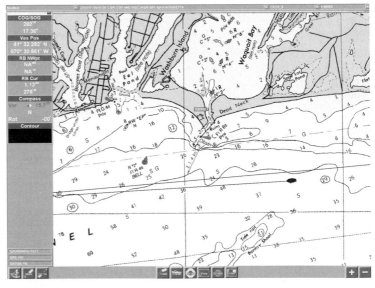

FIGURE 9-5. *Continuing along the Same Route. This screen shows a view comparable to that in Figure 7-8a for a basic chartplotter. This demonstration using Maptech Offshore Navigator with a raster chart shows the effectiveness of the larger screen and clearer chart features available on a computer-based navigation system.*

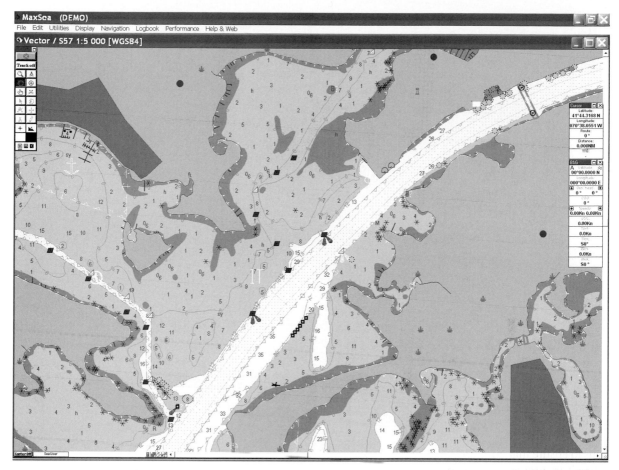

FIGURE 9-6. *More Accurate Details Available with Some Navigation Programs. This MaxSea Yachting program is using NOAA ENC (S-57) cartography to show the fine details being offered for these new charts of the Cape Cod Canal. U.S. Army Corps of Engineers data have been incorporated into the chart to exacting standards. MaxSea is quite easy to learn and use. The floating toolbars are intuitive.*

interesting transition to computer-based navigation, but you may be better off paying more for a more complete program.

Navigation Software Selection

There is a wide range of navigation software. You can narrow down the options by defining what you need and your purpose for the software. The high-end packages are suitable for offshore as well as inland and coastal waters. Obviously, the program you choose should be easy for you to use. Most of these companies have excellent websites and/or trial software. Test out the look and feel. As far as extra features, tide and current data are very useful for coastal

and near-coastal boaters. This generally is available with the more expensive packages. Some companies sell a separate current and tide package, but you may find that you will spend more for the individual parts than for the integrated package.

The accompanying table provides a summary of the key features of popular navigation software packages. This represents a snapshot, and as with most software, features in all of these programs are added and improved continuously. Therein lies one of the advantages to computer-based systems, since you can upgrade parts at will without replacing the entire system.

MaxSea Navigator is one of the easiest programs

Navigation Software Comparison

Features	Nobeltec Visual Navigation Suite	MaxSea Navigator	The Capn Voyager Mosaic	RayTech Navigator	Maptech Offshore Navigator
Platform	PC	PC, MAC	PC	PC	PC
Raster Chart Compatibility	Maptech BSB, Chartpack, NDI, Softchart, Photo	Maptech BSB, Chartpack, NDI, Softchart	Maptech BSB, Chartpack, NDI, Softchart, Photo	Maptech BSB, Chartpack, NDI, Softchart, Photo, Bathymetric Contour	Maptech BSB, Chartpack, Photo, 3-D Bathymetric Contour
Vector Chart Compatibility	Passport CD	C-Map chip	DNC vector (S-57)	C-Map chip or CD	none
Interface	GPS, Autopilot, Compass or Gyro, Depth Sounder	GPS, Autopilot, Compass or Gyro, Depth Sounder	GPS, Autopilot, Compass or Gyro, Depth Sounder	GPS, Autopilot, Compass or Gyro, Depth Sounder, Radar, Instruments	GPS, Autopilot, Compass or Gyro, Depth Sounder
Interface Type(s)	NMEA 0183	NMEA 0183	NMEA 0183	NMEA 0183, SeaTalk, HSB2	NMEA 0183, GARMN
Ease of Use	high	very high	medium	medium	high
GPS Up/Download	both	both	upload only	both	both
Tide and Current Predictions	yes	yes	yes	no	yes
Smooth Chart Scrolling	yes	yes	yes	yes	yes
Seamless Chart Quilting	yes	yes	yes	no	yes
Chart Rotation	yes	yes	no	yes	yes
Split Screen (Tiled Display)	yes	yes	yes	yes	yes
Overzoom	yes	yes	yes	yes	yes
Internet Weather Routing	yes	yes	yes	optional	no
Unlimited Routes, Waypoints	yes	yes	yes	yes	yes
Preplanned Routes (external service)	yes	no	yes	no	no
Drag Zoom	yes	yes	yes	yes	yes
Drag Scroll	yes	yes	yes	yes	yes
Approximate Cost	$450	$450	$350	$450	$180

to use, and one of the most capable marine navigation programs. MaxSea has a strong following among offshore racing sailors and professional fishing-boat captains. Nobeltec's software is considered to be the most feature rich, and their programs are very popular among recreational boaters. The Capn Voyager also has solid features and has been the pick of the U.S. Coast Guard for its boats. RayTech offers the most flexible interfaces with other equipment and integrates with their entire Raymarine line of equipment as well as other equipment via NMEA 0183. Maptech Offshore Navigator is the least expensive; offers an excellent interface with their raster cartography, PhotoCharts, and Contour Professional charts; and has excellent features. Offshore Navigator is in the price range of the stripped-down versions of the other software, which includes Nobeltec Visual Mariner and Capn First Mate.

The Capn Voyager also offers optional pre-planned routes for the Intracoastal Waterway (ICW) and other parts of the eastern United States from Virginia to Maine. These packages are based on the experiences of others cruising these waters and on extensive data collection. Each package includes thousands of waypoints, as well as details on shoals, hazards, daymarks, marinas, anchorages, and more. This is an outstanding concept that may find its way into other packages.

Most of the major suppliers of navigation software have websites that summarize their features, which change with each version and update offered. Unfortunately, the only way to really determine how a given program works and what it does is to talk with others using the same software or get your hands on the program. Most of these companies offer demonstration versions. Unfortunately, the demos may not offer much in the way of cartography, but you at least can get a feel for the screens and how to access functions. Some demos will work with your GPS unit, but most do not. If you are doing any significant cruising, consider one of the high-end packages. If you are simply looking to sample live computer-based navigation, you can try one of the lower-cost packages, which will plot your position on a chart and permit you to enter waypoints and routes. If you buy only one type of cartography and believe you will move up

to a better software package at a later date, go for Maptech or Softchart, since most of the programs will accept their cartography. If you already have a chartplotter using C-Map, it may be wise to choose MaxSea or RayTech, since you can use the same chart chips.

Other navigation software programs that you may wish to explore include Chartview Odyssey by Weems and Plath or NavimaQ for the Macintosh by Quintessence Designs.

Tips on Using Navigation Software

Navigation programs enable you to plan and execute your cruise with ease and to save the results for future use. If you have traditional navigation experience, you will find the techniques familiar, but you can stow the plotter and pencil. There are some things that you can do with the software that you cannot do on paper charts.

For example, the charting software allows you to insert waypoints and adjust routes. You can start with a small-scale chart on your screen, mark your approximate starting and destination waypoints, and plot a route between them. Then, you can zoom in on the route, a section at a time, and add waypoints and adjust the route around hazards and into preferred channels. This process is quicker and allows you to test alternate routes for distance and direction, and to work around currents or other issues. During the cruise, you can adjust the route to take into account changes in plans, overnight stays, or sightseeing. Since the computer-based system typically has an unlimited number of waypoints and routes, you can create complex, lengthy routes without concern over typical chartplotter limitations. With chartplotters, it is recommended that cruises be constructed in route segments to more effectively use the available storage. This limitation does not apply to computer-based navigation systems.

Underway, you can display multiple charts tiled side by side or overlaid on top of one another to be accessed quickly. The program will provide your position and track on each chart simultaneously. For example, you may wish to have two levels of zoom for the same chart—one to view a larger section of the cruise and the second to watch closely around the boat for hazards. Alternatively, you can pair up vector and raster charts, and the corresponding bathymetric data.

If you are using raster charts, you can zoom in quickly to read labels and observe local features, and zoom out again to monitor your progress. Some programs quilt charts together. They will match the scale for adjacent charts, even if they are from different sources. The resultant display appears as if you have a continuous chart of the same scale. This makes scanning across charts far easier and less confusing. Usually, you will see some hints of the borders by changes in color scheme or chart details. Be careful to make sure that the cartography that you are using has the same datum and scale information. For example, some charts will use mean low water (MLW) for depths, and others may use mean lower low water (MLLW) (see glossary). Some display depths in feet, others in fathoms. Do not assume, check!

The better navigation software packages give you the ability to adjust the display to suit your needs. Some have floating toolbars that you can position wherever you want. Some offer floating data displays that you can customize in size and location on the screen to your preference. You may wish to arrange the data fields to match your chartplotter, thus making quick comparisons easier.

If you want to check your position with visual bearings, some programs allow you to annotate with bearing lines that display the angles and distances while not interrupting the ongoing plotted cruise. You can make measurements from your boat to an object and obtain a range and bearing, or you can measure the distance between any two locations to help you plan changes while underway.

Navigation Software Trends

Computer-based navigation systems represent a growing trend. Since many boaters already own a notebook computer, the incremental cost for a high degree of performance is nominal. With the major companies, you can't go wrong, and they will continue to improve their packages. Some of the companies offer upgrades at nominal prices, just as other software manufacturers do.

These programs will increasingly move toward the fusion of data sources. Radar overlay is popular in high-end chartplotters and is appearing in computer programs. RayTech already has that feature on its software. The merging of 3-D images with charts for depth sounder interface and for viewing terrain on the screen as you might see it in real life is coming. Both advancements will facilitate locating harbors and inlets from some distance. Raster and vector data are ready for integration on the same screen. At this time, the vector and raster cartography companies are separate, but joint ventures are logical next steps. Most importantly, the prices have been dropping. The programs described here already have dropped in price significantly with future updates offering more, often with included cartography.

Connecting GPS Units to Other Instruments and NMEA 0183

GPS Connected to
→ *radar display*
→ *"lollipop" display of waypoints*
→ *radar to superimpose GPS data*
→ *autopilot*
→ *DSC transmission of emergency position*

GPS Input from
→ *Differential GPS (DGPS) receiver*

NMEA 0183
→ *industry standard for interfacing components*

GPS Receiver with Radar

The GPS receiver is the primary position sensor on a boat. There are two devices that can make good use of this information. Most radar units can display GPS digital data including position, course over ground, speed over ground, and active waypoint, as shown in figure 9-7. In the figure, the GPS data provide the information for most of the data fields on the screen. In addition, the active waypoint is displayed on the radar screen as a circle. A dashed line extends from the center of the display (the boat) up toward the waypoint.

This display is often called a *lollipop* due to its appearance. Typically, a radar display is oriented "heading up" (rather than north at top) since its frame of reference is the boat. The lollipop display on the radar gives the skipper a clear indication of the direction to steer and the relative position of the waypoint with respect to the boat. The radar shows reflective surface objects, including land, in the same orientation as the skipper's visual horizon. The combination of GPS position and waypoints with the radar presentation is very useful for safe navigation since underwater hazards don't appear on radar.

There are some displays that will show the radar image superimposed over the chart with the GPS position. In order to do this, the radar display and chartplotter display must be the same unit. Radar manufacturers offering this capability include Raymarine, Furuno, and Simrad; more are likely to follow suit.

There are boats on which multiple stations sharing the radar and chartplotter displays are needed, such as a flybridge cruiser with two helm stations. For this application, manufacturers such as Raymarine and Furuno offer proprietary interfaces that allow multiple sharing of radar and chartplotter displays and more. They each employ a proprietary high-speed interconnection network in addition to one that supports NMEA. However, each connected display unit must come from the same manufacturer. Raymarine's approach is called HSB2 for High Speed Bus version 2. Furuno uses Ethernet. With Raymarine, units are daisy-chained from one to the next, while Furuno requires that all devices be connected to a central hub. It is important to consider the environment in which these devices will operate and make sure that the cabling and connections are suitably waterproofed. At this time, Ethernet hardware is not designed for the marine environment, but that is likely to change.

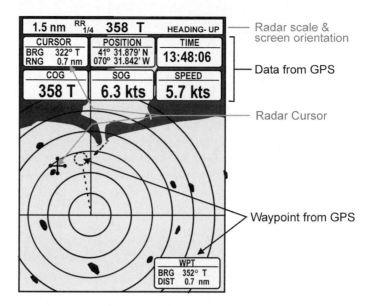

FIGURE 9-7. *GPS Receiver and Radar. A GPS receiver connected to radar is a powerful tool. In the absence of GPS information, the radar screen is useful, but it does not have information about your destination and specific coordinates. This is provided by connecting the GPS output to the radar. A very valuable tool is the* lollipop *display that shows your waypoint enclosed within a circle, with a dotted line extending from your current position up to the waypoint. This display provides you with a physical feel for your path superimposed on objects above the water, such as boats and buoys.*

Radar is a very powerful navigation tool. Unlike GPS receivers, radar senses the environment around you, so the two are very complementary. With the radar data overlaid on a chart, it is easier to recognize fixed objects from moving ones. This also enables the operator to ensure that the GPS data are accurate by correlating them with features on the radar. In order to compare the presentations from the radar and the GPS chartplotter, it is necessary to match both the scale and the orientation of the displays. Once this is done, if features on one are offset, or different, from the other, check your chartplotter.

GPS receivers and radar use inherently different references for their displays. The standard presentation of radar data places the heading direction of the boat at the top of the display. This is commonly referred to as *heading up*. The GPS unit can be set to display "course up" (the actual direction of motion of the boat) or "north up" (true or magnetic). Unfortunately "course up" may differ from "heading up" if there is any wind or current, so the best reference is "north up" (magnetic) for both units. The radar needs an external reference for magnetic north, which is supplied by a fluxgate or gyrocompass.

GPS Receiver with Autopilot

Autopilot is the other electronic instrument that uses GPS input. The autopilot follows the active navigation route within the GPS unit. The autopilot uses the GPS course data to make corrections to the current boat heading. The autopilot also uses an input from the electronic compass to ascertain and display the current boat heading.

GPS Receiver with Digital Selective Calling (DSC)

The latest VHF radios include a feature called *digital selective calling* (DSC). These radios are equipped with an emergency button that, when pressed, sends a coded digital emergency message complete with your boat identity and current coordinates. In order for this feature to function, the radio must be connected to your GPS unit. The appropriate data-out and ground lines from the GPS unit must be connected to the data-in terminal on the radio. Some of the latest chartplotters also incorporate a data input from the VHF radio. When a distress call is made in your area, an indicator will appear on your chartplotter screen showing where the call originated and the coordinates of the boat that sent the message.

VHF channel 70 is dedicated to DSC. The system uses digital signaling to call a designated station. A fully implemented DSC receiver can make four types of calls: distress, urgency, safety, and routine. The concept has been specified by the International Telecommunication Union–Radio (UTI-R) in support of the Global Maritime Distress and Safety System (GMDSS) being implemented for more unified support at sea. Using DSC you can address a call to a single DSC subscriber for routine communications. The signal is heard only on that receiver along with instructions to switch to a specific channel for voice communications. For distress, the sig-

nal is considered to be for "all ships" and sounds an alarm on all DSC-equipped receivers within range. The transmission includes your ship's identity and coordinates provided by your GPS receiver. In order to sign up to use DSC, you must apply for a maritime mobile service identity (MMSI) nine-digit number and mobile station license with the FCC. All ships with DSC will automatically monitor channel 70. The U.S. Coast Guard is in the process of adding DSC capability to each of its stations, but this is not expected to be complete until 2005.

All newly manufactured VHF radio models must provide DSC emergency signaling capability, although older models still can be sold. VHF radios with DSC emergency call capability are now in the price range of a typical fixed-mount VHF (approximately $150 to $300). A fully functional DSC VHF radio that permits selective calling typically costs $300 to $600.

GPS Receiver with a DGPS Receiver

For the most part, the GPS unit sends information to other devices. In one mode it also uses data from another source, the Differential GPS receiver. DGPS is described in chapter 10. Its primary function is to provide correction data to the GPS receiver for each of the satellites within view. When you add a DGPS receiver to the boat, the communication between the DGPS unit and the GPS unit is via RTCM protocol. This protocol was defined by the Radio Technical Commission for Maritime Services (RTCM) Special

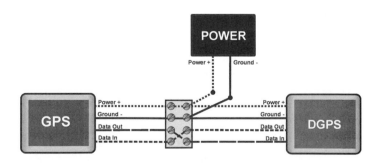

FIGURE 9-8. GPS-DGPS Connection. On board, you can connect your GPS receiver to a Differential GPS (DGPS) unit via the same wires used to connect the GPS receiver to a computer. DGPS, supported by the coast guard, provides improved GPS accuracy. It requires a separate antenna and receiver.

Committee 104 specifically for the communication of satellite corrections. The data-out channel from the DGPS receiver is connected to the data-in line on the GPS receiver. The Interface Setup Menu on the GPS unit must be set on RTCM in and is usually set for NMEA out. Some GPS receivers also need to talk to the DGPS on its data-out line in order to tune the receiver. However, most DGPS receivers are automatically tuned and require no instructions from the GPS. Figure 9-8 shows a typical wiring diagram for the connection between GPS and DGPS receivers. DGPS uses a separate receiver and antenna from that associated with the GPS unit, as is described in chapter 10.

NMEA 0183

The National Marine Electronics Association (NMEA) developed a standard protocol for manufacturers to assure that equipment from different suppliers could work together. This protocol is called *NMEA 0183*. NMEA signals are compatible with serial ports, and can be connected directly to a computer. The information is sent in coded sentences in a standard format. Any unit listening to the NMEA output from another device, as soon as it hears a sentence beginning with the appropriate name, will use the data that follow. All of the digital sentences begin with a "$" followed by a code for the type of device sending the information (GPS, compass, etc.), followed by a three-character code for the type of data being sent (bearing, speed, etc.), followed by the value of the data.

The marine electronic devices are categorized as "talkers" or "listeners" depending upon what they do. Some are both. Interconnection involves ensuring that the talkers are connected to those devices that want to listen to what they have to say. The only problem comes when two or more talkers need to talk to the same listener.

Interconnecting electronics using the NMEA 0183 inputs and outputs is not extraordinarily complicated. Unfortunately, there is little information readily available to the typical boater. This section takes the mystery out of connecting marine electronics. The NMEA connection as described in chapter 8 for connection with a computer uses only three wires. One wire is for data into the device, one wire is for data out, and the third wire is a ground. This concept is very simple in connecting one device to another, but gets complicated as more devices are added. You can connect the output from one talker to multiple listeners, so long as there is enough signal strength for all to hear. However, life becomes complicated when you want to connect multiple talkers to one listener. If you simply connect the wires together, the talkers are likely to interfere with one another. Many manufacturers of GPS receivers and other marine electronic devices anticipated this problem and offer multiple NMEA inputs, usually numbered 1, 2, etc. Simply connect each talker to one of the separate input lines. If the device does not have enough inputs, you will need to purchase an NMEA multiplexer. This device costs between $150 and $200 and typically provides four to eight isolated inputs. The multiplexer listens on each line and saves what it hears. It then provides all the data sequentially to the listening device. Typically, each talker sends new information every second or so.

Conversely, if you have connected too many devices to your talker so that the signal level drops, you need to buy an NMEA expander (amplifier) to boost the signal. An expander typically costs about $150 and offers optical isolation between the connections. Many GPS units come with multiple outputs to avoid this problem. A typical GPS unit will drive up to three listeners on a single output without the expander. If you find that you are losing information on listening devices within your boat, or the information is slow to register, chances are you may need an expander to boost the signal.

Figures 9-8, 9-9, and 9-10 illustrate several typical configurations (refer to figs. 8-1 and 8-2 to see the connection between a GPS receiver and a computer). NMEA 0183 is pin-for-pin compatible with RS-232 protocol used on computer serial ports. The back of the DB-9 serial port female connector appears in the same configuration in figures 9-8 and 9-9.

Figure 9-9 shows a complex configuration of onboard electronics. In this diagram, we have connected a radar, an electronic heading sensor, and an autopilot to the GPS receiver. The GPS unit provides three devices with information: the radar, the autopilot, and

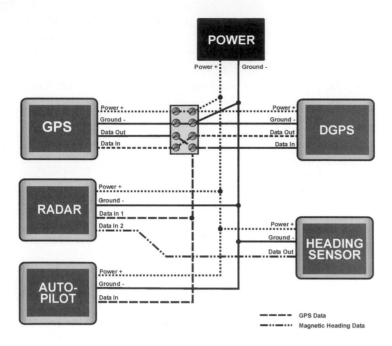

FIGURE 9-9. Integrated System. A GPS chartplotter can be included in an integrated installation. A GPS (or chartplotter) can typically support three devices that listen to its data over the connection. In this installation, the GPS is providing data to the radar and the autopilot. The radar screen will display the GPS data fields and show the plot of the active waypoint. The autopilot accepts the GPS steering commands. The heading sensor provides a digital compass output to drive the radar's magnetic north-up display option.

the DGPS receiver. The heading sensor provides data to the radar for a north-up (magnetic) presentation to match the GPS unit's presentation. In this configuration, the autopilot accepts GPS data for course information. Many autopilots also use heading data. To do that in this diagram, the autopilot needs a second data-in line to accommodate the output from the heading sensor. As you can see by studying the diagram, all listeners (data in) are connected to talkers (data out), and only one talker is connected to any listener line.

Figure 9-10 shows a fully integrated configuration. In this configuration, we have added a computer, a VHF radio, a depth sounder, a wind sensor, and a water temperature sensor. The computer is used as the integrating display unit. Alternatively, a high-end chartplotter can do the same thing. In order to accommodate all of the talkers, we have added a multiplexer (MUX) to concentrate the inputs. The

VHF radio has DSC capability so that it can broadcast your position in the event of an emergency. The position information comes from the GPS receiver. The receiver shown has two data-out lines; otherwise, you might need to use an expander, since there are four listeners to the GPS receiver's output. This diagram has omitted the power and ground wires for simplicity. All devices share these two wires.

The NMEA 0183 specification calls for opto-isolation of devices. An opto-isolator eliminates the direct electrical connection between devices. This prevents potential power surges or ground loops that could damage the equipment under certain conditions, such as poor grounding of equipment. It employs a lamp and a light detector housed in a single device to pass the information from input to output without a direct electrical connection. This can be useful for extensive configurations with many interconnecting devices, as shown in figures 9-9 and 9-10. Most expanders and multiplexers offer built-in opto-isolators, or they can be purchased individually for about $100. Only one is used on any connection between two devices. Typically, the opto-isolator would be used on the computer end of the connection. However, if you seek to upload data, such as waypoints or routes, from the computer to the GPS receiver, you may need to temporarily bypass the isolator with a switch.

NMEA 2000

Since NMEA 0183 was initiated in 1983, there have been many changes in marine electronics, but the open architecture interconnection protocol has remained the same. After many years of review and deliberation, the National Marine Electronics Association released its new specification NMEA 2000 in August 2001. The new standard will have only gradual impact and will not make current equipment designed for NMEA 0183 immediately obso-

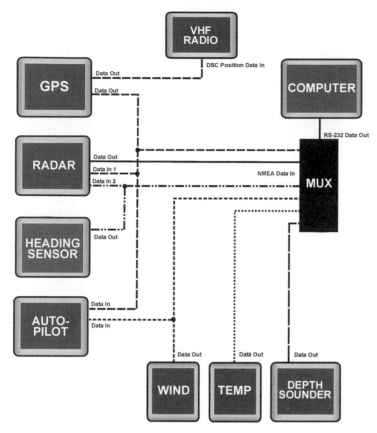

FIGURE 9-10. *Totally Integrated System. The GPS can be used onboard with a computer. The computer serves the chartplotting function with higher power than a typical integrated chartplotter. The GPS unit can be a stand-alone fixed sensor without its own display, or a GPS chartplotter. The computer accepts data from a variety of sensors in this configuration through a multiplexer (MUX). The multiplexer sequentially forwards the data to the computer from each source. Wind, depth, water temperature, radar, and GPS data all can be presented on the computer screen using navigation and other software. The computer then can direct information and commands to the autopilot. Note that power and ground lines are omitted in the diagram for simplicity.*

cal interconnection bus. This makes it easier to add devices by simply tapping into the single bus rather than providing unique point-to-point wiring.

Based on the "CAN bus" standard, which originally was developed for automotive applications, NMEA 2000 supports up to 50 devices connected on a single bus. The bus length can be as great as 660 feet (200 m). The protocol enables devices to listen for their particular information of interest while other data speed along the same path. The connections promise to be self configuring with no setup or master controller required. The bus must be terminated at each end, but devices can be easily added by tapping into the bus. The approach eliminates unique device-to-device wiring in favor of daisy-chained connections that all devices share.

The marine industry is slow to adopt changes. The engine-control segment of the marine business is leading the charge to adopt NMEA 2000. Electronic engine controls are relatively new on the scene, so these companies are looking to the higher-power NMEA 2000 as their connection of choice. Most electronic equipment is still being outfitted with the NMEA 0183 interface. NMEA 2000 is inadequate for demanding applications such as multistation radar/chartplotter displays, and NMEA 0183 works fine for most of

lete. Most electronic manufacturers have opted to stay with NMEA 0183 for the time being. So, the new standard may not gain favor until more boatbuilders begin to offer integrated electronics packages with their boats. NMEA 2000 is 26 times faster than its predecessor, but the most significant change is the ease with which devices can be connected.

While NMEA 0183 allows only one talker to be connected to a listener, NMEA 2000 enables multiple talkers and multiple listeners on the same electri-

today's other needs. Do not expect a change in the near future. Fortunately, in the long run, even users with NMEA 0183 equipment will be able to bridge to the new networks if they become more common. It is possible to use a hybrid approach with your current equipment interconnected on NMEA 0183 and to bridge to the new bus as you add equipment.

Since NMEA 2000 will not support the speeds required for multiple station displays sharing radar and chart data, Raymarine's proprietary HSB2 and Furuno's NAVnet will continue to serve that purpose. These network protocols are 10 to 50 times faster than NMEA 2000 and are better suited to the task. As NMEA 2000 becomes popular, Raymarine and Furuno are likely to add connectivity from their networks to NMEA 2000. As a boater, this new standard may have little impact on you unless you purchase a new boat incorporating this protocol. In any event, you will be able to interface your current electronics.

Integration Considerations

A few tips will ensure that your onboard electrical and electronics connections do not fail when you need them. All cabling used on your boat should be marine grade and should be so labeled. The harsh marine environment may corrode wiring made for automotive or other applications. NMEA cabling wire pairs should be twisted to reduce stray pick-up and interference with other equipment. Shielding the cables is a good practice. Shielded cables have a metallic sheath wrapped around the wires to prevent interference either from or to the wires. The shielding should be

grounded. Any display cabling should use multi-shielded cables with two or more concentric metallic sheaths.

Power is an important consideration. Boats typically have 12-volt DC available. Some notebook computers will work directly from this voltage using a cigarette lighter connection, or you can hardwire an installation. If you use a computer requiring 110-volt AC, you may need to use a sine-wave, or quasi-sine-wave converter. These are more expensive and provide AC that more nearly matches the characteristics found in the wall outlet at home. The less-costly switched converters may not work well with your computer's power supply. You will be able to tell if the computer does not operate well or the lower-cost unit consumes more power than you would expect based on the power rating of the computer. You should also consider using an uninterruptible power supply (UPS). This device provides an extra degree of isolation, and, with an internal backup battery, provides an extra measure of security to keep your navigation system operating temporarily if the boat power fails.

Improving Performance and the Future of GPS

Stated GPS Accuracy
→ *20 to 33 feet (6–10 m) typical (no SA)*

Improving Accuracy
→ *DGPS (10–16.5 ft./3–5 m)*
→ *WAAS (3.3–10 ft./1–3 m)*
→ *antenna performance and placement*

GPS May Be More Accurate than Charts

GPS Receiver Accuracy

Before GPS, electronic navigation was accomplished with the aid of Loran-C. Loran-C uses three fixed ground stations rather than satellites to provide the reference signals. The Loran-C receiver measures the time difference (TD) of the pulses received from pairs of ground stations to locate your position. Many older charts provide Loran-C overprinted TD lines to aid in locating position. Using two sets of TDs you can identify a unique spot on the Earth within the effective range of the transmitters—typically 1,000 to 1,500 miles (1,600–2,400 km). The typical absolute accuracy of Loran-C is about one-quarter of a mile (400 m). The accuracy limitation of Loran-C is largely due to the fact that the signals are affected differently by water and landmasses. Water distorts the precise location of the TD lines and limits the absolute accuracy. However, Loran-C is quite accurate (approaching the accuracy of GPS) in returning to a previously recorded position because the geometry of land and water paths remain the same in both cases. This is why fishing-boat captains still use Loran-C to mark their favorite fishing spots. The termination of loran operation has been delayed several times. In fact, improvements are currently being made to the Loran-C stations. However, only one company still manufactures marine Loran-C sets (Furuno), and these cost over $1,000.

Figure 10-1 shows the comparative absolute accuracy of Loran-C and GPS. The outer circle for GPS indicates the accuracy available to civil users with Selective Availability (SA) turned on. The stated accuracy was 330 feet (100 m) or better 95 percent of

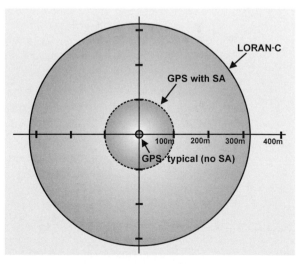

FIGURE 10-1. GPS Versus Loran-C. GPS provides considerable improvement over Loran-C. Loran-C continues to operate, but GPS provides superior accuracy at a much lower unit price.

the time. In May 2000, SA was shut off by presidential order. The resulting accuracy improved dramatically, as is shown in figure 10-1.

The accuracy of a basic GPS unit is so good compared with other navigation tools that you might wonder why we would want to do better. In open water, the advertised position accuracy of 50 feet (15 m) is quite good. If we approach obstacles, we need to stay an extra 50 feet away just to make sure that we are not within the limits of the GPS receiver's accuracy. However, a GPS receiver is not suitable as the primary means of navigating harbors and channels without some improvement. The U.S. Coast Guard has determined that an accuracy of 15 feet (4.6 m) is required for electronic navigation of harbors and channels. Certainly, one would not navigate using a GPS unit alone in channels or harbors unless there was no other choice—such as when in a dense fog or near total darkness.

Figure 10-2 illustrates comparative accuracies for GPS using currently available techniques. In this illustration, imagine that you are operating a 25-foot (7.6 m) cruiser, as shown, to provide a sense of scale. The current civil GPS accuracy, as advertised, is 50 feet (15 m) with no SA. This is the outer circle. However, you can expect to achieve accuracies on the

order of 33 feet (10 m) or better, as illustrated by the "GPS Typical" circle. This is quite good, providing a position within an extra boat length fore and aft. However, this could still be problematic, so two special techniques are available with relative accuracies shown by the inner circles labeled "DGPS" and "WAAS," respectively. Typically, you can expect to achieve these accuracies or better with these enhancements. With DGPS, your circle of uncertainty is nearly the size of the boat, and with WAAS, the accuracy may be *better* than the size of the boat. DGPS is provided by the U.S. Coast Guard, WAAS is provided by the FAA. Mariners can use either DGPS or WAAS, but not both at the same time. Since each is providing a set of corrections for each satellite, the GPS unit has no way of distinguishing which to use. Both systems are described below.

DGPS and Sources of GPS Receiver Error

The coast guard initiated a program called Differential GPS (DGPS) to provide typical 15-foot (4.5 m) accuracy. The coast guard began this program some time before Selective Availability (SA) was shut off. DGPS, in the regions where it is available, overcomes the effects of SA plus some other errors inherent in the system. To better understand how much we can improve GPS, it is useful to understand the various error sources, how DGPS works, and what is available to you.

The sources of navigation error can be broken into several categories, each with some different potential remedies. First, as already discussed, it is important that the user take prudent steps to ensure that the GPS unit receives a good signal. The primary means of doing this is to make sure that the antenna is properly placed and clear of obstructions that mask substantial portions of the sky. The antenna should be mounted in a location as low as possible to minimize the effects of pitch and roll, but high enough to be clear of obstructions. The antenna should be clean and never painted. The location should be within the recommended wiring distance from the GPS unit. If a handheld GPS receiver is used, it should be mounted in a

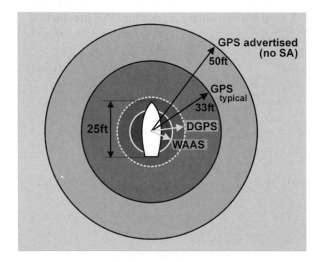

FIGURE 10-2. *Today, GPS Provides High Accuracy. Without SA, basic GPS ("GPS typical" here) is excellent, but not sufficient for harbor navigation. DGPS provides further improvement, and WAAS takes accuracy to the next level.*

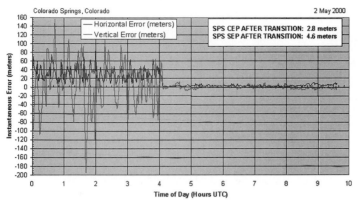

FIGURE 10-3. *The DoD Shuts Off SA. GPS civil performance literally improved overnight when SA was shut off on 2 May 2000.* (U.S. SPACE COMMAND)

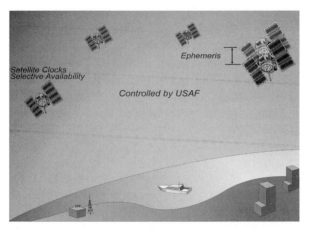

FIGURE 10-4. *GPS Errors Controlled by the U.S. Air Force. The satellites determine the basic accuracy of GPS receivers. The two main errors attributable to the satellites are position and clock accuracy. Both of these are measured and corrected by the air force using the ground control stations. The predicted satellite position over time is provided by an* ephemeris *table. This is the position information that the satellite transmits to the user along with current time. The ephemeris data are computed on the ground and transmitted to each satellite. The predictions are regularly updated to ensure accuracy, since any error in the satellite's position will result in a similar error on the ground. The clocks are checked for accuracy by the ground stations and adjustments are uplinked to the satellites.*

bracket with the top of the receiver facing upward. The antenna is designed to provide near-uniform coverage of the sky with the GPS unit in a position slightly tilted from vertical at a convenient viewing angle. Coverage will be degraded if the receiver is lying flat so that part of the antenna coverage is blocked. Also, make sure that the bracket location is not obscured, particularly by metal objects, and that any antenna or power connections to the GPS unit are secure.

The U.S. Air Force controls GPS satellites and is tasked with minimizing associated error sources. One obvious source of error, SA, was directly under the control of the air force. However, figure 10-3 is a graphic display that plots error over time. It is easy to see significant improvement at the exact moment SA was shut down by the Department of Defense. The other principal error sources include satellite *clocks* and *ephemeris*, as shown in figure 10-4. The clocks, while very precise, do drift. The high degree of accuracy needed requires that the clocks be adjusted regularly. The ephemeris refers to the precise orbit of the satellite. It is the ephemeris data of its position that the satellite transmits to the ground. If this position is in error, the resultant ground position calculation will be in error. Therefore, the ephemeris is continually measured, calculated for future position, and updated to the satellite. If necessary, the satellite is repositioned. These tasks are accomplished by the ground-control segment that monitors all of the satellites. High-powered computers determine corrections and ephemeris tables that are uplinked (transmitted) to the satellites by large communications terminals. It is impossible to minimize these errors, so they are maintained to a sufficient degree to assure the published GPS accuracy limits.

The atmosphere causes the greatest amount of error—almost 40 percent of the total. Radio waves do not travel in straight lines. The atmosphere contains charged particles that cause the waves to bend, as shown in figure 10-5. The degree of bending is not

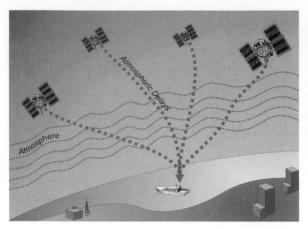

FIGURE 10-5. *The Atmosphere Causes the Greatest Errors. By far, the greatest error is introduced by a satellite signal's path through the atmosphere, where it is bent and shifted to some degree. This error is uncontrollable, although some correction is possible. The military uses a second frequency, L2, to assist. The results can be compared and some adjustments made to refine the error. Future satellites will offer multiple frequencies to the civil user, which will lead to further improvements in accuracy.*

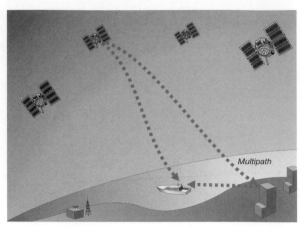

FIGURE 10-6. *Multipath. Sometimes satellite signals are reflected off nearby objects. These objects could be buildings, land features, other ships, other objects on a large ship, or any other large, nearby object. The reflected signal will be delayed at the receiver by the length of the reflected path, and this can cause erroneous indications of those satellites' positions.*

constant with altitude nor with frequency. Consequently, the L2 signal will be affected differently than the L1 signal. The military uses both and can compute some additional corrections by comparing both. Civil users employ the L1 frequency only. Obviously, radio waves that are bent travel a longer path than if they traveled over a straight line. It is possible to minimize these atmospheric errors to some degree using DGPS, as explained later in this section.

The local environment also can cause some significant errors. *Multipath* is illustrated in figure 10-6. Multipath, as the name suggests, occurs when the signal arrives at the GPS receiver via multiple paths. If there are large objects near the boat, the signal may be received by reflection off the object, resulting in a longer path than the direct path. As an example, using a GPS unit on or near large ships or along a mountainous coastline could cause this error. Multipath is not often a concern to recreational boaters, and it is not correctable by DGPS or WAAS since it comes from the user's local environment. Simply be aware that you could have an error if you are near large objects that could reflect the signal. This is especially true if you are in harbors near clusters of tall build-

ings, as might be found in large cities, as the figure illustrates.

Quantitatively, the sources of GPS error are divided into ionospheric effects, clock errors, ephemeris errors, receiver errors, and multipath. Assuming that a total error of 33 feet (10 m) is typical for GPS receivers without SA, the ionospheric propagation effects account for about 13 feet (4 m) of this error. The satellite clocks contribute another 7 feet (2.1 m). The ephemeris contributes another 7 feet. The receiver contributes a mere 1.5 feet (0.5 m) and multipath can contribute another 3 feet (1 m) or so.

The solution to some of these inaccuracies is DGPS. To see how DGPS works, imagine that you have a high-quality GPS receiver at a precisely known location, as shown in figure 10-7. The coast guard ground station receives signals from all satellites in view. The coast guard computes navigation solutions with all possible combinations of satellites. To the extent that these solutions produce positions that differ from the known position, the coast guard is able to compute corrections to each satellite that would produce the right answer. Assuming that your boat is not far from this DGPS ground station, the errors that you experience from each satellite are likely to be very similar. So, the coast guard transmits a table of correc-

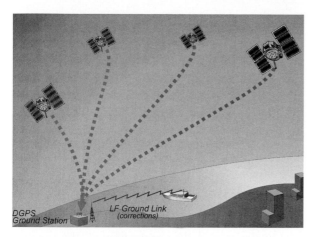

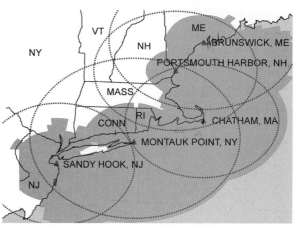

FIGURE 10-7. *U.S. Coast Guard DGPS. Maritime users needed greater accuracy for harbor and channel operations than basic GPS afforded. The Differential GPS satellite signals are received by a fixed ground station. A processor compares the satellite-derived positions with the actual position and computes adjustments for each satellite. The adjustments are transmitted locally using retrofitted transmitters from radio beacons taken out of service. At the time that it was implemented, DGPS offered a great advantage by canceling out most of the SA errors and a good bit of the atmospheric errors. Today, with SA turned off, the DGPS signals still offer an improvement over basic GPS signals from 50 feet (10 m) to about 16 feet (5 m) or better. SA still can be turned back on under conditions of military conflict.*

FIGURE 10-8. *DGPS Coverage in New England. DGPS stations are arrayed around the U.S. coasts and along principal waterways. Each transmits about 90 miles (145 km). They are designed for overlapping coverage. This figure shows the New England coverage. Other forms and types of DGPS are used throughout the world but are not compatible with the USCG DGPS receivers.* (U.S. COAST GUARD)

tions for each satellite. These transmissions go out on radio frequencies around 300 kHz range.

The coast guard has DGPS stations along the U.S. seacoasts, the Great Lakes shorelines, and major navigable waterways, such as the Mississippi River. Each station operates autonomously, receiving signals from all satellites in view, and computes corrections continuously as the satellites move across the sky. Figure 10-8 shows coverage for New England. A list of stations can be found on the U.S. Coast Guard Navigation Center website listed in the resources section.

In order to receive these corrections, you must have a DGPS antenna and receiver, as shown in figure 10-9. This receiver is connected to the GPS unit, which takes the provided corrections and applies them to the position calculations. The disadvantage to DGPS is the added cost (around $300) of the second antenna and receiver, plus installation. The advantage is position accuracy on the order of 10 to 16 feet (3–5 m). A note of caution: the DGPS signals can

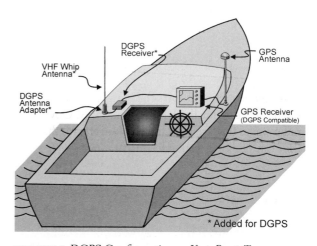

FIGURE 10-9. *DGPS Configuration on Your Boat. To use DGPS, you need a second receiver and antenna to detect the coded signals from the USCG's DGPS stations. The DGPS receiver decodes the data and forwards them to your GPS receiver, where they are used to correct satellite distances and to offer position information that is more accurate.*

only be received up to about 90 miles (145 km) from the station. The antenna must be properly mounted and grounded. Otherwise, the received signal will be too weak to be useful. DGPS works with most GPS receivers, including handhelds; however, DGPS receivers and antennas are not available as handheld.

Various forms of DGPS are available across the globe. The concept of corrections generated and re-transmitted from a fixed ground station to mobile GPS users is used by many companies and government agencies. The method of transmission of the corrections may be unique to each application. For example, some are transmitted by radio stations. Others are transmitted over special channels. GPS is employed in applications such as land surveying and construction. A special-purpose local fixed ground station is used as part of a technique called *real-time kinematic* (RTK) to achieve accuracies on the order of inches or better. GPS receivers used in the transportation industry sometimes require a degree of accuracy measured in feet rather than inches.

WAAS

The FAA, in response to demands from the commercial aircraft industry, developed a program called Wide Area Augmentation System (WAAS). The USCG DGPS was deemed to be inadequate for aircraft for two major reasons: its current coverage is largely coastal, whereas aircraft fly over the entire country and cross oceans; and DGPS is not fast enough. Also, since aircraft usually operate at some considerable altitude, getting the corrections to them is better served by some means other than the coast guard's DGPS.

Actually, WAAS is a form of DGPS. It uses a network of fixed ground monitoring stations with precisely known positions. The processors analyze the satellite signals in a similar fashion as

those for the USCG. However, the WAAS stations are networked together, whereas each USCG station is independent. The master control station, which prepares the corrections, factors the data from individual monitoring stations and computes a more refined set of corrections for each user region. Upload stations then transmit the corrections to the WAAS satellite. The WAAS system for the United States is depicted in figure 10-10. The two WAAS satellites, which are depicted over the oceans in the figure, are in geostationary orbits roughly twice as high as the GPS satellites (depicted between the WAAS satellites over North America). While the GPS satellites move with respect to us on the ground, the geosynchronous WAAS satellites appear to be in fixed positions above the equator, one over the Atlantic Ocean and one over the Pacific Ocean.

The ground monitoring stations for GPS satellites, represented by oval dots on the ground, are located in a grid across the U.S. This is unlike the DGPS stations, which are arrayed along the seacoasts.

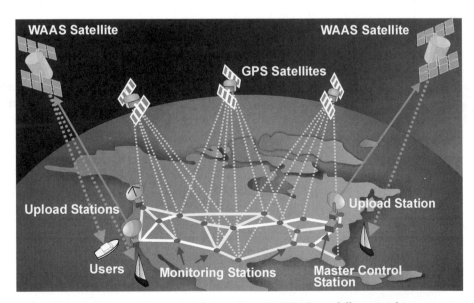

FIGURE 10-10. *Wide Area Augmentation System (WAAS). WAAS is a different implementation of DGPS. It uses a grid of ground stations across the country—instead of just along the coast—to collect data. Greater accuracy is achieved by networking all of the stations and computing an array of corrections. The corrections are transmitted from the ground to two geosynchronous WAAS satellites, one over each ocean. These satellites retransmit the corrections to the boater on the GPS L1 frequency. A WAAS-enabled receiver need only be programmed to listen to the WAAS satellite on one of its GPS channels. No separate receiver or antenna is required.* (ADAPTED FROM AN ILLUSTRATION BY RAYMARINE)

The GPS satellite signals are received by each WAAS ground monitoring station and compared. Rather than compute the corrections and transmit them from each of these stations as is done in DGPS, the data are linked to the WAAS Master Control Station. The corrections are forwarded to three ground uplink stations, two on the West Coast and one on the East Coast. The uplink stations supply the corrections to the WAAS satellites, as shown in figure 10-10.

These corrections are transmitted to the two geosynchronous satellites. These satellites relay the correction and other information to your GPS receiver. Fortunately, the WAAS satellites were designed to transmit this information on the GPS L1 frequency. As a result, virtually any GPS receiver in clear view of a WAAS satellite can receive the signals without any further equipment. However, your GPS receiver must be programmed to accommodate the WAAS information. Unfortunately, most GPS equipment made prior to 2001 cannot be upgraded to decipher WAAS. The software is the primary reason for this problem: it requires larger memories to run than most older GPS units possess. Most new GPS receivers have incorporated the WAAS feature and are designated "WAAS enabled." With the networking approach, WAAS provides accuracy that exceeds that of DGPS—on the order of 10 feet (3 m) or better typical as compared with 16 feet (5 m) for DGPS. The obvious advantage to WAAS is the lack of extra expense for a second antenna and receiver. If you also have access to DGPS, you can use one or the other, but not both, at the same time.

How Do You Use WAAS?

You need to enable the WAAS function within the GPS setup menu. You need to have a clear view of the Atlantic or Pacific above the equator. On the water, this is relatively easy, and the only obstructions are likely to be on the boat. WAAS may be intermittently effective on land due to possible blockage.

Initially, it takes up to 20 minutes to download all the WAAS almanac data—updates are quicker. A newer, WAAS-enabled GPS unit will provide an indication if it is operating with WAAS corrections, usually by inserting a letter D within the satellite bars, or by indicating "3-D Differential" on the Satellite

screen. However, as always, it is recommended that you exercise caution by using other techniques to cross-check your position.

WAAS is rapidly becoming a standard feature on all GPS receivers sold in the U.S. Why not? It is practically free. Remember, this system was developed for commercial aircraft not boats. The FAA is paying for it. Consequently, it will undergo an extended and rigorous set of tests to ensure accuracy for aircraft. In the meantime, mariners are incidental and beneficial users of the system. By all means use it, but ensure that the receiver is operating in differential mode before executing maneuvers in tight areas.

The WAAS capability will become global. The European Union is in the process of implementing a similar and compatible program called EGNOS (European Geostationary Navigation Overlay System). This program will be usable within the next few years in advance of full operational capability.

Is GPS More Accurate than Charts?

Even if you diligently plot your GPS position on your chart, there may be times when you find yourself somewhere other than where you think you are on the chart. Which is correct? More than likely, your GPS position will be accurate, but the chart may not. Many charts date back thirty years or more. The data recorded on the charts were developed using the best tools of the day, which generally were far less capable than your GPS receiver. In North America, the latitude and longitude grid was referenced to a single point near the center of the continent in 1927 and referred to as NAD-27 (North American Datum 1927). With the advent of GPS and other positional tools, it was discovered that NAD-27 did not accurately reflect many coastal features. As a result, a new datum was developed in 1983 and referred to as NAD-83. The following year this standard was adopted as a global reference and renamed WGS-84 (World Geodetic Survey 1984). Today, most navigation charts use the WGS-84 reference. If you happen to use a chart that has not been updated from NAD-27 and plot your GPS position on the chart using WGS-84, you may find that you have mislocated your position by as much as a half nautical mile.

Today, charts are being updated using DGPS as the position reference; however, many charts have not yet been updated. As new information is obtained and verified, it generally is published in the *Local Notice to Mariners*. Charts are updated with that information when they are reprinted. It is important that you examine the legend for the date of the most recent update. These corrections may reflect particular aids to navigation or specific locations, but the entire chart may not have been updated.

In general, you can expect your GPS receiver to be nearly as accurate as the best charts. In many cases, the GPS unit will be much better. A good example is shown in figure 10-11. The entire island was mislocated. Even when features such as buoys were initially plotted accurately, they may drift or be repositioned. Digital charts have the same problems as paper charts, since they are made from paper charts. Some of the vector charts have incorporated additional corrections from other sources, such as channel depths provided by the U.S. Army Corps of Engineers. Various organizations such as the U.S. Power Squadrons and the Coast Guard Auxiliary assist NOAA under the Cooperative Charting Program with updates using GPS. However, it takes time for NOAA to incorporate this information into printed charts. Even with budget constraints, NOAA updates over 300 charts per year, but this means it takes time to get to your chart of interest. The conclusion? Assume your GPS reading is more accurate than the chart that you are using. Do not rely upon the charted location of a hazard and venture too close assuming that you will not be in danger.

For these reasons, you should consider marking

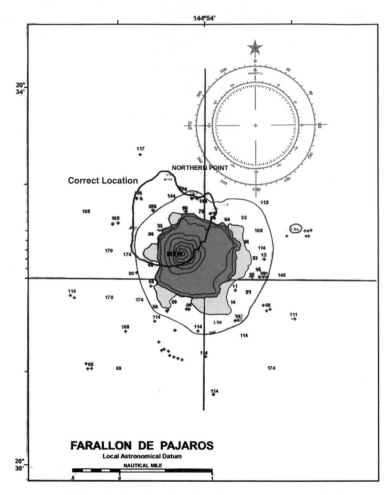

FIGURE 10-11. *Where Did We Put That Island? You can expect your GPS receiver to be more accurate than many charts now in use. Today, charts are updated using GPS data. The National Ocean Service has demonstrated how much charts can be in error with this chart of Farallon de Pajaros (Mariana Islands). Clearly, the entire island is charted more than half a nautical mile from its actual location.* (NOAA)

key features as waypoints in your GPS receiver as you pass them, and to compare these waypoint coordinates with the charts. In addition to buoys, you can mark hazards, such as rocks. If you use fixed landmarks to help you navigate around danger or into a harbor, you can mark the positions of these objects while on land with a handheld GPS unit. Usually the marked GPS positions will be your best reference for locating these features or buoys in the future. A number of groups and companies provide coordinates for objects and aids to navigation. These objects can move over time, or the originator of the data may be in error. Double-check all important waypoints that you use.

GPS is being used for all forms of transportation, including airplanes, trains, trucks, buses, and boats. These many users will continue to insist on accurate, reliable GPS performance. All-in-all GPS will be driving navigation for a long time to come. Happy boating!

The Future of GPS

Several government agencies are involved in further improvements to GPS. The FAA is looking for even greater accuracy for aircraft as they approach airports. To do this, they are implementing LAAS (Local Area Augmentation System), which will provide accuracies closer to 3 feet (1 m). Unfortunately, unlike WAAS, LAAS will offer no assistance to boaters. The local transmitters on the ground will transmit signals upward, line-of-sight to the aircraft. The FAA has little interest in providing similar signals near harbors for boaters.

The U.S. Air Force has issued contracts to refine the next generation of GPS satellites. Civil use continues to gain importance. As a result, the next generation is expected to add additional features, including a civil mode on the L2 frequency. Beyond that, there are plans to add an L5 frequency. One of the concerns expressed after the terrorist attacks in the United States on September 11, 2001, has been the vulnerability of GPS to unintentional and intentional jamming of the signals. So far, jamming of civil users has not been much of a concern. However, with the advent of greater reliance of commercial aircraft on GPS for navigation, the concern is elevated. The extra frequencies make it more difficult for either incidental or intentional jamming to cause a failure of the GPS navigation system. In addition, the extra fre-

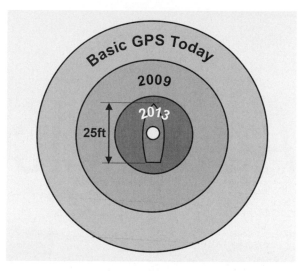

FIGURE 10-12. *Basic GPS Will Become More Accurate. Even without DGPS or WAAS, basic GPS will become more accurate with the addition of new frequencies in future generations of satellites and receivers.*

quencies permit greater processing to reduce the impact of atmospheric effects on the GPS measurement accuracy. Jamming should not be of any great concern to boaters; it is largely limited to line-of-sight. Aircraft at altitude can be seen from great distances; however, the visibility of a boat may be limited to a few miles on the sea. As a result, it is anticipated that a basic GPS receiver capable of receiving these frequencies will have improved accuracy performance. By about 2007, you may be able to achieve accuracy of 16 to 33 feet (5–10 m) with a basic GPS receiver without using WAAS or DGPS. By 2013, you can possibly expect accuracies of 3–16 feet (1–5 m) for basic GPS units with the addition of the L5 frequency. To take advantage of these new frequencies, you will need a GPS receiver that is equipped to receive them. Don't be concerned, however: boaters' L1-only GPS will still work.

Appendices

Appendix 1

Starting in the Simulator Mode

The Simulator mode provides an opportunity to practice with your GPS unit. A GPS device consists of two parts: the GPS receiver and the course computer. The receiver detects the presence of GPS signals and provides the resultant data to the course computer. The course computer converts the data into a set of coordinates based on the selected datum. It also calculates a significant amount of information of interest to the mariner such as speed, bearing, distance, crosstrack error, and velocity made good. In the Simulator mode, the GPS receiver is shut off. Instead a simulated position is provided to the course computer. The user has the opportunity to enter a course, route, or speed to simulate motion.

To get started with your GPS unit and with the Simulator, this appendix provides step-by-step instructions for the Simulator mode in a number of prominent GPS models. It is recommended that you practice with your GPS unit in the Simulator mode as one of the first steps in learning how to use it.

Garmin GPS 12, GPS 48

These GPS units are among the most popular sold to the consumer market. Each of these units shares a common button, screen, menu, and processing structure. Each has a 12-channel receiver, although there are some earlier versions of these models still in use that have 8-channel receivers.

To place these units into the Simulator mode:

- From any screen, as shown in figure A1-1, press the "Page" button until the Main Menu appears.

- On this screen, use the up-down cursor on the central four-way rocker switch to scroll down to the "System Setup" option and then press "Enter" to activate.

- On the resultant Setup Menu, scroll down to "System Setup" and press "Enter" again.

- This brings up the System Setup Menu. Scroll to the first category, "Mode" and press "Enter."

- This provides you with two choices: "Normal" and "Simulator." Scroll down over the "Simulator" field and press "Enter."

- You now are operating in the Simulator mode. Press "Page" to advance to the next screen, which should place you on the Satellite screen. From here, you can "Page" to any other screen to see the simulated operation of your GPS unit.

GPS12/48

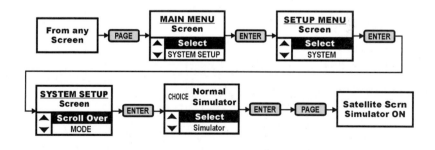

GPS76

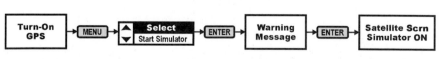

FIGURE A1-1. *Simulator Setup on Garmin Handheld GPS Receivers. The Simulator can be set up by following one of these flowcharts depending upon the model you use. The menu names and button actions are shown.*

Garmin GPS 76, GPSMAP 76, and GPSMAP 176

The newer GPS 76, GPSMAP 76, and GPSMAP 176 have a simpler method to access the Simulator. The easiest way to start is to shut off the GPS unit and restart it. Then:

- As shown in the bottom part of figure A1-1, after the initial disclaimer message, the GPS unit will go to the Satellite screen.

- Pressing "Menu" offers you an opportunity to scroll over "Start Simulator." Do so, and then press "Enter."

- Most units now show a warning message and ask you to press "Enter" again. You are now in the Simulator mode and located on the Satellite screen.

Magellan 320, 330M, 410, Meridian Marine, and Related Units

From any page, as shown in figure A1-2, you begin by pressing the "Menu" button. Then:

- From the choices offered, scroll down to select "Setup."

- Pressing "Enter" again offers you a set of choices, including "Simulator," which you access by scrolling down and pressing "Enter."

- This provides three choices as shown in the figure. For our current purposes, set the cursor over "Auto" and select. This enables simulated navigation on selected routes.

Lowrance GlobalMap 100, EagleMap

Lowrance owns the Eagle brand, so it is no surprise that the two brands share a common layout. Figure A1-3 shows the process for these models.

- To enter the Simulator mode, you begin by pressing "Menu" while viewing any screen.

- From the choices offered, select "Simulator Setup" and press "Enter."

- Select the choice "Simulator Off On" and scroll horizontally until "On" is highlighted.

- Then press "Enter" and you are now in the Simulator mode.

MAGELLAN

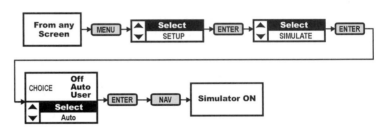

FIGURE A1-2. Simulator Setup on Magellan Handheld GPS Receivers.

LOWRANCE/EAGLE

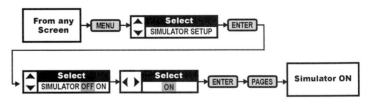

FIGURE A1-3. Simulator Setup on Lowrance/Eagle Handheld GPS Receivers.

Appendix 2

Button Configurations for Popular GPS Handhelds

Most GPS receivers are quite similar in their button configurations. All manufacturers compromise given the relatively small amount of space available to in-

stall controls. This leads to the somewhat complex menu structures used on each receiver. This appendix summarizes the buttons and their functions for a number of popular handheld GPS units. This book uses the Garmin GPS 12 as a baseline; however, most other units, even those from Garmin, have some differences.

The figures in this appendix list the primary functions on the left and identify the comparable button on each GPS unit to the right under the appropriate column.

Figure A2-1 details two Garmin units. The first is the baseline GPS 12, which is the same as the GPS 12XL and the GPS 48. To its right is the GPS 76, which is a newer design. The GPS 76 incorporates a "Menu" button which enables quicker function changes. It also replaces the "GoTo" with a "Nav" button that accesses the "GoTo," "Route," and "Track" functions. It incorporates two buttons for

GPS MODEL	GARMIN GPS12, GPS48	GARMIN GPS76, GPSMAP76
BUTTON LAYOUT / FUNCTIONS	GOTO, PAGE, MARK, QUIT, ENTER (cursor pad)	IN, OUT, NAV, PAGE, MENU, QUIT, ENTER (cursor pad)
POWER	⏻	⏻
BACKLIGHT	Press ⏻ with GPS on	Press ⏻ with GPS on
ENTER	ENTER	ENTER
QUIT	QUIT	QUIT
MENU	Press PAGE to Menu Screen	MENU
PAGE	PAGE	PAGE
GOTO	GoTo	Use NAV submenu
NAV	N/A	NAV
MARK	MARK	Press ENTER twice
MOB	Press GoTo twice	Press NAV twice
CURSOR	✛	✛
ZOOM	On Map Screen press ENTER to access submenu	IN OUT
COMMENTS	GPSMAP12 & GPS12CX have ZOOM IN/OUT buttons	NAV submenus GoTo/Route/Track

FIGURE A2-1. Button Structure for Garmin Handheld GPS Receivers. The common functions (left) and the buttons to access them are shown for the baseline GPS 12 and the GPS 76.

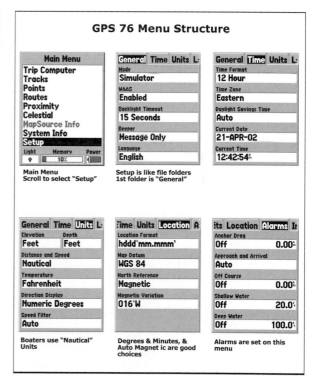

FIGURE A2-2. Menu Structure for Garmin GPS 76 Handheld Receiver. These menu screens for a Garmin GPS 76 are actual screenshots from the GPS receiver. The choices are representative of what will be found on most handhelds today.

GPS MODEL	MAGELLAN 320	MAGELLAN MAP 410
BUTTON LAYOUT / FUNCTION	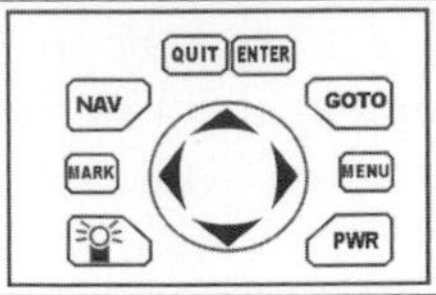 (button layout: QUIT, ENTER, NAV, GOTO, MARK, MENU, PWR)	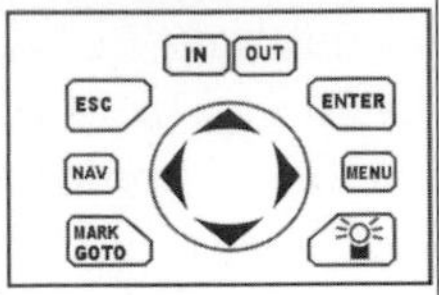 (button layout: IN, OUT, ESC, ENTER, NAV, MENU, MARK/GOTO)
POWER	PWR	(backlight icon)
BACKLIGHT	(backlight icon)	Press (backlight icon) with GPS on
ENTER	ENTER	ENTER
QUIT	QUIT	ESC
MENU	MENU	MENU
PAGE	Use NAV	Use NAV
GOTO	GoTo	GoTo
NAV	Used to access screens	Used to access screens
MARK	Press ENTER twice	Press GoTo twice
MOB	Press GoTo Select MOB ENTER	Press GoTo Select MOB ENTER
CURSOR	(cursor pad)	(cursor pad)
ZOOM	On Map Screen press (cursor pad) L or R to change scale	IN OUT
COMMENTS		

FIGURE A2-3. *Button Structure for Magellan Handheld GPS Receivers. The common functions (left) and the buttons to access them are shown for two types of Magellan handheld GPS units. The button names and functions are slightly different from those used by Garmin.*

GPS MODEL	LOWRANCE/EAGLE MAP	NOTES
BUTTON LAYOUT / FUNCTIONS	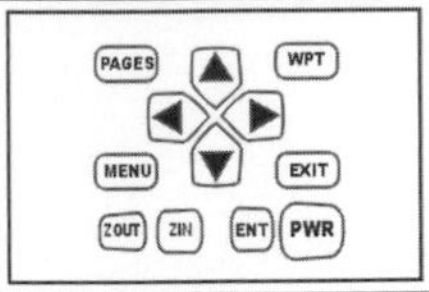 (button layout: PAGES, up arrow, WPT, left/right arrows, MENU, down arrow, EXIT, ZOUT, ZIN, ENT, PWR)	
POWER	PWR	
BACKLIGHT	Press PWR with GPS on	
ENTER	ENT	
QUIT	EXIT	
MENU	MENU	
PAGE	PAGES	
GOTO	Use MENU to submenu	
NAV	N/A	
MARK	Press WPT twice	
MOB	Press WPT twice	
CURSOR	(cursor pad)	
ZOOM	IN OUT	
COMMENTS	Use WPT to enter or edit waypoints	

FIGURE A2-4. *Button Structure for Lowrance and Eagle Handheld GPS Receivers. The common functions (left) and the buttons to access them are shown for Lowrance and Eagle handheld GPS units. The button names and functions are slightly different from those used by Garmin.*

zooming in and out. The GPSMAP 76 has an identical button structure to that of the GPS 76.

Figure A2-2 shows the GPS 76 menu structure, which is accessed by pressing the "Menu" button. This is an example of the extensive and easily accessible menu pages available on a recent-model GPS receiver. The menus are formed into a number of screens and identified by what appear to be tabs on a manila folder. You can scroll left or right to see additional tabs. Each screen is accessed by scrolling onto the appropriate folder tab, and then scrolling down to the item of interest. The Magellan and Lowrance units offer similar structures.

Figure A2-3 presents the button structures for two Magellan handheld GPS receivers, the 320 and the Map 410. Most other Magellan handhelds match one or the other of these two. Magellan uses the "Menu" button to perform the page scrolling function. The Meridian Marine and 400 series add a "Nav" button and two buttons for zooming in and out.

Figure A2-4 presents the Lowrance and Eagle handheld GPS unit button structure. Eagle is owned by Lowrance, and the two are identical.

Sample Exercise Using Waypoints and Routes

This exercise allows you to practice with your GPS receiver and compare your results with the correct answers. We will take a sample cruise on Buzzards Bay near Cape Cod in Massachusetts. To start, you'll set up your GPS unit, enter some sample waypoints, and then construct a route for your cruise using these waypoints.

Setting Up the GPS

Set up your GPS receiver as shown below. From the setup menu, locate the submenu for navigation (on the GPS 76, these are provided under two tabs: "Units" and "Location"). In order to obtain the proper results, your GPS will need to have settings that correspond with the following.

1. **Position (or Location) Format:** Set to degrees, minutes, and tenths of minutes (e.g., h ddd° mm.mmm′). This corresponds to the scales on the chart.

2. **Map Datum: WGS-84.** This corresponds to the chart we are using.

3. **Units (Distance and Speed):** Nautical Miles (nm) and Knots (kn). This permits us to use the latitude scale to measure nautical miles on our chart.

4. **Heading:** Set to Magnetic, Auto Variation (or manually set 016°W). This enables you to relate directly to your compass. Remember that you need to use the inner compass rose on the chart for magnetic directions.

To begin, place your GPS unit in the Simulator mode, using the instructions in appendix 1. If your unit differs from these, consult your manual.

Next, look at the section of a chart for Buzzards Bay near Cape Cod shown in figure A3-1. You will enter three waypoints into the GPS unit giving them easily identifiable and separable names of ZZ1, ZZ2, and ZZ3. (After you have completed the exercise, you will want to remove these three waypoints.) Consult figures 4-17, 4-18, and 4-19 as a refresher on how to enter waypoints. You will need to access your waypoint screen. You can do this following the procedures outlined in chapter 4 in the Entering Waypoints into Your GPS Receiver section. One of the simpler ways to do that is to scroll the cursor on the Map screen. On most GPS models, the coordinates of the cursor position are indicated on the screen. You can scroll to coordinates near those indicated and press "Enter" to get to the corresponding Waypoint screen. While on that screen, you can edit the name and the precise coordinates to match those for the exercise.

As with planning a cruise, you first identify what features you plan to assign to waypoints. On the sample chart shown in figure A3-1, locate the green buoy directly to the west of the channel through Woods Hole. This buoy is identified as G "13" on the chart. The "G" signifies that it is green, and the "13" signifies the number painted on the buoy. Using the "Red-Right-Returning" rule, the green buoy should be kept to your left in returning from sea. You know it is a buoy because it is marked on the chart by a diamond shape with one point intersecting a small circle. Its location is indicated by the center of the circle. You can tell that this buoy is lighted because there is a larger circle around the smaller circle. On the chart, this larger circle is magenta in color. The diamond is green. The buoy's light pattern is described in the line below the buoy ID as "Fl G 4s." This means that at night the buoy displays a green light that flashes at four-second intervals. The last line, "BELL," means that the buoy has a bell to produce a sound.

Entering Sample Waypoints

Note that many current charts provide the coordinates for key aids to navigation. In our current example, we have annotated the coordinates of the selected waypoints. Most NOAA charts do not provide this in-

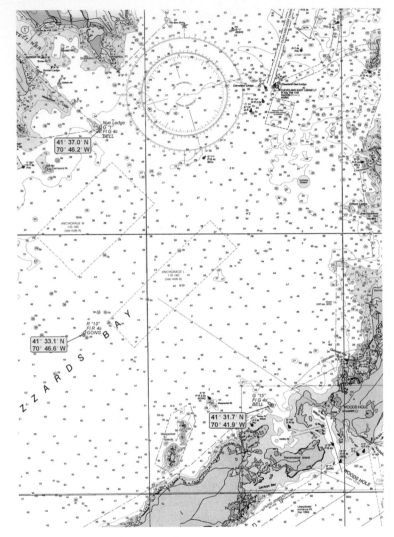

FIGURE A3-1. *Chart Section for Simulated Cruise. This is a section scanned from a NOAA chart for Buzzards Bay, Massachusetts. Starting from Woods Hole, you will use three buoys to enter as waypoints. The coordinates for each buoy are shown.*

tude) scale from the grid line parallel to the scale.

- The point on the scale under the divider marks the minutes and tenths of latitude. Degrees must be read from the scale legend. Make sure you are counting the scale marks in the proper direction. Similarly, longitude is measured from a horizontal grid line. In the Northern Hemisphere, latitude increases upward, and longitude increases westward.

The Selected Waypoints

The first step is to identify the waypoints that will be used. In this example, there are three waypoints that you will use, and they are labeled as follows.

1. We will designate the first buoy waypoint ZZ1.

2. The second point is the buoy Flashing Red, 4-second interval, number 10, with a gong ("Fl R 4s GONG") to the west northwest of the first buoy. We will call this waypoint ZZ2.

3. The third waypoint is Flashing Green, 4-second interval, number 1, with a bell ("FL G 4s BELL") marking Nye Ledge to the north. We will call this waypoint ZZ3.

To summarize, the waypoints and their coordinates are as follows.

formation, but many commercially available chart books provide coordinates and preprinted preferred courses with bearings and distances listed.

- If the coordinates are not given, you must measure to the point from the nearest horizontal grid line using a pair of dividers (see figure 4-2 in chapter 4).

- You then transcribe the same distance using the divider setting along the left or right vertical (lati-

ZZ1	latitude	41°31.7′ N
	longitude	70°41.9′ W
ZZ2	latitude	41°33.1′ N
	longitude	70°46.6′ W
ZZ3	latitude	41°37.0′ N
	longitude	70°46.2′ W

To enter these waypoints into the GPS receiver, first access the Waypoint screen, as shown in figure A3-2 for the Garmin GPS 76.

- Go to the Main Menu (or Navigation Menu on some units).

- Scroll down to highlight "Waypoint" or "Point" and press "Enter." This will bring up the Waypoint screen.

- On the Waypoint screen, scroll down to highlight the waypoint name field and press "Enter."

- Now only the leftmost character in the field will be highlighted. Scroll up (or down) until the character "Z" appears.

- Now move the cursor to the right to highlight the next character and repeat.

- Once the name field shows "ZZ1" you can press

"Enter" to return the highlight to the full name. This is your indication that you can scroll to the next field.

On most GPS units, the waypoint coordinates come next.

- Repeating the same process used for the name field, press "Enter" while the coordinates field is highlighted.

- The F first character in the coordinates field should now be highlighted.

- Latitude will be entered first, followed by longitude.

- Many GPS units place the N-S-E-W designations first, followed by the value in degrees, minutes, and tenths of minutes.

- Enter the appropriate coordinates from the previous table, character by character until both the latitude and longitude have been entered.

- Press "Enter" again to highlight the entire coordinates field. You can now scroll down to another field.

- Most GPS units offer a notes field wherein you can input the features of the waypoint or other data. We will skip this field for now.

- Scroll over the field that indicates "OK" or "Save" and press "Enter."

- The waypoint is stored in the GPS receiver with the name "ZZ1."

You will now enter the information for waypoints ZZ2 and ZZ3 by repeating the preceding steps. After finishing, you can check on your stored waypoints by selecting "Waypoints" from the Main Menu and pressing "Enter." This will display your entire list of stored waypoints. Scroll up or down until you have highlighted "ZZ1" and press "Enter." The Waypoint screen will come up with the data that you have entered.

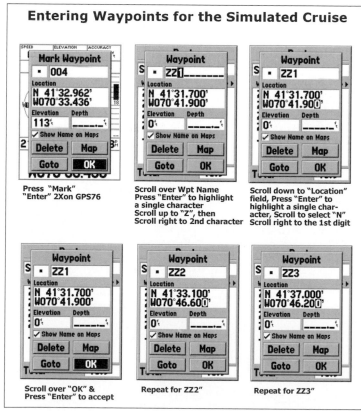

Entering Waypoints for the Simulated Cruise

Press "Mark" "Enter" 2Xon GPS76

Scroll over Wpt Name Press "Enter" to highlight a single character Scroll up to "Z", then Scroll right to 2nd character

Scroll down to "Location" field, Press "Enter" to highlight a single character, Scroll to select "N" Scroll right to the 1st digit

Scroll over "OK" & Press "Enter" to accept

Repeat for ZZ2"

Repeat for ZZ3"

FIGURE A3-2. *The Process of Entering the Selected Waypoints. Using a Garmin GPS 76, you access the Route Menu and enter the waypoints as illustrated.*

Entering a Route

Now that the three waypoints are stored in your GPS unit, you can construct a route.

- The particular route that we are planning begins at ZZ1, goes to ZZ2, then ZZ3, and then returns to ZZ1, as shown in figure A3-3.

- To store a route, you go to the Main Menu and locate the "Route" option. This is shown for the GPS 76 in figure A3-4. Each page corresponds to the following step-by-step instructions.

- Pressing "Enter" while highlighting the "Route" option brings up a list of routes stored in the GPS unit. To make a new route, we need to locate the Route screen. On most GPS units, go to the Main Menu, scroll down to highlight the selection called "Routes," and press "Enter."

- Once the Route screen has been located, scroll to the first waypoint field at the top left of the open list.

- When you press "Enter," the first character is highlighted. In this case, you do not need to enter the entire name. After the first character (in this case "Z") is entered, the first stored waypoint name beginning with that character is shown on the screen. This may not be the waypoint that you want. If not, scroll right to the next character and scroll up or down to change it to the one that you want. The first waypoint name with these two characters now will appear on the line. Still, this may not be the one that you want. In this

case, we used "ZZ" for the first two characters, so we will need to scroll to the third character field and scroll to the proper number.

- Once the correct waypoint name appears in the field ("ZZ1"), press "Enter" and scroll down to the field for the second waypoint in your route.

- Repeat the process for ZZ2, ZZ3, and finally ZZ1 again.

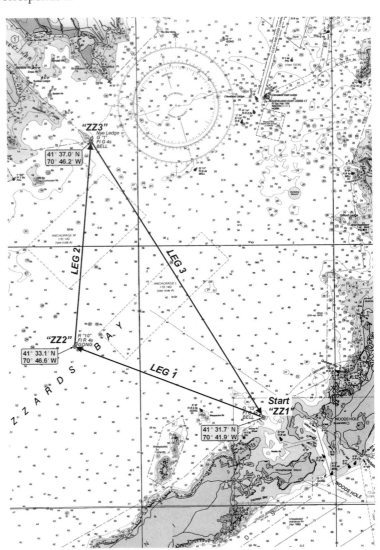

FIGURE A3-3. Chart Section with Simulated Cruise Plotted. The chart section for Buzzards Bay has been annotated with a plot of the intended cruise.

FIGURE A3-4. *Defining the Route for the Simulated Cruise. Using a GPS 76, you access the Route Menu, name your new route, and sequentially enter the waypoints as shown. Many GPS models will assign the names of the first and last waypoints as the name of the route. This can be more meaningful than a made-up name, and it tells you which way the route is being navigated—forward or inverted.*

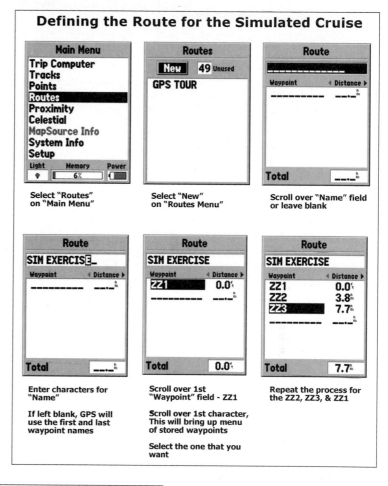

FIGURE A3-5. *Active Route Data Available. The GPS receiver computes various useful data regarding the route, including total distance, and the course and distance for each leg.*

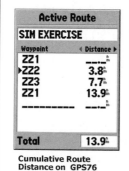

The sample route is summarized as follows.

	Depart:	Woods Hole (ZZ1)
1st Leg	Go to:	Center of Buzzards Bay (ZZ2)
2nd Leg	Go to:	Nye Ledge (ZZ3)
3rd Leg	Go to:	Woods Hole (ZZ1)

The Route screen will show the bearings and distances between the waypoints for each leg of the route. Compare what your GPS receiver indicates with the following. (On the GPS 76, the Route screen provides several columns of data that can be accessed by pressing the right or left cursor key, as shown in fig. A3-5.)

		Course	Distance	Total Distance
1st Leg	ZZ1–ZZ2	308°	3.8 nm	3.8 nm
2nd Leg	ZZ2–ZZ3	020°	3.9 nm	7.7 nm
3rd Leg	ZZ3–ZZ1	165°	6.2 nm	13.9 nm

If your Route screen indicates these course directions and distances, you have succeeded in using the course computer part of your GPS receiver. If there are differences, go back and check to make sure that you have properly entered the waypoint coordinates.

You can see from this exercise that the GPS is a powerful course computer. You no longer need to measure bearings and distances on your chart. The GPS does this for you once you have entered the waypoint coordinates and planned a route.

Simulating the Route

Once you have entered the route, you can simulate sailing this course. To do this, you need to put the Simulator into an active mode.

Setting Up the Route Simulation

The following instructions are to set up the GPS 12.

- Set the unit to the Simulator mode and then activate the route using the Main Menu and Route screen.

- Go to the Position screen. On this screen, you can set the position to that of the first waypoint by scrolling down using the cursor key until the coordinates field is highlighted. By pressing "Enter" you will have the first character highlighted, and you can enter the desired coordinates to start your simulation. In this case, you will enter the coordinates of ZZ1, and press "Enter" again.

- On that same screen, set the speed manually by scrolling over "Speed," pressing "Enter," and scrolling the individual characters to the desired simulated speed.

- As soon as you press "Enter" again, you will be navigating the simulated route.

To set up the GPS 76:

- Go to the Satellite screen.

- Set the unit into the Simulator mode by pressing the "Menu" button, selecting "Start Simulator," and then pressing "Enter."

- Set the initial position by pressing "Menu" and selecting "New Location" as shown in figure A3-6, frame (a).

- Pressing "Enter" gives you two choices, select "Use Map" as shown in (b).

- This will present you with the Map screen and a title "New Location," as shown in (c).

- Scroll to the desired waypoint (ZZ1), which will then be highlighted as shown in (d).

- You may need to zoom out to get near the desired location and then zoom in to refine the selection. Notice on (d) that "ZZ1" appears in a box on the page, indicating that you have selected that waypoint.

- By pressing "Enter," you will be returned to the Satellite screen (e), which now indicates the correct coordinates for ZZ1 as your current location.

- Now, press the "Nav" button, and then select "Navigate Route," as shown in (f).

- This brings up a list of stored routes. We named this exercise "SIM EXERCISE" (which stands for simulated exercise) when we created the route, so we will select that choice as shown in (g). Note: If you did not name the route, most GPS models will name it according to the first and last waypoints in the route (ZZ1–ZZ1 in this case).

- This brings up the Active Route screen as shown in (h). The triangle on the left side of the page indicates the "active to" waypoint as ZZ2.

- If we page to the Highway screen you will see something similar to (i).

- In this example, we are not moving and we are not pointed at ZZ2, as shown in (i), but we can see the legs of our route on the Highway screen.

Running the Simulated Route

- You initiate navigation of the route by pressing the cursor upward while on the Highway screen or the Compass screen. Each time you press upward on the cursor, the speed will increase by 10 knots. It helps to have speed as one of the data fields on whichever screen you are using to monitor the speed setting—see frame (a) of figure A3-7.

- You are now navigating the simulated route. Your screen now will appear as in frame (b).

- As you proceed along the first leg of the route, the Highway screen will show your progress, as indicated in frame (c). You are on course and heading straight for ZZ2 at a speed of 40 knots; your current distance is 2.9 nautical miles. The Map screen is shown in frame (d) for a short time later (note that the distance to ZZ2 is now 2.2 nm). The Compass screen is shown in frame (e) for a short time later. The black arrow (the direction in

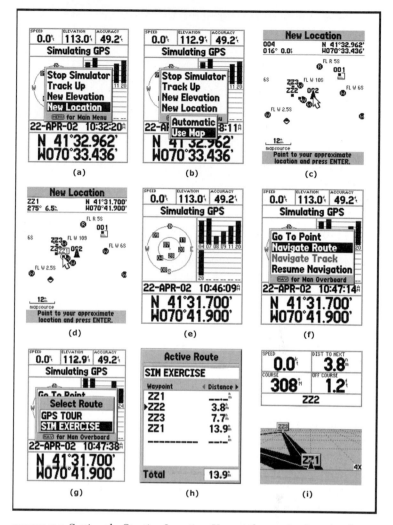

FIGURE A3-6. Setting the Starting Location. You set the starting location for the cruise (a), using the map option (b), on the map (c) and (d), which results in the starting coordinates on the Satellite screen (e). You set the Simulator to activate the selected route (f) and (g). The Active route shows that you are about to cruise on the first leg (h). The initial Highway screen shows you pointing in a northerly arbitrary direction (i), since you are not yet moving.

which you must go) aligns with the gray line at the top, indicating that you're on course. The compass rose shows that you are headed in a direction of 308°. The VMG data field indicates 40 knots, the same as your speed, indicating that you're heading directly for ZZ2.

- Frame (f) shows what would happen if you were to veer off course: the black arrow indicates that you need to steer left to 304° and that you are now headed almost to magnetic north. Your VMG is now only 22 knots, reflecting that you are no longer headed directly toward ZZ2. Off-course simulation is presented in the next section.

- In figure A3-8, you have reset the simulation and restarted at ZZ1. In the left frame, you are heading directly toward ZZ2 shortly after starting the simulated route at a speed of 30 knots. Once the GPS has determined that you have arrived at ZZ2, it changes course for ZZ3, as shown in the center frame. Here you can see that the GPS switched to the second leg a bit too early, and you are 267 feet (81.4 m) to starboard (right) of your intended course line. The higher zoom level (16x) in the center frame magnifies this effect. This demonstrates the arrival circle issue discussed in chapter 6. In the right frame of figure A3-8, you are on the third and final leg, heading back to ZZ1.

Deviating from the Route

It is also possible to deviate from our set route.

- Start the simulation again on the Highway screen, as shown in the left and center frames of figure A3-8.

- As you progress along the first leg, the Map screen will appear as shown in frame (d) of figure A3-7.

- Page to the Compass screen and you will see that you are on course, as shown in frame (e) of figure A3-7. The black arrow indicates the bearing to the waypoint while the gray bar indicates the current course over ground.

- You can alter your course on the GPS 76 by pressing the cursor key to the right (or left) on either the Compass or Highway screens. On the GPS 12, you can set the course on the Position screen. On other models, you may need to access

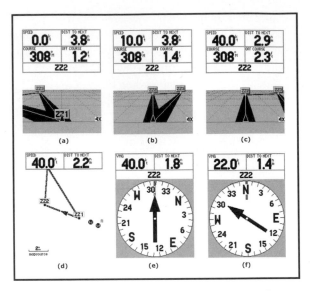

FIGURE A3-7. *Simulating the Actual Cruise—Leg 1. Before starting, your Highway screen (a) is the same as (i) in the previous figure. As soon as you apply some speed, the GPS receiver begins navigating on leg 1 to ZZ2 (b). As you progress along leg 1, the boat moves on the highway (c). The equivalent Map screen (d) and Compass screen (e) are shown. If you were to venture off course sharply to the right, your Compass screen would appear as in (f).*

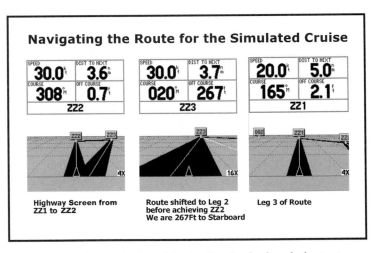

FIGURE A3-8. *Simulating the Actual Cruise. Starting back at the beginning, the three Highway screen shots show each leg of the cruise. Notice that the GPS receiver shifted the course to leg 2 before it actually reached the first waypoint, ZZ2. This can be demonstrated by your position to the right of the highway centerline in the center frame.*

simulated motion (speed and course) on one of the setup menus.

- If you press the cursor key to the right while on this page you can change course.

- In frame (f) of figure A3-7, you have turned to the north. After some time along this new course, as shown in frame (a) of figure A3-9, we see that you're heading toward ZZ3 rather than ZZ2 as indicated by the route. The corresponding Map screen is shown in frame (b) of figure A3-9. ZZ2 is now abeam to port.

- In frame (c) of figure A3-9, the Compass screen indicates a short time later that you are beyond abeam of ZZ2, and the VMG is negative. This indicates that you actually are moving farther away from your selected active waypoint, ZZ2.

- If you decide to return to your original route and turn toward ZZ2, your Compass screen will show that you again are on the proper bearing for ZZ2 at 229°, as shown in (d). Note that the GPS cannot tell you if this path is safe. You need to refer to the chart for that information.

- A short time later, the corresponding Highway screen shows that you indeed are heading toward ZZ2, as shown in (e).

- Once you have reached ZZ2, the simulator automatically takes over again and switches your course toward ZZ3, as originally intended.

These examples provide a sense of how the GPS receiver functions, the corresponding screens, and what they tell you. In the absence of a chart on a chartplotter, the Highway screen is perhaps one of the most meaningful for navigation. Its graphic represen-

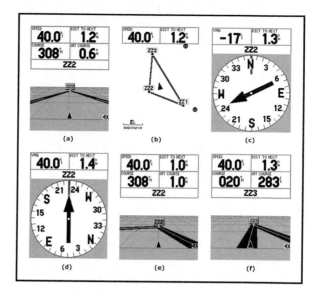

FIGURE A3-9. *Simulating a Deviation from the Route. Instead of following leg 1 all the way to ZZ2, you decided to change course toward ZZ3 at mid-leg to see what would happen. After a short time, you find yourself in the middle of the triangular route looking at ZZ3 dead ahead (a). On the Map screen, you can see your relative location (b). The Compass screen (c) indicates that your active waypoint is to your port and you actually are moving away from the waypoint (negative VMG). You turn toward your waypoint using the Compass screen (d). The Highway screen shows you returning to the active waypoint (e). After you achieve the waypoint, the GPS simulates returning you to your route (f).*

tation provides a good sense of your situation without deep concentration on the display. In addition to the waypoints shown in this example, other waypoints, such as hazards that you enter into the GPS receiver, also will show on the Highway screen, alerting you to areas of concern.

Remember, this is only an exercise—*never navigate in the Simulator mode!*

Glossary

Terms in italic are defined elsewhere in the glossary.

2-D mode. A two-dimensional *position fix* that includes only horizontal *coordinates* (*latitude* and *longitude*). It requires adequate signals from a minimum of three visible satellites.

3-D mode. A three-dimensional *position fix* that includes horizontal *coordinates* (*latitude* and *longitude*) plus *elevation*. It requires adequate signals from a minimum of four visible satellites.

accuracy. The level of match between the GPS-measured *position*, time, and/or velocity and its true position, time, and/or velocity. GPS system accuracy is usually stated as a statistical measure of system error, characterized by three measurements:

> **predictable accuracy.** The anticipated accuracy of a radionavigation system's position solution as compared with the corresponding charted solution. The position information for both must be based upon the same geodetic datum.

> **repeatable accuracy.** The accuracy with which a user can return to a *position* using the previously measured *coordinates* on the same navigation system.

> **relative accuracy.** The accuracy with which a user can measure *position* relative to that of another device or reference at the same time.

acquisition time. Amount of time required for a GPS unit to lock onto three satellites to provide a 2-D *fix* of present *position*.

active antenna. An antenna that amplifies the GPS satellite signal before it sends it to the receiver.

active leg. The segment of a *route* currently being traveled starting at the active "from" *waypoint* and traveling to the active "to" waypoint.

alarm radius. The distance set from a proximity (or danger) *waypoint*, or on an *anchor watch* location for an alarm. The distance is equivalent to the radius of a circle with that point at its center. If the GPS records entry into a *distance* within this radius for a proximity waypoint, if set, an alarm will sound and a note will be displayed on the screen.

almanac data. Information transmitted by each satellite on the orbits and state (health) of the entire constellation. Almanac data allow a GPS receiver to acquire satellites rapidly as soon as it is turned on.

analog. An indication that is presented on a continuous scale as opposed to digits.

anchor watch. This is an alarm function within some GPS models. A radius can be set from a given location at anchor. If the boat should move beyond this set limit, an alarm will sound indicating the potential that the anchor is dragging and a note will be displayed on the screen. See also *alarm radius*.

approaching waypoint. This is an alarm function available on many GPS models. Often this *distance* and an alarm can be set by the user. Whenever the GPS *position* indicates that the boat has come within that distance, an alarm will sound briefly and a note will appear on the screen.

ARCS (Admiralty Raster Chart Service). The United Kingdom Hydrographic Office produces approximately 2,800 digital raster charts (ARCS) with extensive coverage of shipping lanes. These charts are based on the British Admiralty paper charts, long respected for international navigation. Chart coverage is excellent for northwestern Europe, Scandinavia, Africa, the Mediterranean, the Caribbean, and the North American East Coast. Chart services are available for both commercial and leisure boaters. A number of navigation programs, including MaxSea and SeaPro 2000, are certified to accept these charts.

arrival radius. This is the *distance* from the precise *waypoint* location, that the GPS uses to recognize that the waypoint has been reached. Once this occurs, the GPS will indicate the next *leg* in an active route and provide steering directions for that leg.

atomic clock. A precise clock that operates using the elements cesium or rubidium. A cesium clock has an error rate of one second per million years. GPS satellites contain multiple cesium and rubidium clocks.

azimuth. The horizontal direction from one point on the Earth to another point, measured clockwise in degrees (0–360) from a vertical reference line (generally *true north* or *magnetic north*). An azimuth is more commonly known as a "*bearing.*"

beacon. A beacon, sometimes called a "nondirectional beacon," is a stationary transmitter that emits signals in all directions. In *Differential GPS* (*DGPS*), the beacon transmitter broadcasts correction data to nearby GPS receivers, which allows the receivers to achieve greater accuracy.

bandwidth. The range of frequencies in a signal.

bearing (BRG). The direction (in degrees) from your present *position* to the next *waypoint*, measured clockwise from either *true north* or *magnetic north*.

Block I, II, IIR, IIF satellites. The sequential generations of GPS satellites: Block I was the prototype version of the GPS satellites first launched in 1978 for testing; Block II satellites were the first operational satellites, and 24 Block II satellites formed the fully operational GPS constellation, achieved by 1995; Block IIR consists of replenishment satellites; and Block IIF satellites will make up the next series generation of GPS satellites. Block III satellites are on the drawing board. Each block adds new features.

carrier. The base frequency of a modulated signal that is radiated from the GPS satellites. The current frequencies are identified as *L1* (1,572.42 MHz) and *L2* (1,227.60 MHz).

cartography. The art or technique of making maps or charts. Many GPS receivers have detailed mapping, or cartography, capabilities.

CEP (Circle Error Probable). CEP defines the radius of a circle inside which there is a 50 percent probability that the actual *position* reported by the GPS will be located. Also known as *Circle Error Probability*.

channel. A channel of a GPS unit represents the receiver and associated circuitry necessary to receive the signal from a single GPS satellite.

chart chips. Chart cartography used in most *chartplotters* is provided by removable modules, usually referred to as chart chips. Usually, these chips store vectorized versions of the charts for a region defined by its manufacturer. Typically, only one brand and type of chart chip can be used in any given chartplotter.

chartplotter. A display and processing device that overlays sensor data, such as provided by a GPS, onto a chart. Many chartplotters incorporate internal GPS receivers into the same unit. Others are designed to accept inputs from external sensors, including GPS, *Loran-C*, radar, and depth sounders.

circle of position (COP). A circle on the surface of the Earth surrounding a known object at a fixed distance (radius). You know your position to be somewhere on that circle within the limits of the accuracy of the distance measurement.

clock error. Clock error is the amount by which the internal clock in an electronic device differs from the standard. In the case of GPS, the satellites, while having very precise *atomic clocks*, do drift and need to be adjusted. GPS receivers use crystal-controlled clocks that, although as accurate as good *digital* watches, are inadequate for GPS position measurements. The needed *accuracy* is derived from the received satellite signals.

coarse/acquisition (C/A) code. The standard positioning signal the GPS satellite transmits to the civilian user. It contains the information the GPS receiver uses to fix its *position* and time. This code is a sequence of 1,023 pseudorandom binary biphase modulations on the GPS carrier at a chipping rate of 1,023 MHz, thus having a code repetition period of 1 millisecond. The code was selected to provide good acquisition properties. The C/A code is also known as the "civil code."

cold start. The process of powering up a GPS receiver for the first time or at an entirely new location. The receiver searches out and locks onto the satellites automatically, without the benefit of *initialization* cuing from the operator. This procedure is slower and may require several minutes for initial satellite acquisition. Many newer GPS models assist the user by prompting the selection of a starting point, such as a state or geographic region.

compass card. Typically, instead of a needle, most marine compasses use a compass card that rotates within a fluid to indicate *magnetic north*. These cards are calibrated in degrees and cardinal points to facilitate setting and reading a *course* or direction.

control segment. A worldwide network of GPS *monitor stations* and control stations that maintain the accuracy of satellite positions and their clocks.

Cooperative Charting Program. NOAA maintains this program in cooperation with the U.S. Power Squadrons and others such as the U.S. Coast Guard Auxiliary in order to collect data regarding charted or uncharted objects that should be added or corrected on charts. The supporting organizations supply the required information on the appropriate forms which NOAA uses in updating its charts.

coordinates. A set of numbers that represents a precise location anywhere on Earth. Usually stated as a *latitude* and a *longitude* for maritime applications.

Coordinated Universal Time (UTC). Replaced Greenwich Mean Time (GMT) as the world standard for time in 1986. It is based on atomic measurements rather than the rotation of the Earth. Greenwich Mean Time (GMT) is still the standard time zone for the *prime meridian* (zero *longitude*) near Greenwich, England. Another term, UT (Universal Time) is used by astronomers and is based on the actual rotation of the Earth, which is not uniform from day to day. On average, UTC and UT are nearly the same. GPS uses UTC.

course. The direction from the starting *waypoint* or location to the destination waypoint, measured clockwise (in degrees) from *true north* or *magnetic north*.

course deviation indicator (CDI). A technique for displaying the distance and direction of *crosstrack* *error* (XTE or XTK). Simply stated, CDI is the display of the amount of lateral (port or starboard) deviation of the current location from the intended course.

course made good (CMG). The *bearing* from the "active from" *waypoint* (your starting point) to your present *position*, independent of the path taken to arrive at the current position.

course over ground (COG). Direction of movement relative to the Earth (ground), as differentiated from course through the water.

course plotter. A course plotter is a template or device used by navigators to measure *course* angles and to plot course lines on a chart. Typically, course plotters are made of clear or frosted plastic and have a compass rose and other calibrating marks printed on them.

course up. The orientation of a display (e.g., radar or *chartplotter*) such that the *course over ground* of the boat is on top of the screen.

course to steer. The *heading* you need to maintain in order to reach a destination.

crosstrack error (XTE/XTK). The lateral *distance* in either direction (port or starboard) you are off the desired *course*.

danger bearing. A danger *bearing* is one predetermined by the navigator and used to define a region within which danger may be present. Usually, the danger bearing is drawn from a known and visible landmark across the edge of the region to be avoided. The helmsman, by careful attention to the bearing to the landmark ensures that he never ventures past that bearing designated as a danger bearing. In addition to a bearing angle, the danger bearing must designate whether the actual bearing maintained by the helmsman must be NLT or NGT (not-less-than or not-greater-than) the listed number for safe passage.

datum. A reference to which measurements are related, such as the North American Datum 1983 (NAD-83) and the World Geodetic System 1984 (WGS-84). *Latitude* and *longitude* lines on maps are referenced to a specific map datum. Generally, the terms "datum" and "*grid*" are merged on a GPS receiver. Technically, a datum is the reference from which the grid is developed. The grid is the mathematical model by which parallel lines, such as latitude and longitude, are fitted on a flat representation of the Earth's surface, using the datum as the reference. Since the Earth is not a perfect sphere, the specific coordinates are dependent upon a good mathematical match to your current location. The map datum for a GPS

receiver needs to match the datum listed on the corresponding paper or electronic chart.

dead reckoning (DR). The process of navigating from a known location using only direction, speed, and time to derive current position. Dead-reckoning navigation is based on the formula Distance (nautical miles) = Speed (knots) x Time (hours).

desired track (DTK/TRK). The *course* (based on *true north* or *magnetic north*) between the "active from" and "active to" *waypoints*.

deviation. Deviation is a term associated with a magnetic compass. On the boat, the magnetic compass is affected by local objects such as engines, wires, structures, and others. The difference between the actual magnetic direction and the compass is called "deviation" and it is stated separately for each direction (typically in 15° increments). The compass usually can be compensated for many of these errors. The remaining error is printed as a deviation table that, if the remaining number is significant, must be applied to the compass reading to adjust for these errors.

Differential Global Positioning System (DGPS). A technique used to improve positioning or navigation *accuracy*. DGPS first determines the positioning error at a known fixed location and subsequently transmits corresponding corrections to other GPS receivers. The local GPS receiver applies the corrections to each of the identified satellites in order to improve local accuracy. DGPS reduces the effects of *Selective Availability*, propagation delay, etc., and can improve position accuracy to less than 33 feet (10 m).

digital. Generally, information is expressed, stored, and transmitted by either *analog* or digital means. In digital form, information is seen in a binary state as either a one or a zero, a plus or a minus. Computers use digital technology for most actions.

digital selective calling (DSC). DSC is a *digital* channel dedicated to VHF channel 70. Using a DSC-enabled radio, the operator can signal selectively to another radio, or globally to all others. In the event of an emergency, the DSC radio, at the press of a button, automatically transmits a distress-coded digital signal to all other radios along with its coordinates which are obtained from a connected GPS unit. The user must register the radio with the FCC in order to have the boat information associated with the radio.

dilution of precision (DOP). A description of the purely geometrical contribution to the uncertainty in a *position fix*. Standard terms for the GPS application are *GDOP* (geometric—three position coordinates plus clock offset in the solution), *PDOP* (position—three coordinates), HDOP (horizontal—two horizontal coordinates), VDOP (vertical—height only), and TDOP (time—clock offset only).

distance. The length (in feet, meters, miles, etc.) between two *waypoints* or from your current *position* to a destination waypoint. This length can be measured in straight-line *(rhumb-line)* or great-circle (over the Earth) terms. GPS normally uses great-circle calculations for distance and *desired track*.

distance off. The navigator can use a predetermined value of *distance* from a designated landmark or *waypoint* to assist in safe navigation. This is similar to the *danger bearing*; however, the region defined by distance off describes a circular arc. If an arc is drawn on a chart using a drawing compass with the waypoint as its center and a collection of dangerous objects are included within the radius, the distance off can by used to stay away from that region. Alternatively, distance off can be used with a single waypoint along with a plotted *bearing* to mark current *position*, or used with two or more landmarks with the intersection of the distance off arcs indicating the current location.

distance root mean square (drms). A measure of GPS *accuracy*, the *root-mean-square* value of the distances from the true location point of the *position fixes* for a collection of measurements. As typically used in GPS positioning, 2 drms is the radius of a circle that contains at least 95 percent of all possible *fixes* that can be obtained with a GPS receiver at a fixed location.

distance value. This is the numeric value of a *distance* expressed in *nautical miles*, feet, meters, or other linear measure.

DoD. The U.S. Department of Defense. The DoD manages and controls the *global positioning system (GPS)*.

Electronic Charting Display Information System (ECDIS). A system based on standards established by the International Hydrographic Organization with sufficient precision that commercial navigation can be accomplished without the aid of paper charts.

electronic navigation chart (ENC). An ENC is a *vector chart* complying with standard *S-57* of the International Hydrographic Organization. It is sufficient for navigation with an *ECDIS*, and use of one on commercial ships removes the requirement for backup paper charts.

elevation. The distance above or below *mean sea level*. Mathematically, the vertical distance above the *geoid*.

ellipsoid. A geometric surface whose plane sections are either ellipses or circles.

ephemeris. A list of the precise *positions* or locations of the GPS satellites as a function of time. Available as "broadcast ephemeris" or as postprocessed "precise ephemeris."

estimated position error. A measurement of horizontal *position error* in feet or meters based upon a variety of factors, including *dilution of precision (DOP)* and satellite signal quality.

estimated time of arrival (ETA). The projected time of day of arrival at a destination based on current speed and course.

estimated time en route (ETE). The time remaining to destination based upon current speed and course.

fix. Your known position on the surface of the Earth based on a quality reading from a GPS receiver, or the intersection of any of the following based on simultaneous observations: two or more *lines of position* separated by no less than 45° in angle; a line of position and a *circle of position* wherein the angle between the line and the tangent to the circle at the intersection is separated by no less than 45° in angle; two intersecting circles of position with tangents at the intersection separated by no less than 45° in angle.

fluxgate compass. An electronic device used to measure magnetic direction. It employs multiple coils of wires to compare the effects of the magnetic field on each coil. The differences can be related to the Earth's magnetic field. Fluxgate compasses are subject to the same onboard influences as a mechanical compass; however, internal electronics are employed to automatically calibrate the fluxgate compass to a high degree of *accuracy*. Accuracies of 0.5 to 1.0° are typical for these devices.

form factor. This term is used to describe the way a device is constructed, such as its shape.

frequency band. A particular range of frequencies. The GPS receiver transmits in what is referred to as the "*L-band.*"

frequency spectrum. The distribution of signal amplitudes as a function of frequency.

GARMN (or GRMN) protocol. Garmin uses a proprietary protocol for communicating with its GPS models. The protocol is a predetermined set of standards for signal levels, signaling characteristics, and codes for specific information. Many software suppliers have designed their products to interface directly with Garmin GPS devices using the Garmin protocol. Others, in addition to Garmin, use *NMEA 0183* for the same function.

geodesy. The science related to the determination of the size and shape of the Earth (*geoid*) by direct measurements.

geodetic datum. A mathematical model designed to best fit part or all of the *geoid*. It is defined by an *ellipsoid* and the relationship between the ellipsoid and a point on the topographic surface established as the origin of *datum*.

geographic information system (GIS). A computer system or *software* capable of assembling, storing, manipulating, and displaying geographically referenced information (i.e., data identified according to location). In practical use, GIS often refers to the computer system and software, as well as the data-collection equipment, personnel, and actual data.

geometric dilution of precision (GDOP). Geometric *dilution of precision* is the broadest form of DOP. It represents the amount by which the inherent *accuracy* of GPS is degraded for a specific geometry of satellites. At a value of 1, there is no dilution. At a value of 2, the accuracy is degraded by a factor of two. Other forms of DOP include HDOP (horizontal dilution of precision) for only the horizontal effects, and VDOP (vertical dilution of precision) for the vertical effects. Typically, HDOP is of the greatest importance to boaters. HDOP and VDOP generally have different values with HDOP being the lower of the two.

geosynchronous orbit. A specific satellite orbit at the same rotational speed as the Earth. A satellite rotating in geosynchronous orbit appears to remain stationary when viewed from a point at or near the equator. It is also referred to as a "geostationary orbit."

geoid. The particular equipotential surface that coincides with *mean sea level* and that can be imagined to extend through the continents. This surface is perpendicular to the force of gravity.

geoid height. The height above the *geoid* is often called "elevation above *mean sea level*."

global positioning system (GPS). A global navigation system based on 24 or more satellites orbiting the Earth at an altitude of 11,000 *nautical miles* and providing very precise, worldwide positioning and navigation information 24 hours a day, in any weather conditions. Also called the "NAVSTAR system."

GLONASS. The Russian *global positioning system*.

Global Navigation Satellite System (GNSS). Organizing concept of a European Union system that would incorporate GPS, *GLONASS*, and other space-based and ground-based segments to support all forms of *navigation*.

GoTo. A route consisting of one *leg*, with your present *position* being the start of the route and a single defined *waypoint* as the destination.

GPS sensor. Usually a GPS receiver device, absent the display and button controls. It often will be packaged with the GPS antenna and mounted externally. The GPS sensor is controlled via wires connecting it to the display device, often a *chartplotter* or computer.

grid. A pattern of regularly spaced horizontal and vertical lines forming square zones on a map used as a reference for establishing points. Typically, grid lines on nautical charts indicate meridians of *longitude* (*true north*–south) and parallels of *latitude* (true east–west). GPS units are equipped to process a number of other grid systems representing different mathematical models for the shape of the Earth. Examples include the Swiss Grid, Swedish Grid, Taiwan Grid, and UTM.

gyrocompass. A device used for determining direction. Typically, using a high-speed rotating gyro device, the gyrocompass is present for a given direction. The gyrocompass maintains that reference with a relatively high degree of precision for some period of time. One advantage to a gyrocompass is that it is unaffected by local metallic objects on the boat and does not require a *deviation* table. On the other hand, gyrocompasses tend to drift over time and need to be recalibrated on a regular basis.

hand-bearing compass. A magnetic compass mounted into a package designed to be held in the hand and aimed at objects to sight a *bearing*. (Fixed ship's compasses do not present an easy way to sight directions of objects other than those referenced to the boat, such as the bow.) As with any magnetic compass, the hand-bearing compass is subject to local metallic devices, but they are not designed to be compensated. It is wise to use one near where the fixed compass is located and compare the bow bearings of both. You can adjust the readings of your hand-bearing compass readings to be consistent with your ship's compass.

hardware. The physical components of a system. Reference is often made to "hardware" and "*software*"; in that context, "hardware" consists of the receiver, computer, input and output devices, and other peripheral equipment.

heading. The direction in which a ship or an aircraft is pointing. Heading is indicated by a compass that is fix-mounted to the ship. It refers to the bow-on direction. This may differ from *course over ground* (COG) due to winds, sea conditions, etc.

heading up. The orientation of a display (e.g., radar or *chartplotter*) such that the *heading* of the boat is on top of the screen.

Highway screen. Shows a graphic "highway view" of the GPS user's *course over ground*. Provides helpful instructions as to how far you are off course and which direction to steer (right or left) to make corrections, and displays related navigational data pertaining to *waypoint*.

initialization. Refers to the first time a GPS receiver orients itself to its current location. After initialization, the receiver retains and uses this location information, making subsequent requests for information faster.

initial location start. The process of centering the GPS signal on a specific starting *position*.

integrated chartplotter. A GPS receiver that incorporates the *GPS sensor* into the same unit as the chart display and processor. Usually, an integrated chartplotter will employ an external antenna.

invert route. A function within the GPS receiver that reverses the sequence of *waypoints* in a saved route so that the user can navigate from the end point back to the beginning point.

I/O (input/output) interface. The one-way or two-way transfer of GPS information with another device, such as a nav plotter, autopilot, or another GPS unit.

ionosphere. The band of charged electrons 80 to 120 miles (130–190 km) above the Earth's surface. The ionosphere alters and disperses the paths of radio signals passing through it. The density of charged particles is dependent upon the position and activity of the sun.

ionospheric refraction. The change in the propagation speed and direction of a signal as it passes through the *ionosphere*.

Kalman filter. A numerical method used to track a time-varying signal in the presence of noise.

L1 signal. The primary *L-band* signal transmitted by each GPS satellite at 1,572.42 MHz. The L1 broadcast is modulated with the C/A and P-codes and with the *navigation message*. Civil users are limited to using the less accurate C/A (*coarse/acquisition*) *code* rather than the *P-code* (P for *precise*), which is restricted to military use.

L2 signal. The second *L-band* signal is centered at 1,227.60 MHz and carries the *P-code* and *navigation message*.

L5 frequency. Beginning with *Block IIF*, the GPS satellites will include a third frequency at 1,176.45 MHz. It will include a civil code that can be used by the general public. L5 was conceived to reduce the vulnerability of commercial aircraft to jammers by providing an independent signal channel.

L-band. The radio frequencies designated by the Military Radar Band extending from 1,000 to 2,000 MHz. The current GPS carrier frequencies are in the L-band (1,227.60 MHz and 1,575.42 MHz).

latitude. Measured as an angle from the Earth's equator (0°) to the North Pole (90° North) or South Pole (90° South). Parallels of latitude are imaginary circles that run parallel to the equator's plane and grow progressively smaller as they get closer to the poles. One minute of latitude measured north or south equals one *nautical mile* measured.

leg. A portion of a *route* consisting of a starting (from) *waypoint* and a destination (to) waypoint. A one-way route that is comprised of waypoints W1, W2, W3, and W4 would contain three legs. The route legs would be from W1 to W2, from W2 to W3, and from W3 to W4.

lithium. A soft, silvery, highly reactive metallic element that is used in batteries for which weight and cold weather conditions are concerns.

line of motion. The plotted line intended to reflect the boat's motion.

line of position (LOP). A straight line on the surface of the Earth with a fixed *bearing* to a known object. Your position is somewhere on that line within the limits of the *accuracy* of the angle measurement.

line of sight (LOS) propagation. Propagation of an electromagnetic wave in which the direct transmission path from the transmitter to the receiver is unobstructed. The need for LOS propagation is most critical at GPS frequencies.

liquid-crystal display (LCD). A method of displaying information—as on a screen—produced by applying an electric field to liquid crystal molecules and arranging them to change its reflectivity or transparency.

listener. Using *NMEA 0183*, it is the data input of a device that is "listening" for coded information from another device called a "*talker*."

Local Area Augmentation System (LAAS). The implementation by the FAA of a specialized type of *DGPS* to support aircraft landings in a local area (20-mile/32 km range). LAAS is of little value to mariners.

Long Range Radio Direction Finding System (Loran). A *radionavigation* aid operated and maintained by the U.S. Coast Guard. It is used as a supplemental system for harbor approach and inland navigation. Loran-C is used in civil aviation as well as by some mariners.

longitude. The angular distance (measured in degrees) east or west from the *prime meridian* to another meridian. Grid lines running north–south through the poles are meridians of longitude. Each meridian is a large circle.

magnetic north. The direction a compass needle shows as north. Magnetic north differs from *true north* by varying degrees, depending on location. The magnetic North Pole is located in northern Canada.

magnetic north-up display. A GPS receiver's display screen that always shows *magnetic north* on top.

magnetic variation. The angular amount by which *magnetic north* differs from *true north* at any location on the Earth. The compass, subject to its own errors, points to magnetic north. The compass reading must be adjusted by variation to compute true north, adding easterly and subtracting westerly variation.

map display. A GPS display screen that provides an overhead bird's-eye view of current position relative to the *waypoints* and marker icons saved. A dotted line marks the shortest route to the chosen waypoint, and a recorded plot trail displays the path just traveled.

mean low water. The average level of the ocean's surface, as measured by the level only at low tide.

mean lower low water. The average level of the ocean's surface, as measured by the level only at the lower of two daily low tides.

mean sea level. The average level of the ocean's surface, as measured by the level halfway between mean high and low tide.

Mercator projection. This projection, attributed to Gerhard Kremer, a Flemish *cartographer* whose Latin name was Gerhardus Mercator. His projection is designed for mariners and accurately represents direction from north. The projection can be visualized by wrapping a cylinder around the Earth and aligned with the poles. If you project from the center of the Earth and trace the resultant chart on the cylinder, you will get a Mercator projection. As you head toward the poles, landmasses become larger, but represent their relative shapes. This produces a distorted view of the Earth, but is most acceptable for local boating. The projection maintains the integrity of angles so a compass can be used. A straight-line course on a Mercator projection is called a *"rhumb line."* It generally is not the shortest path between two objects, which is reflected by a great circle path, but it represents the path that you sail if you maintain a constant course. Meridians (lines of constant *longitude*) extending through the poles are great circle paths since their centers coincide with

the center of the Earth. Measurements along meridians (*latitude* measurements) reflect an accurate representation of distance at a given latitude and can be used for distance measurements with one-minute of latitude (arc) being equal to one *nautical mile* for region of that latitude.

monitor stations. The worldwide group of stations used in the GPS *control segment* to track satellite clock and orbital parameters. Data collected at monitor stations are linked to a Master Control Station at which corrections are calculated and from which correction data are uploaded to the satellites.

multichannel receiver. A receiver containing multiple independent channels. Each channel tracks one satellite continuously, so that position solutions are derived from simultaneous calculations of *pseudoranges*. Typical GPS receivers offer 12 channels to monitor 121 satellites, 4 of which are selected for a navigation solution.

multipath. Interference caused by reflected GPS signals arriving at the receiver, typically as a result of bouncing off nearby large objects or other reflective surfaces. Signals traveling longer paths produce longer (erroneous) *pseudorange* estimates and, consequently, *position errors*.

NAD-27. North American Datum, 1927.

NAD-83. North American Datum, 1983.

nanosecond. One billionth of a second.

National Differential Global Positioning System (NDGPS). A network of ground- and beacon-based differential stations that increases GPS *accuracy*.

National Marine Electronics Association (NMEA). A U.S. standards committee that defines the data message structure, contents, and protocols that allow GPS receivers to communicate with other electronic equipment.

nautical mile. An international unit of length used in sea and air navigation, based on the length of one minute of arc of a great circle. A nautical mile is equal to approximately 6,076 feet (1,852 meters).

navigation message. The 1,500-bit message broadcast by each GPS satellite at 50 bps on the *L1* data link. This message contains system time, clock correction parameters, ionospheric delay model parameters, and the vehicle's *ephemeris* and health. The information is processed by the GPS signals to give user time and position.

navigation. The act of planning the course or heading of movement from one location to another, and monitoring position.

NAVSTAR (Navigation Satellite Timing And Ranging). The official U.S. government name given to the GPS satellite system.

NMEA 0183. A standard data communications protocol established by the *National Marine Electronics Association (NMEA)* and used by GPS receivers and other types of navigation and marine electronics. Most shipboard electronic devices interface via NMEA 0183.

NMEA 2000. A new standard data communications protocol that will permit up to 50 devices to be connected together to share marine data. Released in August 2001 by the *National Marine Electronics Association (NMEA)*, this standard will gradually be incorporated into electronic equipment. *NMEA 0183* will be supported for some time and will be capable of being bridged into NMEA 2000.

NMEA expander. The NMEA expander is a device used to amplify the data-out signal from a marine electronics device such as a GPS. This ensures that adequate signal level arrives at the listening device. Expanders generally are used only when a single data-out line is used for a number of *listeners*, or the cable runs are long. See also *National Marine Electronics Association (NMEA)*.

north-up display. A GPS receiver's display screen always showing *true north* on top.

parallel channel receiver. A continuous tracking receiver using multiple circuits to track satellites simultaneously.

patch antenna. An antenna based on a plated section of metal on a circuit board and attendant electronics used for receiving GPS signals.

P-code. The precise or precision code of the GPS signal, reserved for use by U.S. and allied military receivers. P-code is a very long sequence of *pseudorandom* binary biphase modulations on the GPS carrier at a chip rate of 10.23 MHz, which repeats every 267 days. Each one-week segment of this code is unique to one GPS satellite and is reset each week.

piloting. The process of navigating using charts and sighting of visual landmarks or aids to navigation, as well as radio, sound, and electronic means.

pixel. A single display element of a *liquid-crystal display (LCD)* screen. The more pixels, the higher the resolution and definition.

position. A geographic location on the Earth commonly measured in *latitude* and *longitude*.

position dilution of precision (PDOP). A unitless figure of merit expressing the relationship between the error in user position and the error in satellite position, which is a function of the configuration of satellites from which signals are derived in positioning (see *DOP*). Geometrically, PDOP is proportional to 1 divided by the volume of the pyramid formed by lines running from the receiver to four

observed satellites. Small values, such as 3, are good for positioning, whereas higher values produce less-accurate position solutions. Small PDOP is associated with widely separated satellites.

position error. A false indication of *position* on a GPS unit, usually caused by insufficient GPS satellite signal strength or poorly positioned satellites.

position fix. The GPS receiver's computed position *coordinates*.

position format. The way in which the GPS receiver's *position* will be displayed on the screen. Commonly displayed as degrees, minutes, and thousandths of a minute, with options for degrees, minutes, and seconds; degrees only; or one of several *grid* formats.

Position screen. One of the primary GPS navigational data screens showing the present position *latitude* and *longitude coordinates*, as well as other helpful navigational information.

precise positioning service (PPS). The highest level of military dynamic positioning *accuracy* provided by GPS, using the *P-code*.

present position. Current location on the face of the Earth, in terms of the specific *latitude* and *longitude coordinates*, displayed in degrees, minutes, and thousandths of a minute on a GPS unit. A thousandth of a minute represents a *position* with a resolution of approximately 6 feet (2 m).

PRN/pseudorandom noise. A sequence of *digital* 1s and 0s that appear to be randomly distributed like noise but that can be reproduced exactly. Their most important property is a low autocorrelation value for all delays or lags, except when they coincide exactly. Each GPS satellite has unique *coarse/acquisition (C/A)* and *P-codes*.

prime meridian. The zero meridian, used as a reference line from which *longitude* east and west is measured. It passes through Greenwich, England.

proximity waypoints. *Waypoints* (often called "danger waypoints") that have an additional feature—they have an associated radius that can be set around the waypoint. Usually, an alarm can be used in conjunction with these waypoints to indicate if the circle of the set radius has been penetrated indicating the potential for danger.

pseudorandom code. The identifying signature signal transmitted by each GPS satellite and mirrored by the GPS receiver in order to separate and retrieve the signal from background noise.

pseudorange. A distance measurement, based on the correlation of a satellite-transmitted code and the local receiver's reference code, that has not been corrected for errors in synchronization between the transmitter's clock and the receiver's clock.

quadrifilar helix antenna. A type of GPS receiver antenna in which four spiraling elements form the receiving surface of the antenna. For GPS use, quadrifilar antennas are typically half-wavelength or quarter-wavelength size and encased in a plastic cylinder for durability.

radionavigation. The determination of *position*, or the obtaining of information relative to position, for the purpose of navigation by means of the propagation properties of radio waves. GPS is a method of radionavigation.

Radio Technical Commission for Maritime Services (RTCM) Special Committee 104. A committee established for the purposes of establishing standards and guidance for interfacing between radiobeacon-based data links and GPS receivers, and to provide standards for ground-based *Differential GPS* stations.

range rate. The rate of change between the satellite and receiver. The range to a satellite changes due to satellite and observer motions. Range rate is determined by measuring the Doppler shift of the satellite beacon carrier.

raster chart. A *digital* chart that has been scanned from an original master. The term "raster" refers to the scanning approach whereby closely spaced parallel lines are scanned and stored. The raster chart reflects the characteristics of the original with a high degree of fidelity; however, the file sizes tend to be large. Compare *vector chart*.

real-time kinematic (RTK). RTK is a technique for precision positioning both horizontally and vertically. Typically, RTK is used in applications such as road surveying and agricuture. In its simplest configuration, a high-accuracy local monitoring station is positioned with great precision at a known position at a local site. It then transmits precise corrections to RTK GPS units in the immediate area, usually within 6 *statute miles* (10 km). These corrections are then applied to the GPS receiver solution. To resolve the signals to a high degree of precision, the fixed and mobile GPS receivers compare the actual phase of the incoming carrier signal at each location, and the GPS receives carrier signals on both the *L1* and *L2* frequencies. RTK has been an area of significant development over the past decade and will continue to grow in importance and applications.

relative bearing. The *bearing* measured to an object from a boat referenced to the boat's *heading*.

relative navigation. A technique similar to *relative positioning*, except that one or both of the points may be moving. A data link is used to relay error terms to the moving vessel or aircraft to improve real-time navigation.

relative positioning. The process of determining the relative difference in *position* between two locations, in the case of GPS, by placing a receiver over each site and making simultaneous measurements by observing the same set of satellites at the same time. This technique allows the receiver to cancel errors that are common to both receivers, such as satellite clock and *ephemeris* errors, propagation delays, and so forth.

reliability. The probability of performing a specified function without failure under given conditions for a specified period of time.

rhumb line. A line of the surface of the Earth that crosses all meridians with at a constant angle. In other words a rhumb-line course always has the same heading with respect to the North Pole. A rhumb line generally is not the shortest path on the surface of the Earth—those are great-circle paths. A rhumb line, other that one exactly east or west, continued to its limits will spiral around the Earth and terminate at one of the poles.

route. A sequence of *waypoints* that combine to mark a proposed route.

RTCM protocol. A signal protocol, by the Radio Technical Commission for Maritime Services (RTCM), to be used between *DGPS* GPS receivers. This protocol defines the signaling and information structure for the coded corrections from the DGPS. The format for basic DGPS receivers is specified as RTCM, *SC-104*.

RS-232. A serial *I/O (input/output)* standard that allows for compatibility between data-communication equipment made by various manufacturers. Typically used for a computer serial port.

S-57. The charting standard of the International Hydrographic Organization for *electronic navigation charts (ENCs)* used in *ECDIS*.

satellite status display. An information screen that shows technical data about each satellite in view. Information includes receiver channel numbers; actual satellite ID numbers; status of satellite tracking (T) or searching (S); satellite elevations and azimuths; signal-to-noise ratios (SNR) (the higher the number, the better); and *dilution of precision* ratings (*GDOP* is most important). The smaller the number approaching 1, the better potential accuracy.

satellite reacquisition time. The time, usually measured in milliseconds, it takes for a GPS receiver to request and receive current information.

SC-104 format. This is the specific *RTCM protocol* used for communication between the *DGPS* receiver and the GPS unit.

Search the Sky. A message shown when a GPS receiver is gathering data from satellites to compute a position without *almanac data*.

Selective Availability (SA). A *DoD* program that controls the *accuracy* of *pseudorange* measurements, degrading the signal available to nonqualified receivers by dithering the time and *ephemeris* data provided in the *navigation message*. SA has now been switched off.

serial communication. The sequential transmission of the signal elements of a group representing a character or other entity of data. The characters are transmitted in a sequence over a single line rather than simultaneously over two or more lines, as in parallel transmission. The sequential elements may be transmitted with or without interruption.

software. A set of instructions that direct a computer to perform a particular task, usually called a "program." System software controls the computer and application software performs a task for the user.

space segment. The portion of the GPS system that is located in outer space, that is, the GPS satellites and any ancillary spacecraft that provide GPS augmentation information (differential corrections, integrity messages, etc.).

speed over ground (SOG). The actual speed the GPS unit is moving over the surface of the Earth (ground). This may differ from nautical speed due to sea conditions such as wind and currents.

spherical error probable (SEP). The radius of a sphere within which there is a 50 percent probability of locating a point or being located. SEP is the three-dimensional analog of *CEP*.

spread spectrum. Communications techniques in which a signal is transmitted with a much greater bandwidth than necessary for the content of the original information. In GPS, *PRN* code is used to spread the signal. This technique permits the satellites to share the same frequency while adding a degree of immunity to noise and *multipath* for the received signal. The GPS receiver gains an advantage over noise since it has a priori knowledge of the code.

Standard Positioning Service (SPS). The normal civilian positioning accuracy obtained by using the single-frequency *coarse/acquisition (C/A) code*. Under *Selective Availability* conditions, SPS is guaranteed to be no worse than 330 feet (100 m) 95 percent of the time (2 drms).

static positioning. Location determination accomplished with a stationary receiver. This allows the use of various averaging or differential techniques.

statute mile. A unit of length equal to 5,280 feet (1,609 m) used in the United States and other English-speaking countries.

Steering Page. An alternative term for a GPS receiver's *Highway screen*.

straight-line navigation. The act of traveling from one *waypoint* to another in the most direct line and with no turns.

talker. Using *NMEA 0183*, a "talker" is a device that is sending coded information to another device, called a *"listener."*

time to first fix (TTFF). The time it takes to find the satellites after the user first turns on the GPS receiver, when a GPS receiver has lost memory or has been moved over 300 miles (480 km) from its last location.

Track Back. A Garmin feature that converts data from your current track log into a *route* to guide you back to a starting position.

track (TRK). Your current direction of travel relative to a ground position. Track is the same as *course over ground* (COG).

Track. A series of points (defined by a *latitude, longitude*, and time) on a GPS receiver that shows a history of where the user has been.

track-up display. A display screen on which the direction to travel to reach the next *waypoint* is always located at the top.

true north. The direction that points directly to the North Pole. Magnetic compasses show *magnetic north*, which differs from true north by varying degrees, depending on location. The difference is called "variance."

turn (TRN). The degrees which must be added to or subtracted from the current heading to reach the *course* to the intended *waypoint*.

Universal Transverse Mercator (UTM). A worldwide coordinate projection system utilizing north and east distance measurements from reference point(s). The UTM is the primary coordinate system used on U.S. Geological Survey topographic maps. UTM is not used for marine navigation.

uplink. A transmission path by which radio or other signals are sent from the ground to an aircraft or a communications satellite.

user interface. The *hardware* and operating *software* by which a receiver operator executes procedures on equipment (such as a GPS receiver) and the means by which the equipment conveys information to the person using it: the controls and displays.

user range accuracy (URA). The contribution to the range-measurement error from an individual error source (apparent clock and *ephemeris* prediction accuracies). This is converted into range units, assuming that the error source is uncorrelated with all other error sources. Values less than 10 are preferred.

user segment. The part of the whole GPS system that includes the receivers of GPS signals.

UTC. See *Coordinated Universal Time*.

vector chart. A vector chart is created from a master chart (the reference chart maintained by a hydrographic office) by digitizing the key features into a sequence of points. Coastlines and other lines are converted into a series of short straight-line segments by saving the points between the lines. The resulting *digital* file is significantly smaller than a *raster chart* file representing the same area.

velocity made good (VMG). The rate of closure to a destination *waypoint* based upon current speed and course. Velocity made good is particularly useful to sailors who may tack due to the wind rather than sailing directly toward the destination waypoint. The same is true for powerboaters tacking to avoid heavy seas. VMG provides a measure of success toward achieving the end objective.

warm start. The process of requesting and acquiring a new signal when a GPS unit is already on, or if it is restarted at the same location shortly after it has been shut down usually within 300 miles (480 km).

waypoint. A geographical point stored in the memory of a GPS receiver, representing a position to which to navigate.

WGS-84 (World Geodetic System 1984). The mathematical *ellipsoid* used by GPS since January 1987. Most current nautical charts use this datum.

Wide Area Augmentation System (WAAS). A U.S. Federal Aviation Authority (FAA) system to supplement GPS accuracy. The system employs a linked network of fixed ground stations that determine corrections for each satellite that will produce a more accurate ground *fix*. These corrections are adjusted to provide a table of corrections by region and transmitted to geostationary satellites over the Atlantic and Pacific Oceans. The system, which was developed for aircraft en-route navigation, is applicable to mariners and provides excellent precision enhancement. Since the corrections are transmitted to the Earth on the *L1* frequency, no additional receiver or antenna is required.

World Geodetic System. A consistent set of parameters describing the size and shape of the Earth, the positions of a network of points with respect to the center of mass of the Earth, transformations from major *geodetic datums*, and the potential of the Earth (usually in terms of harmonic coefficients).

Resources

The Internet is the best source of information regarding GPS. There are several categories of websites, many of which were used to check information contained in this book, particularly the government sites. Although a wealth of information is available on the Web, the greatest challenge is often interpreting it and resolving inevitable differences from multiple sources.

GPS Equipment Manufacturers

The websites of major manufacturers of GPS equipment are listed below. The principal handheld GPS manufacturers are Garmin, Magellan, and Lowrance/Eagle. The leading manufacturers of marine-integrated chartplotters are Garmin, Lowrance, Furuno, Raymarine, Icom, and Standard Horizon. The leading manufacturers of chartplotters without GPS include Raytheon and Furuno.

Brooks and Gatehouse	www.bandg.com
Cetrek	www.cetrek.com
Computrol	www.bottomlinefishfinders.com
Datamarine	www.sea-dmi.com
Eagle	www.eaglegps.com
Furuno	www.furuno.com
Garmin	www.garmin.com
ICOM	www.icomamerica.com
Interphase	www.interphase-tech.com
JRC	www.jrcamerica.com
Leica	www.leica-geosystems.com
Lorenz Electronics	www.lorenz-electronics.com
Lowrance	www.lowrance.com
Magellan	www.magellangps.com
Navman	www.navmanusa.com
Northstar	www.northstarcmc.com
Raymarine	www.raymarine.com
Simrad	www.simradusa.com
Si-Tex	www.si-tex.com
Sodena	www.sodena.net
Standard Horizon	www.standardhorizon.com
Trimble (professional)	www.trimble.com
VDO Kienzle GMBH	www.vdokienzle.com

Government Resources

The best website for boaters is the U.S. Coast Guard Navigation Center site. The FAA website is a source of WAAS information. The U.S. Air Force, Aerospace Corporation, and U.S. Navy sites are the best government sources for basic GPS information, including facts about the satellites.

Aerospace Corporation	www.aero.org/publications/GPSPRIMER/
Australian Hydrographic Office	www.hydro.gov.au/
Canadian Hydrographic Office	www.chs-shc.dfo-mpo.gc.ca/chs
FAA	gps.faa.gov
French Hydrographic Department	www.shom.fr/
Japanese Hydrographic Service	www.jhd.go.jp/jhd-E.html
Land Navigation New Zealand	www.linz.gov.nz/
Local Notice to Mariners (LNM)	www.navcen.uscg.gov/lnm
NOAA	www.noaa.gov
NOAA Online Charts	chartmaker.ncd.noaa.gov/mcd/enc/download.htm
Office of Coast Survey NOAA	chartmaker.ncd.noaa.gov/
Royal Netherlands Navy	www.mindef.nl/marine/hydro.htm
Smithsonian	www.nasm.edu/galleries/gps/
U.K. Hydrographic Office	www.hydro.gov.uk/
U.S. Coast Guard	www.uscg.mil

US Coastline Extractor	rimmer.ngdc.noaa.gov/coast/
U.S. Air Force GPS Joint Program Office	gps.losangeles.af.mil/
USCG Navigation Center	www.navcen.uscg.gov/
USCG Office of Boating Safety	www.uscgboating.org
U.S. Navy	tycho.usno.navy.mil/gpsinfo.html

Independent GPS Sites

The following sites are maintained by individuals with personal interests in GPS. Many of these sites are excellent and well maintained. One of the best is Joe Mehaffey's. His site is heavily weighted toward Garmin, with some information for Magellan and Eagle. This site also links to many other sites. Mehaffey's site is oriented toward the novice to intermediate user. Sam Wormley's site is oriented toward more advanced users. There are many other sites covering GPS, but they tend to be for more specialized applications and may be of lesser interest to boaters. Most of the sites listed below have excellent links, including manufacturers, stores, software sources, shareware, and current reviews.

Dale DePriest's Nav and GPS Articles	www.celia.mehaffey.com/dale/
GPS Nuts	www.gpsnuts.com
Joe Mehaffey GPS Information	www.joe.mehaffey.com
Sam Wormley's GPS Information	www.cride.iastate.edu/staff/ swormley/gps/
Tom's Garmin GPS Pages	www.lurge.de/GPS/

Educational Site

This site offers solid technical data as a background to GPS. For most boaters, this information is incidental to using GPS.

University of Colorado	www.colorado.edu/geography/gcraft/ notes/gps/

Cartography and Navigation Software

The websites of the companies providing chartplotting software are listed below. Comparative data can be gathered from these sites; however, it is best to talk with individuals who actually use these packages before making a purchase. The information and specifications provided on these sites begins to sound as if they are all the same.

C-Map	www.c-map.com
Fugawi	www.fugawi.com
Garmin	www.garmin.com
Global Navigation Software	www.globenav.com
GPSS	www.gpss.com
Jeppesen	www.jeppesen.com
Maptech (BSB charts)	www.maptech.com
MaxSea	www.maxsea.com
Nautical Technologies (The Capn)	www.thecapn.com
Navionics	www.navionics.com
Nobeltec	www.nobeltec.com
Ozi Explorer	www.oziexplorer.com
Quintessence Designs (NavimoQ)	www.quintessencedesigns.com
RayMarine	www.raymarine.com
SoftCharts	www.softcharts.com
TopoGrafix	www.topografix.com
Weems and Plath	www.weems-plath.com

GPS Upload/Download

The websites listed below provide information and/or downloads for some of the popular software packages used to interconnect a GPS receiver with a computer. These programs do not offer real-time navigation, but enable the user to upload and download waypoints, routes, and tracks. Several of these packages are shareware or freeware.

Easy GPS	www.topografix.com

G7towin	home.attbi.com/~g7towin/
Garmin MapSource	www.garmin.com
GarTrip	www.gartrip.de
Waypoint+	www.tapr.org/~kh2z/Waypoint/

Other Useful Websites

The websites listed below provide information relating to boating safety, weather, marine organizations, and related subjects.

Boaters Against Drunk Driving	www.badd.org
Boating Safety	www.boatingsafety.com
Hurricane Hunter	www.hurricanehunter.com
Incident News	www.incidentnews.gov
Marine and Oceanographic Tech	www.motn.org
Mariners Guide	www.marinersguide.com
MarineWaypoints.com	www.marinewaypoints.com
National Marine Electronics Association	www.nmea.org
National Safe Boating Council	www.safeboatingcouncil.org
United States Coast Guard Auxiliary	www.cgaux.org
United States Power Squadrons	www.usps.org

Index

Numbers in **bold** refer to pages with illustrations. The glossary and resources have not been indexed.